Unbreakable Valor

A Special Forces Medic's Fight to Heal What War Left Behind

By
Drew Webb

Dedication

To my wife and all my children, your love was the anchor through every storm.

You bore the unseen burdens with quiet strength and never let go.

You endured the silence, the distance, and the darkness that followed.

To those who never made it home, we remember you not just in silence, but in the lives we live because of your sacrifice.

To the brothers who came back, changed, scarred, carrying more than gear…

You carried each other.

You carried me.

This book is for all of you.

Julie, thank you for holding the line when I could not.

© 2025 by Drew Webb
All rights reserved.
This is a work of fiction based on real events. Some names, locations, and identities have been changed for privacy and narrative flow.
ISBN: 9781967866083
Library of Congress Control Number: 2025940113
Printed in the United States of America
No part of this book may be reproduced without permission from the author.

For those who came home quietly… and the ones who never did.

Reflections

Unbreakable Valor is a raw, unflinching meditation on the unseen wounds of war—those carved not by shrapnel, but by shame, guilt, and the quiet erosion of one's moral compass. Drew Webb, a Special Forces Medic, reveals the paradox of being both a healer and a warrior—trained to save lives while often forced to take them. The memoir fictionally reconstructs his lived experiences in combat areas like Kandahar, Gardez, Paktika, Parwan, where the line between right and wrong often dissolved in the red dust and adrenaline. Each chapter unveils the emotional residue left behind by morally ambiguous decisions, such as performing trauma care on a dying civilian with nothing but his trauma bag and instincts or realizing he had inserted a chest tube unnecessarily—all moments where the cost of survival was a piece of his own humanity. Through these stories, Webb exposes a haunting truth: that moral injury, unlike PTSD, stems not from fear but from a betrayal of what one believes is right. And that betrayal doesn't end with the mission—it follows veterans into hospital hallways, clinical metrics, and sleepless nights.

Beyond the battlefield, Webb extends the conversation to include the systemic failings of military and medical institutions that too often overlook the soul's suffering. He names and frames moral injury as a distinct and urgent psychological wound—one that isn't listed in diagnostic manuals but claims lives through isolation, self condemnation, and silence. In calling out how moral injury is misdiagnosed and mistreated, he critiques a system that prioritizes checkboxes and productivity over real healing. Yet within this brutal honesty lies hope: Webb insists that redemption is possible not through medication, but through acknowledgment, trust restoration, and narrative truth. His reflections are not just personal—they are a call to action for veterans, clinicians, and leaders to recognize, validate, and respond to the ethical injuries left in war's wake. Unbreakable Valor is more than a story of survival—it is a testament to the strength required to carry invisible scars, and the bravery it takes to name them.

Table of Contents

Dedication ii

Reflections v

Introduction 1

Author's Note 9

Part I – The Weight We Carried 16

    Chapter 1: Kandahar Airfield 17

    Chapter 2: Lessons Learned 21

    Chapter 3: The Red Tomb 26

    Chapter 4: Blood on the Tailgate 30

    Chapter 5: Cold Blood 33

    Chapter 6: The Call to War 40

    Chapter 7: Two Scars on the Throat 44

    Chapter 8: The Soldier's Hands 50

    Chapter 9: Arachnophobia 55

    Chapter 10: The Boy from the Wrong Village 57

    Chapter 11: The Other Side of the Wire 61

    Chapter 12: Two Seconds to Decide 64

    Chapter 13: The Fat of the Land 69

    Chapter 14: Close Enough to Kill 72

    Chapter 15: The Clinic Chronicles 78

    Chapter 16: The Morning After 83

    Chapter 17: The Last Warning (Part I) 88

    Chapter 18: The Weight That Remains (Part II) 92

    Chapter 19: Dreams of Home 98

Chapter 20: The Mistaken Family	104
Chapter 21: The Making of a Ghost	109
Chapter 22: The Hunt for Truth	114
Chapter 23: A Line in the Dust	120
Chapter 24: Smelling Like Roses in Orgun-E	125
Chapter 25: The Morality of the Hunt	131
Chapter 26: The Things You See in the Dark	139
Chapter 27: The Standoff	143
Chapter 28: The Commander's Plaything	152
Chapter 29: The Cost of Mercy	158
Chapter 30: The Deadly Chaos	165
Chapter 31: Don't Cry for Me but for the Widows	171
Chapter 32: The Triangle of War	177
Chapter 33: The Quiet Debrief	185
Chapter 34: The Boy with the Grenade	190
Chapter 35: The Price of Survival	195
Chapter 36: The One Who Froze	197
Chapter 37: The Consequences	202
Chapter 38: Not Here. Not Now.	206
Chapter 39: Rotor Wash and Razor Wire	211
Chapter 40: Five Empty Tents	218
Chapter 41: The Weight of Leadership	224
Chapter 42: In the Dust	230
Chapter 43: The Night Riders	236

Chapter 44: Stand Down 240

Chapter 45: The Cheat Card 247

Chapter 46: Smoke and Silence 252

Chapter 47: Through Quiet Valleys 256

Chapter 48: The Specialist 261

Chapter 49: Four Feet from Home 265

Chapter 50: Developing an Asset 268

Chapter 51: The Cow 271

Chapter 52: The Afghan Commander's Bargain 275

Chapter 53: Ice, Vodka, and Donkey Races 279

Chapter 54: Unconventional Warfare (UW) Hospital 283

Chapter 55: Shoulder to Dust 287

Chapter 56: Blackout Days 289

Chapter 57: The Neckline 292

Chapter 58: The Light Behind the Wall 297

Chapter 59: The Bridge They Built 303

Chapter 60: Parachutes in the Dark 307

Chapter 61: Big Mike Said No 312

Chapter 62: Don't Stare at Hector's Junk 316

Chapter 63: When the Uniform No Longer Fits 322

Part II – The Fire That Never Went Out 326

Chapter 64: Reflection Without Return 327

Chapter 65: The One Who Bit Down 332

Chapter 66: Blood in the Dust 336

Chapter 67: Carrying What's Left 339
Chapter 68: The Rule of Three 343
Chapter 69: The Tower Still Stands 347
Chapter 70: The Flyover 351
Chapter 71: What You Keep 355
Chapter 72: Coming Home With Honor 361
Part III 366
Chapter 73: The Line We Don't Cross 367
Chapter 74: Behind the Red Door 372
Chapter 75: Red Light, Blue Light 378
Chapter 76: Double Exposure 380
Chapter 77: The Kill Box 384
Chapter 78: What Will Become of Us 392
Chapter 79: The Final Exfil 399
Chapter 80: The Final Mission 404
Chapter 81: Waiting for Your Heart 409
Chapter 82: The Funeral 416
Chapter 83: The Last Round 424
Chapter 84: Home 427
Chapter 85: A Road Too Fast 432
Chapter 86: SERE School The Box 439
Chapter 87: A World Apart 444
Chapter 88: The Weight of the Slide 449
Chapter 89: Not a Saint 453

Chapter 90: Trigger Discipline 456
Part IV 462
Chapter 91: 3rd Special Forces Group (Airborne) 463
Chapter 92: Firestorm 467
Chapter 93: Blue on Blue 472
Chapter 94: The Oath 479
Chapter 95: He Never Screamed 483
Chapter 96: Wrist Shot 487
Chapter 97: Echoes of the Wrong Name 491
Epilogue I: The Weight We Carry 495
Epilogue II: Reflection On Moral Injury 501
Epilogue III: My 18-Year-Old Baby Girl 504
Final Truth 511
Song and music for Unbreakable Valor 513
For My Family 517
Epilogue IV: The War After War 519
Part V: The Fire That Never Went Out Dedication 521
Honor Roll – 3rd Special Forces Group (Airborne) 523
Glossary of Terms 529

Introduction

Unbreakable Valor

By Drew Webb
Retired U.S. Army Major, Former MSG, 3rd SFG(A)
18D / 18Z /65D Physician Assistant

In the unforgiving mountains of Afghanistan, a U.S. Army Special Forces Medical Sergeant walked the razor's edge between duty and damnation.

He wasn't just a warrior—he was a healer. Trained to save lives, ordered to take them. On missions that blurred the line between right and wrong, Drew carried both a rifle and a trauma bag— never knowing which he'd need first.

Dropped into the blackness of night by helicopters, Drew faced choices that textbooks never prepared him for. He operated under the weight of moral complexity—developing intelligence assets, treating Afghan villagers and militants, and bearing witness to decisions no man should have to make.

All while thinking about home—his wife Julie, their daughters, and the life he tried to protect from half a world away.

But war leaves fingerprints. On bodies. On souls.

Unbreakable Valor is not just a story of combat. It's a story of restraint, of brotherhood, of nights spent cleaning blood off concrete floors in a goat shed turned into an Unconventional Warfare hospital. It's about Green Berets in pressed uniforms standing in silence at Arlington and the weight of a folded flag in a widow's lap.

It's about what happens when the war doesn't end after the last bullet is fired—and what it takes to carry the memory of the fallen without losing yourself in the process.

For every Soldier who returned home with ghosts…

For every family who waited for a man who came back changed…
This is for you.
From Drew……

Veterans

If You're Reading This and You're in The Fight—Don't Go Alone

If you've ever thought,

"I don't want to die… I just don't want to live like this anymore."

You're not broken.

You're not weak.

You're not the only one.

Combat doesn't always kill.

Sometimes, it follows you home—quietly, relentlessly, waiting for silence to do what the bullets couldn't.

If you are thinking about taking your own life… or someone else's… Stop.

This book can wait.

The mission now is you.

There are people who will understand.

They won't judge you.

They've seen the same dark.

Some of them walked through it.

Get Help—Right Now:

Veterans Crisis Line

Dial 988, then press 1

Text: 838255

Free. Confidential. 24/7

Healthcare Providers

Unveiling the Unseen Wounds: The Urgent Need to Address Moral Injury in Veterans and Healthcare Providers As a nation, we have spent two decades at war.

Men and women have returned.

Some whole.

Many broken.

And before we can help them heal, we must understand what "broken" really means.

For years, we've treated the signature wounds of war through the lens of Post-Traumatic Stress Disorder (PTSD). It has become a catch-all—clinical, codified, and reimbursable. But what happens when we treat the wrong injury?

What happens when the cause isn't trauma from fear… …but a betrayal of values?

The Name of the Wound We Couldn't See

Recently, the term "Moral Injury" has emerged in both military and medical circles.

It isn't listed in the DSM-5, the American Psychiatric Association's manual for diagnosing mental disorders. But make no mistake—it is real. And it is deadly.

Coined by psychiatrist Jonathan Shay and further developed by Litz et al., moral injury describes the psychological, emotional, and spiritual harm that results from perpetrating, failing to prevent, or witnessing acts that violate one's moral code.

Where PTSD stems from fear, moral injury stems from guilt, shame, and betrayal.

And when misdiagnosed, the treatments intended to help—like exposure therapy—can reignite guilt rather than resolve it.

This isn't semantics. It's survival.

The Military Consequences of Misdiagnosis

Combat veterans often carry wounds that don't show up on scans or fit neatly onto a chart.

A medic who couldn't save a child…

A sniper who hesitated for half a second—or didn't…

A Soldier who followed an order his soul knew was wrong…

When we treat a moral injury like PTSD, we focus on triggers instead of meaning.

We manage symptoms instead of restoring trust.

We offer pills when what's needed is ethical repair, spiritual counsel, and reconnection to moral identity.

Left unaddressed, moral injury erodes the soul.

It isolates the veteran.

It convinces them they are unworthy of forgiveness, unfit for redemption, and unneeded in the world they protected.

And that's when we lose them—not to war, but to suicide.

Moral Injury Is Not Just a Military Problem

I didn't leave moral injury in Afghanistan.

I brought it home.

As a Physician Assistant, I entered clinical medicine expecting to continue serving.

But what I found was a system more committed to documentation than healing.

Productivity quotas. Time limits. Metrics over meaning.

I was judged not by how many lives I saved—but by how many boxes I checked.

Eventually, I was part of a jury in a military court-martial process that had nothing to do with justice—and everything to do with protecting the institution.

And when I returned to the clinic, I watched a brilliant Army physician—dying of cancer—still working until his final CPT code. That was when I knew:

The battlefield didn't end at the wire. It followed me into the clinic.

I wasn't burned out.

I was morally injured.

The Cost of Silence

If you are reading this as a healthcare provider, and you've:

- Sat through mandatory wellness lectures that didn't touch your pain...
- Watched good colleagues pushed out while you kept your head down...
- Endured the death of patients, the pressure of litigation, and the betrayal of institutions that once claimed to value you... Then maybe you know the feeling.

Not trauma.

Not fear.

But ethical violation.

The wound that forms when you are forced to act against what you believe—or punished for standing your ground.

A Call to Clinicians, Leaders, and Lawmakers

Moral Injury demands its own path to healing.

Group therapy may help. So may narrative writing. Ethical discussion. Chaplain support.

But first—we must recognize it exists.

We must compensate it as a real injury.

We must guarantee confidentiality to those who speak its name.

And we must train providers to see it—not just medicate it.

When moral injury is misdiagnosed as PTSD, we don't just treat it ineffectively—we compound the injury.

We gaslight the soul of the person trying to survive.

We Can Still Change the Ending

This isn't about psychiatric coding.

It's about giving our veterans—and our providers—a way home.

This isn't about rewriting doctrine.

It's about breaking the silence.

You cannot medicate a soul.

But you can listen.

You can bear witness.

You can restore moral trust.

To the healers still carrying their own wounds: You are not broken. You were betrayed.

This is not burnout.

This is Moral Injury.

And you're not alone anymore.

Author's Note

From a Green Beret Medic who never stopped carrying the weight
This book is fiction. But the pain is real.

The blood, the dust, the restraint—it all happened.

I served as a U.S. Army Special Forces Medical Sergeant, an Operations Sergeant, and later as a Physician Assistant. I trained to save lives. I was also trained to take them. And I've lived every day since trying to reconcile those two truths.

Unbreakable Valor is not about one man. It's about all of us.

Every 18D who dragged a man back from death while getting shot at.

Every quiet operator who called in a 9-line, knowing the patient was already gone.

Every teammate who lived when someone else didn't—and still wonders why.

It's about moral injury.

A wound that doesn't bleed doesn't get a Purple Heart and doesn't always show up on a clinical checklist.

It's the moment you didn't shoot… or did.

It's the body you couldn't save… and the one you had to carry anyway.

It's not a weakness. It's the cost of being fully human in an inhuman war.

If this book found you at the right time—whether you're a young medic, a survivor, a leader, or someone trying to understand what your father/brother/husband still won't say—I hope it gave you words when there were none.

And if you're one of the ones still in it…

I hope you found something in these pages that reminded you:

You're not alone. You were never alone.

We don't all get out clean.

But we can still come home.

De Oppresso Liber,

—A Green Beret who remembers everything

Understanding the Green Berets: Crest, Code, and the ODA

This section is for readers who want to know what it means—truly means—to be a U.S. Army Green Beret. Before you enter the stories, here is the code, structure, and legacy that define the Soldiers behind the missions.

What Does "De Oppresso Liber" Mean?

The motto of the U.S. Army Special Forces is De Oppresso Liber, Latin for "To Free the Oppressed."

It is not just a phrase—it's a mission statement.

It means that a Green Beret is trained and trusted to go behind enemy lines, work with indigenous forces, and help people stand up against tyranny and oppression. Not by invading—but by enabling, training, and fighting alongside.

This is the foundation of Unconventional Warfare (UW): working with local populations to resist enemy control and restore sovereignty from within.

Green Berets don't conquer. They empower.

The Meaning Behind the Crest

The Special Forces crest, or "DUI" (Distinctive Unit Insignia), is more than a symbol. Every element has meaning:

- Dagger: Represents elite skill and silent strength. The weapon of close quarters, quiet professionals.

- Arrows: Crossed arrows signify Special Forces' origins with the Office of Strategic Services (OSS) and their deep-rooted relationship with indigenous and guerrilla forces.

- Motto Scroll: "De Oppresso Liber" appears on a banner beneath the arrows and dagger—a reminder that every mission is for someone else's freedom, not personal glory.

The crest isn't ornamental. It's earned.

And it's worn with the understanding that every Green Beret has a duty to uphold its meaning—on and off the battlefield.

What Is an ODA?

ODA stands for Operational Detachment Alpha—the foundational unit of U.S. Army Special Forces.

It's not a squad. It's not a fire team. It's a 12-man Team designed to operate independently in hostile environments, often with little or no support.

Each man has a specialty:

18A – Detachment Commander

A Captain who commands and plans missions.

180A – Assistant Detachment Commander (Warrant Officer)
Assistant ODA Commander, tactical and operational planner.
18Z – Operations Sergeant

Senior enlisted leader; maintains team readiness and mission oversight.

18F – Intelligence Sergeant

collecting, processing, and analyzing intelligence for special missions.

18B – Weapons Sergeant (x2)

Experts in U.S. And foreign weaponry.

18C – Engineer Sergeant (x2)

Responsible for demolitions, construction, and mechanical skills.

18D – Medical Sergeant (x2)

Combat trauma experts trained in advanced medicine and surgery.

18E – Communications Sergeant (x2)

Satellite, HF/UHF/VHF, encryption, and electronic warfare.

ODAs can train local forces, lead combat patrols, run humanitarian aid missions, or conduct surgical strikes—all while operating in politically sensitive, remote, and dangerous locations.

Every ODA is a team of experts—not just Soldiers.

They rely on each other. They know each other's strengths, weaknesses, and scars.

When one falls, the others carry on. They finish the mission.

They finish it for him.

The History That Binds Them

The origins of U.S. Army Special Forces trace back to World War II's Office of Strategic Services (OSS)—the predecessor to both the CIA and modern Special Forces. These were men who parachuted into occupied France, trained partisans, conducted sabotage, and helped bring down the Nazi regime from within.

In 1952, the 10th Special Forces Group was formally activated under Colonel Aaron Bank.

Then came Vietnam.

Green Berets became a household name through the MACV-SOG program and remote A-camps spread across South Vietnam. They trained South Vietnamese, Montagnard tribesmen, and other local forces to resist the North Vietnamese Army and the Viet Cong.

Many never came home.

Their legacy lives on in the quiet professionalism still demanded of every man who wears the tab.

This book was written by one of them.

And now that you know what those words and symbols mean—you'll understand what's really at stake when you turn the page.
The Origin Of 3rd Special Forces Group (Airborne)

Activation Date: June 5, 1963 – originally activated at Fort Bragg during the height of the Cold War to support missions in Africa, the Middle East, and the Caribbean.

Deactivation: Inactivated in 1990 during the post-Cold War drawdown. Big mistake.

They thought the war was over.

Reactivation: July 1, 1990, just in time for history to correct them.

When the towers fell on 9/11, 3rd Group didn't dust off boots— they were already laced up.

Other Groups got caught in drawdowns, geography, or policy.

But 3rd Group?

We owned the dirt in Africa, and now the Middle East.

Where did the men come from?

They came from every broken pipeline in the Regiment.

The castoffs.

The transfers.

The "too intense" guys.

Men who weren't at home in Germany, Panama, or Okinawa.

But in Kunar? In Helmand? In Bagram and Paktika?

They became legends.

Why Is the Beret Flash Different?

The beret flash consists of four distinctive colors.

Yellow: 1st SFG(A)

Black: 5th SFG(A)

Red: 7th SFG(A)

White: Special Forces Training Group

Hence its original motto: "From the rest, comes the best." **Who Are These Men?**
These are the men who had nowhere else to go.

They didn't get the sunny assignments.

They didn't want them.

They didn't sleep in hotels in Qatar—they slept in tents and mud huts, often under fire.

They carried rifles, not laptops.

They flew into war every six months, not one mission a tour.

They never stopped rotating.

While 10th Group hit the gym in Stuttgart— While 1st Group studied language tapes in Japan—
While 7th Group drank mojitos in Colombia—

3rd Group was dying in Africa and Afghanistan, bleeding into gravel, packing each other's wounds, calling in fire on their own positions, and coming home just long enough to go back.

Part I – The Weight We Carried

Before we knew what, it would cost, we bore it all—dust, blood, silence. This is where the journey began.

Chapter 1: Kandahar Airfield

The heat in Kandahar never left. Not with the sunset. Not with the wind. It clung to your skin like sweat you couldn't wipe off. Radiated from the tarmac long after the sun dipped behind the jagged mountains. It was a second atmosphere—dry, relentless, heavy.

By day, the airfield was a storm of motion: dust devils spinning across the concrete, diesel smoke curling from idle generators, the rising scream of C-130s, and Chinooks launching into the void. Rotor wash whipped the fine Afghan dirt into our eyes, into our mouths, into every weapon we cleaned twice a day. Dust coated the world.

Beige tents stretched like temporary cities. Plywood shacks slapped together with urgency, camo netting sagging under the weight of sun and gravity. Some structures had spray-painted call signs or American flags flapping against rebar. Most were just numbers, half-faded. There was order but no comfort.

You could smell the war.

Burning trash. Jet fuel. Grease from the motor pool. Sometimes—if you were lucky—a hint of grilled meat from the makeshift DFAC line. Even the scent of chow felt tactical, like something that could vanish at any moment.

The showers were either scalding or glacial if they worked at all. Water pressure barely qualified as functional. The latrines were lined in blue plastic, no-flush, and hot as ovens inside. But no one complained. We'd seen what happened to units that forgot hygiene.

You didn't need a firefight to lose combat strength—just bad sanitation.

Hesco barriers boxed us in. Concertina wire curled along the perimeter like barbed punctuation marks. Beyond them: the unknown. Sometimes distant explosions rolled in from the hills—

maybe an Apache lighting up a cave, maybe an old Soviet shell detonated by EOD. We never knew for sure.

But we always knew this: the enemy was watching.

At night, the sky changed.

It didn't go quiet—it became surgical.

Above us, the low hum of an AC-130 Spectre gunship would circle like a god in orbit. Somewhere out there, a team had made contact. Invisible to the naked eye, the IR strobe blinked. A fire mission was inbound.

"Cleared hot."

The M61 Vulcan cannon barked first—short bursts, surgical. Then the Bofors 40mm, thudding deep into the rock. And finally, the 105mm Howitzer. A hammer from heaven. It didn't just shake the earth—it made it feel like the bones beneath your feet were cracking in sympathy.

Every flash lit the underbelly of the clouds. Every boom rewrote the skyline. The enemy didn't run. They scattered. Then they died.

The flight line never slept.

Crews worked under harsh floodlights, patching the Chinooks hit over Takur Ghar. You could still see the holes—clean entry, jagged exit. Mechanics crawled over their skin like ants, replacing panels and testing rotors.

Apaches returned, rotors still warm, optics still smeared with dust from the fight. Fuel trucks hissed and groaned. Forklifts hauled pallet after pallet. Then Riggers would attach them to parachutes—water, ammo, MREs, T-rations—destined for the Forward Operating Bases (FOB), the real Special Forces outposts. The ones where men didn't have backup.

That's where we came in.

Beards-some with grey, Oakley sunglasses, longer than regulation hair—some shaved heads. We didn't wear unit patches. No name tapes. No identifiers. Some of us wore civilian baseball caps with the Special Forces crest, others shemaghs. I wore an NY Yankees hat. Not for fashion. For the memory of 9/11. For identity. A little piece of home in a place where everything else felt foreign.

We all wore our secondary weapons low in Safariland drop rigs. Every man trim, lean, ready. Some tucked their DCU tops into their pants—faster access to the sidearm if everything else failed. Within six months, we all had new rigger belts with steel D-rings sewn in—after the lesson learned during Operation Anaconda, when a Navy SEAL fell out of a CH-47. The Predator feed showed his last stand—and his execution.

A grim reminder that we were fighting a ruthless enemy and a confirmation that we would fight to the death, never submitting to capture.

We remembered. We always remembered.

Inside the TOC, the walls were lined with maps. Red and blue lines. Kill boxes. Known IED hotspots. Friendly grids marked in grease pencil. The radios never stopped. Somewhere, always, someone was calling for help.

We monitored it all.

And we waited.

One night, after the pre-combat inspections were complete and the gear was staged, I sat outside our tent with a lukewarm glass bottle of Coke in my hand and a rifle across my lap.

The stars over Kandahar were different.

Sharper. Closer.

It was like the war had burned away everything that clouded the sky. Like this place—this unforgiving, beautiful, cursed place—had cut through the veil between heaven and hell.

The war would outlast us. So would the mountains. But at that moment, beneath the burning stars, I realized something:

We were never the center of this world.

We were just men trying to survive in it.

And the airfield, for all its noise and violence, was just another heartbeat in a war that would never really end.

Not for us.

Chapter 2: Lessons Learned

Kandahar Airfield was deceptively quiet that morning.

The kind of quiet that didn't last. The kind that always came before something went wrong.

The heat pressed down like a hand on your back—thick, oily, relentless. Even in March, it was already rising off the tarmac in waves, soaking into our gear, our uniforms, our bones. The air smelled like diesel, burning trash, and the distant ghost of old cordite. I was thinking how it felt heavier than usual and wishing I had brought my medical bag.

Jim and I were walking the outer edge of the base, near the Soviet wreckages. Decades-old MiGs sat stripped and gutted, skeletal reminders of a previous war. Their rusted frames looked like carcasses abandoned by time, bulldozed into piles to make way for the new war—the one we were now fighting.

We weren't geared for a fight. No M4s slung across our chests, just our Berettas holstered in Safariland drop rigs, secondary weapons we treated like lifelines. Mine was always chambered, selector on fire, mag seated clean. I didn't trust safeties. I didn't trust anything but muscle memory.

I always focused on the details, like draw angle, thumb pressure, or transition drills. Maybe because I'd been burned once—an 18B had unloaded my pistol during a training lane, and when I reached for it mid-drill, nothing happened. I never forgot that moment. Since then, my holster has become an extension of me. Quick thumb break. Draw up, close, press out. One motion. No hesitation.

I wasn't the best shooter on the Team. That wasn't my job. I was the medic. But I was good enough to survive long enough to do what mattered.

Most regular army officers wore their primary weapon, the M9, tucked in a nylon-issued holster. It was secured by multiple safeguards. Always unloaded, rarely a magazine in the well, unless outside the wire. Clipped in with a snap-button thumb break. The secondary strap was wrapped around the handle and required the thumb and forefinger to unclip the plastic buckle. The butt of the weapon was secured by a lanyard, and some had upgraded to a cord similar to the old telephones. The cord was tied to their issued belt or to their equipment. If a magazine was seated, rarely would they chamber a round. Safety selector never on fire. They were terrified to lose their weapon or have an unauthorized discharge. Gone were the days of training. The vocabulary had changed. No more "Accidental." Even in combat, "unauthorized" was a career killer…… Fuck that. I couldn't even imagine trying to get that thing undone in time before the enemy tattooed an AK-47 muzzle to their forehead. Different army, different leadership, different training levels. It wasn't their fault. They just followed orders.

We walked in silence. Brown DCU shirts soaked through with sweat. Dust kicked up from our boots, turning into a fine paste that stuck to the leather. Our convoy to Paktika province was already staged—trucks loaded, ammo stacked, water and fuel secured, trailers hooked up, winches tested, "I Love NY" sticker firmly secured to the front of the ammo carrier. U.S. Flag waiving proudly from the rear. A message to the enemy, "U.S. Army Special Forces have arrived; here we are."

We had nothing left to prep.

Just time to kill.

And that's when it happened.

It wasn't a loud explosion. No fireball. No mushroom cloud. Just a low, angry thump. A sound with weight.

Jim and I turned at the same time. Instinct. No words. Just a shared look.

A plume of dust hung low near the old Soviet munitions pit, where EOD had been clearing out old ordnance. We ran—boots hammering hard-packed earth, pistol holsters bouncing hard against our thighs, powerful legs transporting us rapidly toward the explosion.

By the time we got there, everything had already slowed.

The Danish Soldier was still on his knees.

His face… wasn't a face anymore.

The blast had gone under his ballistic face shield and turned his lower jaw into a pulp. His nose was gone. Lips shredded. Cheeks were torn open, like meat peeled back from the bone. Blood, thick and arterial, pumped out and streamed down his front in ribbons. His teeth—those that hadn't been shattered—were slick with red. His eyes were still open, unseeing.

And he was trying to breathe.

That sound will never leave me.

Wet. Gurgling. Half-choked. It came in short spasms, his head tilting forward, his body instinctively trying to keep the airway open. But there was no airway to save. His throat was drowning in his own blood.

I reached for my med bag.

Nothing.

Fuck.

Nothing but my holstered pistol and hundreds of hours of training—and not a damn thing that could help him.

Jim and I locked eyes.

We didn't speak.

We didn't need to.

He wasn't going to make it.

Other medics ran in—Americans, multinational forces. Someone shouted for a stretcher. Another screamed into a radio for a medevac bird. But deep down, we all knew the truth: this man was already dying. We were just witnesses.

Jim dropped beside him anyway. One hand on his shoulder. A gesture. Human. Final.

His uniform was soaked. The Danish flag patch was smeared with blood. He was coalition, but in that moment, he was ours.

I stood there, fists clenched, guilt pounding behind my ribs. I had walked out that morning thinking I didn't need to carry medical gear.

Thinking Kandahar was "safe."

Thinking wrong.

His breaths slowed.

Then stopped.

The last sound he made was a soft exhale—less a breath, more a surrender.

And then… silence.

Jim stood up. Blood on his hands. Eyes unreadable.

No words. No tears. Because Green Berets don't cry.

But we remember.

We watched as other allied medics and doctors transported his dead body to their military hospital. Conducting useless chest compressions, even as their vehicle disappeared down the dusty road.

No words were spoken between me and my junior 18D. We both knew what we could have done, what needed to be done, what we failed to do.

That's Moral Injury. The chipping away of values, the erosion of humanity, and the inability to act. Our minds didn't react to the brutality of the injuries, as in PTSD; our minds packed away the memory of preventing a man from dying.

After that day, I never walked anywhere without lifesaving medical supplies carried on my person.

I packed a cut-down #6 endotracheal tube, 10cc syringe, scalpel blade, 1" tape, and an NPA, all in my left shoulder pocket.

In my right shoulder pocket, I stuffed it with Kerlix, ACE wraps, hemostat clamps, and CAT tourniquets. I looked like Popeye the Sailor with spinach-infused biceps. Not as strong but always saving the weak.

I always had trauma tools within reach. Always ready. Even in the wire. Even on a "safe" base.

Because the truth is this: You're never safe.

And when the blood hits the dirt and the breath turns wet and ragged, the only thing worse than watching a man die…
…is knowing you could've saved him. And didn't.

Green Berets never forget. But we always learn.

Chapter 3: The Red Tomb

Gardez, March 2002. Just after Operation Anaconda.

We arrived late afternoon. The compound was CIA-owned, roughly 20 feet high, boxed in by mud walls and ringed with sandbags.

We were given a quick tour of the compound, shown the guard towers, and given an orientation of the compound security plan. We were shown Chief Harriman's red Hilux. The one he had been in when it was ripped apart by a Spectre gunship. The hood was riddled with large caliber holes and looked like it had been clawed by a god—torn open, edges blackened. Jagged holes continued up to the roof. A shredded orange marker panel was still taped to the roof with black 100mph tape. An X made from IR glint tape had been added on top of the panel. Another safety feature to ensure no friendly fire incidents. Metal was torn as rounds had punctured through the thin metal. The truck bed was full of AK-47 brass and human tissue from dead Northern Alliance fighters riding in the back when they were cut down, alongside their American counterparts.

We looked inside the twin cabs. Absent windows and windshield, shattered glass was strewn everywhere—blood stains, black and dried, painted the seats and ceiling. There were pockmarks across the panels—already rusting silver tears, where rounds had entered, warping the metal, chewing through steel.

5.56mm brass littered the floorboards—hundreds of casings. Signs of firefights they'd fought before they died. The backseat was streaked with dried blood. The passenger door was half-ripped off, punched through by shrapnel of the AC-130 strike. The stench of oil, cordite, and death spilled from the cab.

That was CW2 Harriman's truck.

That was his last ride.

That was a tomb parked, awaiting a full Army investigation to figure out if a friendly fire incident was at fault.

I never understood why the Hilux was outside the compound. Like it was on display for everyone to see. I guess the compound occupants didn't want to be reminded of their vulnerability to accidental death. Harriman was an American, our brother, but not a CIA man. And this wasn't a Special Forces compound…. Not yet.

We continued to be shown around the outer perimeter. The CIA had hired local workers to bulldoze tank fighting positions alongside the outer walls. They didn't have the engineering experience of a Special Forces ODA. They had inadvertently disrupted the drainage and natural flow of the compound's runoff.

There were old Soviet tanks and vehicles parked all over the landscape. Northern Alliance vehicles and militiamen who had supported Operation Anaconda.

Back inside the compound, a large tarp was nailed to the mud wall and spread over dozens of duffle bags. Inside the musty green nylon, stuffed full of outdated U.S. Military-issue cold-weather gear. Parkas, fleece layers, gloves, boots, and below-zero sleeping bags. The CIA guys told us flatly to take what we wanted—but we had to take entire bags, not pick through them. No sorting. No trading. Just grab and go.

It wasn't charity. It was a necessity. We hadn't been issued freezing weather gear back at Bragg. The sleeping bags were a lifeline. Thick and warm old green type, with drawstring hoods you could cocoon into when the wind screamed through the gaps in the wall.

A few of us ensured everyone had a warm bag and hauled them into our tent. Grateful didn't begin to cover it. We could always count on each other to ensure no one missed out. If one ODA member got a new knife or sunglasses, everyone got them.

That first evening, we were tired. Still adjusting to the altitude. Some of the guys were inside USAID tents, stashing their rucks on top of cots, laying out gear. Others were under tarps strung between the HMMWVs, cleaning rifles and crew-served weapons. I heard soft voices in a corner of the compound. Hector and Jim were working quietly, piecing together several busted AKs to build complete ones. I asked what they were doing. Jim looked up and smiled. "Can never have too many guns, Brother." The kind of thing Green Berets do when there's no mission and too much silence.

The sun set and soon the sky had darkened to block out the stars. I was quietly talking to another Teammate. I had a habit of talking louder than I should. After all, we were behind 20-foot solid walls.

"Webby???? Is that you?" I heard a familiar Australian accent. It was my old Aussie Reconnaissance patrol commander. Fifteen years prior, I had been in his platoon when he was a senior NCO. I embraced him like family. We chatted and reminisced. He handed me a jar of Vegemite and one of his coins. I couldn't see it in the dark, but I appreciated his gesture.

It wasn't until he bid me farewell and walked away that another Aussie who knew me said, "You know that's the Regimental Sergeant Major of 22 SAS out of Perth, Australia?"

Small world. I had come halfway across the world, in a remote American CIA safe house and run into an old mate. It wasn't the last time I would meet up with an Aussie digger who had entered the world of Special Forces.

Later that night when the air smelled like wet stone and rusted metal. No stars. Just fog. The radio stayed on. One man is always up. Tourniquets prepped. Rifles close. We didn't trust the quiet. We never did……the rain came.

Not all at once. Just a steady, cold drizzle that soaked through tarps and tents and boots, crawling up cots and down backs. Afghan mud doesn't drain. It thickens. Swells. Turns into something alive.

Most of us didn't sleep that night. I awoke at about 0330. I shined my headlamp towards the tent entrance. I could see the water was up to our cots. Tents sat in the center of a rising pool. I kept an eye open every few minutes to see how high it would rise. Others were awake, but no one complained.

And then, sometime before first light, the wall gave way.

No explosion. No shouting. Just a deep, grinding groan.

Then, a huge boom rocked the compound. It was right next to our tent. The only thing that should have been there was the 20-foot-high wall that towered above our tent.

Zippers tore sleeping bags open. Boots hastily put on. Men jumped into rapidly draining water that had flooded the tent. Rifles were grabbed, and plate carriers were thrown over heads. We rushed the perimeter, expecting contact.

Instead, we found absence.

A massive section of the mud wall had collapsed outward, melted by the water, and undermined by the poorly placed fill. The rubble stretched a dozen meters wide several deep. The wall would have crushed us if it had fallen inwards. A miracle it had fallen in the right direction.

At first, we didn't even realize what was missing.

Until someone said: "Where's Harriman's truck?" Gone.
Not stolen. Not moved. Buried. His red Hilux.

When the sun came up, we realized it was completely buried. Gone. As if the war had come back to claim it one final time.

It was gone like him. No ceremony. Just swallowed.

Chapter 4: Blood on the Tailgate

The next morning, the rain stopped.

Steam rose from the dirt. The compound felt bruised. Nobody said much.

Until the grenade went off.

An explosion cracked the air. Close. Too close.

We grabbed our gear. I had my rifle. Aid bag over my shoulder. Beretta on my hip. The ODA was moving before the smoke settled. We followed the Afghan militia through the wall opening, still soaked with runoff.

A silver Hilux had taken the blast. One of theirs. A few grenades we're tossed inside while it idled. Four men inside. Two in the bed. All dead.

The interior was shredded. Blood sprayed across every surface.
Human tissue in the vents. A boot sat where a man's leg should've been.

I leaned in. The smell hit first—iron, diesel, sulfur, bile, urine, and feces. The release of bodily fluid is never kind to the deceased.

We weren't just Soldiers. We were eyewitnesses.

In the bed of another truck, two bodies had been thrown like trash. One shot point-blank, skull peeled back. One eye was detached, and the face ripped open. Pieces of the skull were missing. The other's face was gone, only one eye left, wide and useless.

Our 18F and Team Leader were snapping photos to include in an intel report. I walked over to two teammates standing off to the side. I asked them quietly if they could give me a hand to move the bodies.

They hesitated but followed my lead.

"Use gloves. Pull them out. Position for photos. Respect the dead. This was prep. Not punishment."

When they lifted the first man, his brain slid out and landed with a wet thump onto the tailgate.

One gagged. Another cracked a joke to mask the nerves. In hindsight, we should've shown more respect. They weren't our teammates, and no bond existed between us—but they were still human beings, not garbage.

Someone grabbed the wrist of the second terrorist. The limb tore free at the shoulder with a sickening pop. He stared for a second—expressionless—at the piece of flesh in his grip. Then he dropped it beside the other body, face-up in the wet dirt, and moved on.

No simulation training could ever truly prepare you for the feel of a human body when it falls apart in your hands.

Our men didn't stop because one day, they'd have to do this during future operations. Search a dead enemy. Clear weapons. Ensure no explosives. Confirm the man was dead. No prep. No pause. Just function.

Better they learn now. We finished the work.

The militia unceremoniously loaded the enemy dead back into their vehicle. Someone muttered a prayer. Someone else lit a cigarette.

That night, back at the tent, the guys didn't speak about the incident. That's how we survived. Move on to the next task, don't dwell on the moment, box it up, and put it on the shelf. It'll always be there. Especially when you least expect or want to revisit those memories.

That's moral injury. The slow suppression of emotions…until you feel nothing at all.

The wall took his truck. The blast took theirs. And the flies took everything else.

That was Gardez. A brief stopover. Little to no sleep. Brief encounters with death. And the last Americans to see CW2 Harriman's truck.

It wasn't a positive experience, but a necessary one.

Chapter 5: Cold Blood

Before I ever learned to save a life, I learned how to take one.

I was a boy in Australia then. Fourteen. Maybe a little younger. The bush stretched for miles around our trailer, or caravan as we called it—red dirt, dry scrub, heat that baked the land by day and stripped it cold by night. The air smelled of eucalyptus, rusted iron, and distant smoke. The kind of place where even the silence felt like it had teeth.

Everything out there was built to survive or to kill—spiked grass, biting flies, trees that peeled bark-like skin. Frilled-necked lizards that sprinted on back legs. Spiders that could kill you with a single bite. Snakes, able to paralyze or end a life with speed and precision. You could walk for hours and see nothing but wallabies darting through the scrub, small kangaroo-like animals built to vanish. Emus patrolled the fields like sentries. Fences half-consumed by the land they tried to tame.

It was wild. Beautiful. And cruel.

My father had fought in the jungles of Papua New Guinea during World War II. He carried the war inside him long after the uniforms were folded away. When he wasn't silent, he drank. And when he drank, he hit. My older brother took the brunt of it—he was just a kid. My father would wake him by clamping a hand over his nose. I got my share of it too. I always felt guilty that my brother had it worse. Later, when I grew older, our little brother became the new target. Moral injury had already begun to slither into my soul.

My father used to tell me:

"You've got to learn to kill in cold blood, boy. If you can't, you won't last. It's the only way a man can survive."

At the time, I thought he meant animals. Kill animals to eat so we could survive.

Now, I know he wasn't talking about animals at all.

I had a .22 rifle I rebuilt myself. Stripped the stock and re-varnished it in the backyard. Bought a cheap Hong Kong scope with the money I earned from selling newspapers. I had to hide a portion of my tips from my parents. If they found out, I'd be subject to another heavy-handed assault. I bought one box of rounds—twenty bullets. I handled them like gold.

One morning, I spotted a kangaroo just beyond a clearing. Grey coat. Ears twitching like antennae. Chewing rhythmically, listening to the sounds of the bush. I dropped to a knee and cradled the rifle like I'd seen in WWII comic books. I drew a slow breath and held it. Not too long, or the crosshairs would start to waiver. I pressed the trigger back and held it. There was almost no recoil.

The shot hit low.

The kangaroo fell—but didn't die.

When I got close, I saw its eyes. Wide. Thrashing. Growling. Most people don't know kangaroos can do that—but they can. Deep, guttural, feral. Like a dog dying in slow motion. Its back legs were ruined. Chest heaving. Every breath a shudder.

I didn't have any more bullets.

I couldn't leave it, so I picked up a heavy piece of wood.

My hands were steady. My mouth was slightly dry. My father's words echoed in my ears—slurred and final.

"Kill in cold blood." So, I did.

I brought the wood down.

Again.

And again.

Until it stopped moving.

Until the growls stopped.

Its head was caved in, distorted, white bone visible, teeth bared.

I didn't feel stronger. I didn't feel older. Just guilt and the silent realization, that I could never take it back.

Then I discarded any emotions—until I felt nothing at all.

After that, I had to gut and dress the body. The sun was going down, shadows stretching long and thin across the red dust. No water. Just a razor-sharp knife and an old shirt.

The blade I carried wasn't a pocketknife anymore. It was a bush knife—fixed blade, scarred steel, sheathed in leather, always on my hip. I'd used it since I was seven—learned to shape the edge with an iron file. I used it to skin rabbits to help feed my family. I was small and hungry back then, but I could strip a rabbit clean in one motion.

I used to dry out the skins on our caravan steps. They became trophies and decorations. Felt like we were moving up in the world.

Skinning a kangaroo was different.

Thicker hide. Hotter blood. Muscles that didn't give up easily.

I slit the belly, cut around the ankles, opened the throat. Twisted the head off.

My hands worked.

My mind took in everything, burned every detail into my memory.

No one taught me how to do any of it. No one watched. My older brother was off somewhere. My younger brother was too small to understand.

My father didn't join me. He was off in his own jungle—beer or wine in hand, fists not far behind. He only taught me what pain and shame felt like.

Later, I found a different man—a quiet and kind one who lived out past the ridge. He let me shoot his Mini-14, a .223 with the rear sight broken off. I learned to shoot it like a shotgun. Just the front post and feel.

He had military cans of ammo, a black dirt floor scattered with sleeping dogs, and a table made from eucalyptus boards.

Never asked for anything in return. Never tried to touch me.

Not like the other men in the bush.

The ones we knew to avoid.

The ones you didn't have to be told about.

You just knew.

They said the kind man choked on his own vomit one night. Died alone. Cockroaches in his mouth when they found him.

I never saw it.

But the story stayed with me.

Truth didn't matter. The story was a warning about alcoholism.

A line one day I would cross.

After I killed and dressed the kangaroo, with the sun starting to go down, I sat in the dust.

Staring at what was left of it.

Trying to understand what was wrong with me.

I had done what I was told.

I had killed in cold blood.

But I didn't feel like a man.

I felt hollow.

Years later, wearing the Green Beret, I remembered that day.

When I patched holes in men still bleeding.

When I pulled a trigger in the dark without hesitation.

When I heard someone scream for a medic, I ran toward the sound.

I remembered the paradox of it all.

How I could save a life with one hand and end one with the other.

Not a contradiction.

A balance.

And I've lived in that balance ever since.

———

They teach you to shoot.

They teach you to heal.

But no one teaches you what it's like when you realize you're good at both.

No one warns you what it means to be both a protector and destroyer.

No one tells you how to carry that weight when the war gets quiet.

———

That's what moral injury is.

Guilt and shame, and the slow erosion of something you didn't know you could lose.

Something like… innocence.

Or mercy.

Or the ability to cry over the life you just took.

———

The boy who beat a kangaroo to death in the bush never cried.

And maybe that's what scared me the most. The ability to suppress my emotions so easily.

Sometimes, during the silent hunt for the enemy…

Or in the quiet hour between cleaning blood from a floor and writing a medical note…

I'd still hear that growl.

Not from an enemy.

Not from a battlefield.

But from the place in me that never made peace with what I'd done.

And I'd remember what it meant to kill in cold blood.

Chapter 6: The Call to War

The land used to be beautiful.

I tried to remember it that way—before the wire, before the blood-soaked dust. Before, we gave it a thousand names: AO, grid, hot zone. But the mountains had no memory for dreamers. They swallowed men whole and spit out their bones.

I stood on the edge of the firebase, sun warming my face. The wind carried the scent of diesel, sweat, human waste—and something else.

Iron. Wet iron.

A Forward Surgical Team (FST) from Kandahar, had been assigned to our location at Camp Harriman. They had moved into our Unconventional Warfare (UW) hospital building after our Team Sergeant had requested additional medical support. Our firebase was treating the majority of casualties in theater. Several miles from our location, at a different Special Forces outpost, a psychological operations team was ambushed. One of their members had been wounded. Due to weather constraints, the medevac helicopter couldn't get to him in time, and he succumbed to his wounds.

Our location was approximately 20 kilometers from the Pakistan border. We were close enough to deliver surgical interventions, yet far enough to avoid the threat of cross-border al-Qaeda attacks. It was critical to maintain medical capabilities within reach of frontline operations. By this point, we had established a large gravel HLZ and a massive refueling capacity. Support came from Soldiers of the 101st Airborne—highly trained and experienced in Landing Zone operations. Their senior leadership assumed responsibility for all helicopter traffic. Together, the FST and 101st Airborne significantly enhanced our Special Forces capabilities and helped save countless lives.

Footsteps approached behind me—measured, heavy. I knew the sound before I turned. My Team Sergeant. No one walked like him. Boot heels crunching in the dirt and gravel.

His face was already telling the story.

"Our boys got hit," he said.

"Hard. Fast. They've got wounded—one might not make it." I didn't need further instructions. I was already prepared.
My aid bag was always packed. Tubes pre-cut. Tape pre-torn. Morphine and Valium dates checked. 14-gauge 3.25-inch needles and catheters. Kerlix, Coban, and ACE wraps were staged in outside pockets. IV fluids, administration sets, needles, syringes, scalpels, Vaseline-impregnated dressings, benzoin tincture, IV antibiotics, naloxone, flumazenil, lidocaine, diphenhydramine, epinephrine. Chest tubes, suture material, Heimlich valves.

On one mission, a casualty started slowing his breathing after morphine and Valium were administered under stress. I watched his chest rise... then hesitate. I knew that look—respiratory depression. I reached into the aid bag, snapped open a naloxone ampule, and gave him 0.4 mg IM into the deltoid. Thirty seconds later, his breathing steadied. Eyes fluttered open. He came back. That dose bought us enough time to keep him alive until extraction.

I was armed to the teeth with weapons and medical equipment.

"I trust you, Drew," he said, eyes locked with mine.

"Wouldn't send another man. If anyone can save them—it's you." I gave a silent nod, turned, and jogged to the landing zone.

The rotors were screaming by the time I walked up the ramp and into the belly of the Chinook. We lifted off, and a calm came across my body. The more intense the situation, the slower my heart rate seemed to beat. My body always relaxed when highly stimulated, like administering Adderall to a hyperactive kid. My gear dug into my shoulders, but it wasn't the weight of armor that pressed on me—it was the silence. The kind of silence where you're already rehearsing failure, and you're not allowed to let it show.

Seated across from me was an orthopedic surgeon—a high-ranking National Guard officer. He'd walked away from his civilian practice the week after the Towers fell, volunteering to lead a Forward Surgical Team in Afghanistan. Now, for the first time, he was getting into the fight.

His Kevlar helmet was cinched down so tight it looked like he was trying to vanish inside it. His body armor shifted awkwardly with every bump. No aid bag. No trauma shears. No IV kits. Just wide eyes and rank.

As I jogged to the LZ, he stepped in beside me and said he wanted to help. I didn't have the authority to say "No," but I did tell him, "Before we hit the ground, rip that rank off your Kevlar—unless you want a sniper to take you out." He looked at me like I was joking.

I wasn't.

Now, in the bird, he clutched the seatbelt strap like a lifeline. His knuckles were white. When he leaned close to yell over the engines, spittle hit my cheek.

"I think I'll stay on the bird."

Smart choice. Allowed me to not babysit and do my job.

The Crew Chief turned, eyes wide behind ballistic goggles.

"One Minute!"

The twin blades allowed the helicopter to flare before slamming into the ground.

I tightened my gloves. Checked my straps. Rehearsed the med sequence again—massive bleed, airway, respiration, circulation, head trauma.

"Go! Go! Go!"

The ramp dropped.

The sound hit like a tidal wave. Gunfire. Not scattered. Not wild. Directed. Someone out there wanted us dead.

I hit the ground—civilian hiking boots sinking into loose, Afghan dirt.

The rotors spun faster and allowed the Chinook to lift upwards. The bird pulled away. Just like that—I was alone.

I started running toward the chaos. Wondering which tools, I would use first: rifle or tourniquet?

Chapter 7: Two Scars on the Throat

I was walking around the local village with my translator and several of my company militia. Shopping for the monthly food supplies for our battalion of Afghan fighters. I was bartering over sacks of rice, large drums of cooking oil, and other cooking supplies. Negotiations were going well. We could have paid whatever the local merchants asked, but that wasn't the goal. We were here to stimulate local businesses, not crash their economy. Not every ODA practiced this technique, and certainly not the regular army. Some would inflate prices so high that they paid American prices for goods and services. This made an extremely small portion of the population, very rich and an even larger percentage live in poverty. We were issued Afghani cash from Kandahar, but the OGA had an unlimited supply of USD. The money to buy our fighter's food, supplies, and salaries came from our OGA counterparts. So, I paid for everything with crisp, new $100 bills.

Behind me, there was a sudden commotion. My men formed a wall of protection between me and the loud shouting. I turned to investigate what was happening. A pickup truck had stopped at the market's edge in a cloud of dust and irritated driver. After a quick assessment of the situation, I realized that the vehicle contained two wounded Afghan men.

Both shot up. Angry, dying, or close to it. I called Mark on the handheld radio. This was prior to us building a 75-foot antenna tower. Comms were sporadic and broken at best. I tried to relay to Mark that I had encountered two wounded Afghanis with gunshot wounds. The broken message got through as "Afghan… gunshot… urgent-surgical… need…"

Our firebase reacted instantly. Drew's men had been in contact and received casualties. They were on their way back. Need the QRF to mount up and provide support.

I got frustrated with comms and made the decision to load them up and treat them immediately. Medical decisions were made without regard for the consequences of my decisions. After the wounded men were evacuated by helicopter, Mark ripped into me. I made a tactical decision without regard for the larger picture. He had assumed from my radio message that U.S. forces had been in contact. That went up to battalion. Everyone scrambling. Second and third-order effects. I learned a valuable lesson that day. I couldn't drop everything just to save a random civilian. We could easily turn the local populace into relying on U.S. Forces casualty support. This actually takes away vital assets from supporting U.S. And Coalition forces. A lesson the regular army failed to understand for years in Iraq.

We arrived back at Orgun-E with the casualties. It had started as a land dispute and ended in a gun battle—AK-47s at close range, neither of them good enough to kill cleanly.

One had taken rounds to the limbs, and the other one a bullet to the face.

I was slightly flustered as I had just had a chewing out by my Team Sergeant. Jim arrived on the scene to assist with treatment. We moved them into our UW hospital. Four army litters were always set up and ready for a mass casualty situation. Jim took the extremity injuries while I focused on the GSW to the face.

The first thing I thought: This is the one. This is my chance at a real cricothyrotomy.

I'd practiced it a dozen times on goats. Studied the anatomy in cadaver labs. Memorized the layout of the neck like a roadmap. But this was the first time I had a real patient, still conscious, whose life was hanging on what I remembered.

His face was torn. Beard matted with blood. Muzzle tattoo around the entry wound. He couldn't speak, but his eyes were open. He was tracking me. Trusting me. Somehow.

His airway was compromised. I knew it the moment I laid him back. And even as I tilted his head to open the neck, I thought of a story a fellow 18D told me once—about a teammate shot in the jaw, naturally sitting up, choking on blood. The medic had forced him flat to get a better position and nearly drowned him.

That haunted me later.

But this Afghan man… he didn't panic. He didn't fight.

Maybe he knew he was going to die.

Maybe he knew I was his only chance not to.

———

I extended his head and exposed his throat. The neck gets long when you do that—tendons stretch, shadows deepen. I felt for the cricothyroid membrane, that soft spot between the thyroid and cricoid cartilages.

Or so I thought.

I made a horizontal incision through the skin. It looked… off. The anatomy didn't match what I'd seen in training. No soft window. Just white cartilage, striated muscle, and bloodless layers that looked like the wrong page in a manual.

So, I cut wider. The man didn't flinch.

Still no membrane window.

That's when I called for Jim.

———

Jim walked over calmly, sleeves rolled, covered in blood from his own casualty. He looked once, didn't flinch, and pointed lower.

"Right there," he said.

No scolding. No lecture. Just accurate, direct correction.

I had been too high.

With a man choking beneath me, I had mistaken the thyroid cartilage for the cricothyroid membrane. Amateur error. Under pressure. Ass recently chewed. Feeling butt hurt.

I swallowed my pride, pinched my cheeks together, and made a second cut.

This time, the tissue gave. A small pop. Like the skin releasing its grip on something deeper.

I inserted the tube—a full-size 6.0 ET tube that hadn't been trimmed down. It slid into place, a little deeper than ideal. I inflated the cuff with a small amount of air. Not too much, as it was way below the epiglottis. The patient improved immediately. His breathing evened. His pulse slowed. Oxygen saturation climbed.

Success.

For a moment, anyway.

I continued the trauma assessment. MARCH—Massive hemorrhage, Airway, Respiration. The airway was good. But when I listened to his lungs, I heard something that didn't sit right.

Clear breath sounds on the right.

Nothing on the left.

Collapsed lung? Pneumothorax? Maybe. It was textbook. I opened a chest tube tray. Made the incision. Blunt dissection. Finger sweep. Inserted the tube. Secured it. It was perfect. No mistakes this time. I felt I had redeemed myself from the unnecessary QRF spin-up and the missed cricothyroid membrane.

I was so wrong. I remembered something the next day.

Something the instructors had drilled into us at Fort Bragg's Combat Medic Course.

If an endotracheal tube goes too deep, it'll likely pass into the right main bronchus. You'll only oxygenate one lung. No trauma. Just a placement error.

That's what I'd done. Gave him a chest tube… for nothing. I later remembered the rule: deep ET tubes favor the right bronchus—leaving the left silent. No trauma. Just error.

And I never forgot it.

That Afghan man lived.

He was medevaced to the Spanish-run hospital at Kandahar, treated, reconstructed, and returned home months later. I have a photo—of me standing next to him. He's missing teeth and disfigured but smiling.

Two scars on his throat.

The upper one is wide and jagged.

The lower one is clean and precise, corrected.

He never knew I made a mistake. Never fought me. Never once panicked. He just lay there and let me work.

And he lived.

Only Jim and I knew that I had made a mistake. But I learned and never repeated the error.

That day taught me more than any textbook ever could.

How long the neck gets when someone's dying.

How quiet the room gets when you're unsure.

How much trust can one man place in another—without saying a word?

The importance of accurate radio communication messages.

I was the baddest 18D in the village that day, but I had failed at 18E cross-training.

———

Chapter 8: The Soldier's Hands

Afghanistan, 2002. I was thirty-six years old.

Older than most. Young enough to move fast. Old enough to know the difference between duty and justification.

This wasn't my first war. But it was the first one that followed me home.

The UW hospital had once been a goat shed.

Stone walls, patched with plywood and canvas. Eventually, we hired local workers to repair the building. They replaced the roof, closed the holes in the walls, installed windows, widened the doorway to accommodate two men carrying a stretcher, and carved a solid wooden door. Supplies were stocked on wooden shelves. The small plastic drawers of our metal MES trunks were filled with sick-call medications and minor surgical kits. Gauze, IVs, trauma shears, dressings, and bandages were strategically positioned. Bleach wiped down every surface after every patient. The air always smelled like bleach, as the smells from the Afghan kitchen wafted through the window. We had decided to paint the building white with a huge Red Cross. Hopefully, even the worst-trained enemy would miss the brightly painted building with their Russian-made recoilless rockets.

I didn't wear scrubs, and our DCUs were becoming faded and thin. Sometimes I wore faded jeans and a grey T-shirt. A rifle slung across my chest. A Beretta on my hip in a pancake holster. My name wasn't stitched on a coat, but my hands saved lives every day.

Sometimes, I worked with conviction.

Other times—with calculation.

That's the part they never teach you in trauma lanes.

Two Afghan men walked in late one afternoon. Rough men. Hardened faces. The kind that didn't recoil when they bled. One held his hand to his chest, fingers swollen and discolored, a thin red line creeping toward the elbow.

The infection was bad. Another few days, and he'd be septic.

I smiled and motioned for him to sit on the wood bench outside the hand-carved wooden door. My translator whispered reassurances. I asked where he'd been and where he was going. Who he knew.

His friend answered for him—careful, polite.

I nodded, listening. But behind my smile, a mask of deceit, I was searching for intel.

I invited him inside and cleaned the wound with saline and betadine.

I injected Lidocaine, and his shoulders relaxed. A sigh of relief escaped his mouth.

I debrided the dead tissue. He didn't squirm, but his eyes tracked everything.

That was when I started to press.

Casually. Softly. Names. Roads. Towns. Faces.

He gave me pieces. He didn't know he was helping us. But he did.

And when I wrapped his hand and handed him antibiotics, I thanked him in Pashto. Smiled again. He returned the nod. His hand would heal.

And soon, he'd meet someone darker than me. Someone who'd take what I'd found and do what I couldn't.

The next morning, I was called to the LZ.

Two Chinooks thundered in low over the valley, their rotors chewing up dust, drowning out the call to prayer. I grabbed my aid bag and sprinted across the rocks.

When the rear ramp dropped, a team of bearded men ran out. Green Berets. Hard eyes. They had something between them—a boy, limp and soaked in blood.

Maybe sixteen. Maybe younger.

He wasn't screaming. He was drowning.

A chest wound. Through-and-through. Sucking sound with every shallow breath. Blood was pooling on his shirt. Bubbles at his lips.

I dropped beside him as the bird lifted off. My knees hit metal. I opened my bag.

Chest tube. Heimlich valve.

My hands moved fast—faster than I thought they could. I cut through his side. Pushed past the rib. Threaded the tube. Blood poured. Then hissed. Then cleared.

He gasped—sharp and ragged. His lungs filled.

He lived.

And as he stared up at me, I saw it:

Not hate.

Not fear.

Just confusion.

He didn't know who I was.

Didn't know why I'd saved him.

Didn't even know if he wanted to be saved.

When we landed, I climbed down, my jeans streaked with blood that wasn't mine.

The dust clung to me. The heat wrapped around my shoulders like a judgment.

I had saved a boy who might've tried to kill us the day before.

And I had manipulated a man with a wounded hand—used medicine as a lure for intelligence.

Was I the hero?

Or just efficient?

That night, I sat on my cot and stared at my hands.

Calloused. Steady. Familiar.

They'd packed wounds and pulled triggers. They'd held frightened children and interrogated tribal elders.

They were healer's hands.

And interrogator's hands.

And sometimes… executioner's hands.

I whispered a prayer I wasn't sure God still heard.

I thanked Him for the boy who lived.

For the man with the healing hand.

And for the silence that hadn't broken me—yet.

The next morning, I woke up and did it again.

Because that's what we do.

We build. We break. We bandage. We bury.

And we carry the weight.

With the same hands.

Chapter 9: Arachnophobia

There was a family of camel spiders living in the ammo bunker. Wind scorpions. Solpugids. Whatever name you gave them, they were fast, hairy, and too damn close. They're not venomous, can move up to 10 mph, and are actually good for eating small rodents and insects.

I thought I was a tough son of a bitch, but I did not like spiders. Especially large, hairy ones.

Having grown up in Australia, I was taught to be wary of dark, cool places. That's where the majority of deadly redback spiders live. I respect them so much that I have a tattoo of one between my shoulder blades.

When I was a teenager living in the hills of Woolloongabba, Australia, we had many encounters with huntsman spiders—big, brown, and hairy. You could hear them scurrying across ceilings and wood floors, pausing to pulse their abdomens like something out of a nightmare.

As a teenager, I was taught to hate spiders.

One morning, I was leaving for high school. I knew there were huntsmen in and around our apartment. I walked out the back door and had to pass through an overhang to reach the garden staircase and get to the bus stop. As I walked under the overhang, a mammoth huntsman spider jumped from the ceiling and landed on my head.

It felt like someone had dropped an entire hand on top of my skull. I could almost see brown legs hanging over my eyebrows. I ripped my sweater off and scrunched it into a ball. I stomped and kicked it as chills of arachnophobia ran down my spine.

Suddenly, the thing scurried out of my sweater—unharmed.

I'll never forget that day.

That's PTSD… not moral injury.

And if I was going to make it through the summer months in Orgun-E, I needed to stay out of the ammo bunker.

Sometimes, I loved being the medic.

Let them clear the bunkers. I'll stick to saving lives—and avoiding spiders.

Even the toughest Green Beret has something that makes his skin crawl. Mine just happened to have eight legs.

Chapter 10: The Boy from the Wrong Village

He was maybe fifteen. Thin. Quiet. Carried an AK like it weighed more than he did. Eyes too old for his age. He stood a little back from the other fighters in the Afghan militia company. He was assigned to another ODA, barely speaking, never smiling. That's what caught my attention.

He didn't act like the others. Didn't joke. Didn't posture. He avoided the older men. Ate alone. Kept his weapon clean but never slung it with pride. That rifle was a burden to him, not a badge.

I started watching more closely.

He wasn't from their village. That mattered here. These militia groups weren't armies. They were family clans with guns. If you weren't blood, you were a tool. Something to use.

After two weeks of observation—and quiet questions asked through our translator—I learned the boy had been assigned to his militia company by a local elder. No choice. No vote. No kinship. Just dropped into a unit of older men who viewed him as little more than property.

He was being abused.

Not in the way command would document, not in a way that made it into an incident report. But the signs were there. Isolation. Shame. Fear clung to him like smoke. And a quiet plea in his eyes every time he caught mine.

I brought it to our senior NCO.

"He wants out," I said. "Wants to be with fighters from his home village. He says he knows them. Trusts them."

That sparked a long silence. In Special Forces, you don't interfere with another man's Afghan company. Those relationships are sacred. Each Green Beret owns the trust, control, and chaos of their assigned militia. You don't cross that line lightly.

But this wasn't about turf. It was about a kid. A human being.

Our Team Sergeant listened. He thought about it. Told me, "If this blows back in our faces, you own it". I agreed and was thankful for his support.

Two weeks later, after quiet negotiations and a few cups of bitter tea, the boy was transferred.

The new company welcomed him like a stray dog that had returned to the pack. They were from his village—men who knew his name, who'd known his father. The boy's shoulders lowered. He started to smile. He trained harder. Ate with the group. He looked… like a kid again.

And that's when it happened.

One afternoon, as I came out of the clinic, three of the fighters from the boy's unit approached me.

They were grinning. Waving me over. Behind them, the boy stood, looking at the ground.

The fighter said something in Pashto that made the other men laugh. I didn't catch it. My translator frowned.

"He says they want to offer the boy to you," he said quietly. "As a gift. For what you did." I felt sick.

The boy wouldn't meet my eyes. Just stared at the dirt. His hands trembled at his sides.

I stepped forward. My voice didn't rise, but every syllable cut.

"No. Absolutely not. We don't do that. Not ever. Not here. Not in America. Not anywhere."

The laughter stopped. Eyes dropped. The air changed.

"You disrespect me," I said, staring at the fighter who made the offer. "You disrespect the boy. You disrespect every American here."

My interpreter translated. Word for word. The fighter's face shifted. Shame. Maybe. Or just the realization that he'd crossed a line.

He nodded. Mumbled something. They walked away.

The boy lingered.

He looked up at me. For just a second. And then he smiled. Small. Sad. Grateful.

I never saw him mistreated again.

But I still wonder.

Had I been played? Was the abuse real? Or was this some long game of manipulation for better status? Was the boy smarter than we thought, or just lucky to have someone notice?

It doesn't matter.

What matters is that sometimes, the only line between right and wrong is the one you draw yourself.

We weren't there to parent a culture. We were there to win a war. But you can't fight for freedom and ignore the people trapped in its absence.

And if doing the right thing cost me, influence cost me trust, cost me something I never even saw?

Whatever happens, happens.

That boy walked taller when he passed me after that.

Maybe that's all I needed.

Maybe that's all he needed.

And maybe—just maybe—we both came out a little cleaner.

Chapter 11: The Other Side of the Wire

From the northern wall of our compound, you could see the whole valley.

The jagged mountains bled into the horizon like broken teeth. Below, a muddy road wound through the terrain—carved not by machines but by generations of boots, hooves, and worn-out tires. To the east, clusters of white tents flapped in the wind. USAID issue—frayed, patched, housing two to four men in each, if they were lucky.

Between the tents, battered Hilux trucks idled like resting animals. Cracked windshields. Doors held shut with wire. Tires bald, engines rattling, patched together with duct tape, scrap metal, and sheer willpower.

They weren't just militia.

They were survivors.

Every morning, before the sun cleared the ridgeline, they formed a line—neat, single-file, just outside a small brick hut we'd converted into their chow hall. It hadn't always been that way. The first few weeks had been chaos. Shoving. Barked commands. Fights over portions.

But we'd taught them the system—our system.

Not for control.

For dignity.

An old man served the food. Face like cured leather. Fingers darkened from years of handling spice and fire. He stood behind a makeshift walk-up window, ladling out rice and goat into dented metal plates with practiced rhythm. Each man received one round of flatbread—two if the old man was in a good mood, which wasn't often.

The food wasn't much, but it smelled like home. Cumin, smoke, and oil. It stuck in your nostrils, in your sweat, in your gear. We smelled it when we worked out when we cleaned weapons, when we slept. And none of us minded.

They were paid through us—via OGA funding, processed in spreadsheets and signed off in pencil. We tried to make it fair. The warlords skimmed, of course. Always did. But we fought for transparency where we could. Fought for routine.

Because in a war built on betrayal, the routine became its own kind of loyalty.

Some of the companies had helped dig a well just outside the cement slab that served as the kitchen. No machines. Just hand tools, pickaxes, buckets, and backbreaking hours under the sun. They didn't complain. It gave them ownership. A stake. Something to call their own.

We taught them to line up single-file. To wait their turn. Not because we demanded discipline but because fairness was a kind of strength. They caught on quickly. Older fighters mentored younger ones. Teenagers learned to wait. Meals were carried back to the tents and shared—like a family dinner.

They didn't need to become us.

They just needed the tools to be a little better version of themselves.

And we gave them that.

Quietly. Respectfully.

Sanitation was another fight.

We tried to implement slit trench latrines—covered pits, ground level piping, drainage. Logical. Efficient.

Some units adapted. Others dug their own pits and burned the waste with diesel and tradition. Wrapped in burlap screens. The way their fathers had done. And their fathers before them.

You can't strong-arm tradition in a place like this.

You don't win trust by issuing orders.

You earn it.

By listening. By building. By sweating in the sun while holding the other end of the shovel.

That's what makes Special Forces different.

Over time, the other side of the wire started to feel less like a separate world—and more like an extension of our own.

Still chaotic. Still foreign. But organized chaos.

A patchwork village of dust, canvas, prayer mats, and pride. Fighters who might not understand us—but respected us. Not because we paid them. Not because we armed them.

Because we treated them like men.

And in war, that's rarer than innocence.

Chapter 12: Two Seconds to Decide

We were moving down a hard-packed dirt road—flat and exposed, with farmland stretching wide on either side. Patches of scrub, wire fences, and the occasional mud-walled compound slid past in a blur of dust and tension.

I was standing in the turret of the second Humvee in a four-vehicle Special Forces convoy. First tour, early in the war. We didn't know what the rules were yet because there weren't any.

My M9 rode tight in the drop-leg holster on my thigh, safety off. My M4 rested on its side on the roof below me, buttstock wedged between two protrusions bolted to the vehicle's frame. It couldn't roll off, but it could be grabbed and shouldered in one clean motion.

It was my go-to for targets past 25 meters.

But is anything closer? That was pistol range.

And in this war, the threats came close.

We passed dozens of vehicles a day. Nondescript Hilux trucks, sometimes packed with men. Most just moved over and kept driving. But I had developed a habit.

Every time a vehicle approached, I'd draw my 9mm and rest it against my chest—close to the body, low and ready. I could engage point-blank targets without needing to fumble for the M4.

I did that every day for a week. Hundreds of vehicles.

No threats.

No incident.

Until one day, it wasn't nothing.

A white Hilux came fast around the bend—mud-caked, packed with four men. One in the bed, standing.

We passed each other at speed. It was routine. But just as we did, the young man in the bed made direct eye contact with me—and mimed throwing a grenade.

He acted it out in slow motion. Pulled the invisible pin. Tossed it into the Humvee—right into our open door. No doors on our vehicles then. Just a gap wide enough for death to enter.

He even mimicked the explosion—mouth puffed, hands flared.

It was all a joke to him.

To me, it was a dry run.

We kept moving. Dust kicking up behind us. My heart pounding. I didn't say anything over the radio.

Could we have stopped? Sure.

Turned around? Interrogated him?

Maybe.

But what would we have done? Arrested a teenager for acting out a grenade toss?

We were moving too fast. And maybe—just maybe—I didn't want to admit how close it came.

A year later, almost the same thing happened again. Different convoy. Different Team.

Only this time, it wasn't a joke.

The grenade went in.

And then you're out of time.

———

I've thought about it a thousand times.

If that kid had thrown a real grenade into the cab, what would we have done?

The driver couldn't stop. Not fast enough.

The Truck Commander (TC) might have jumped out.

Maybe someone in the backseat would've scrambled to throw it out.

Maybe the gunner—me—would've just braced for the blast.

What would you have done?

———

Those are the moments that define your legacy.

He who leaps on the grenade is a hero.

He who leaps out and survives is a coward…

…or maybe just lucky.

Everyone else just braces for impact and hopes not to die.

———

That's why I believed—still believe—that turret gunners have to be fit. Agile. They have to be able to carry their own body weight and move as if their life depends on it.

Because it does.

You're exposed. First to see. First to be seen.

You need to be fast, balanced, and brutal.

I trained for that. I adjusted everything—kit, armor, body composition—for the role.

First tour: lean, fast, minimal load. I stripped down my gear to just what I needed. Body armor cut slim. Nothing on the front that would catch when diving into or out of the hatch. A chest rig only when clearing buildings. Everything tailored.

Second tour: we were muscle-bound animals. Thick wrists, swollen traps, grip strength like iron. Built for speed and violence in close quarters.

But mountain air at 9,000 feet doesn't care how much you bench. Lugging 260 pounds of meat and gear up a hill, teaches you that real strength is adaptive.

That's what made Special Forces different.

We weren't clones.

We weren't told what to wear or how to carry it.

We adjusted to the fight.

Autonomy wasn't a gift.

It was earned.

And so was that memory—burned into me.

A pretend grenade.

A smirk from the bed of a Hilux.

And the silence that followed.

We moved on.

But I never forgot.

Because sometimes it's not the moment itself that haunts you.

It's the two seconds you had…

To decide what kind of man you'd be.

Chapter 13: The Fat of the Land

The sun had just dipped behind the hills, setting the sky on fire with that strange orange haze that only seemed to happen in Afghanistan—dust, diesel fumes, and the last light of day blending into a smoky gold. We'd wrapped up a mission—nothing flashy, just a quiet win. The kind that doesn't make the reports but keeps your men alive.

I presented my Afghan company with a goat. No ceremony, no speech. Just a nod to say: You held the line. You earned this.

They took it like it meant something—and it did. A few hours later, I was invited to a meal.

I ducked through the doorway into a courtyard that stank of latrine runoff and woodsmoke. The smell of unwashed bodies mingled with tobacco, old canvas, and the earthy sweetness of boiled meat. We sat on a plastic tarp stretched over the cracked ground. A single bulb hung from a cord above us, powered by a battered car battery. It flickered every few seconds like it was unsure if it had the strength to keep going.

The stew was already cooking. A shallow metal pot balanced on three stones over a small fire. A boy fanned it with a flattened ammo box lid, sending up sparks and ash.

The oldest man in the group—gray in his beard, AK slung over one shoulder—handed me a tin bowl with both hands and a quiet smile. Inside was their best. Thick broth slick with yellow fat. Chunks of goat meat that were so soft they collapsed when I stirred. And floating on top—white strips of gristle, fat, and cartilage, like jellyfish washed ashore.

This was the honor piece. This was what they saved for guests. And I was the guest of honor.

I forced a smile, dipped the naan they handed me, and took a bite.

The flavor hit like a punch. Smoky, gamey, with a hint of dirt and the tang of whatever metal the pot had leached into the stew. The fat coated my mouth like grease under a vehicle—but it was warm, honest, and given without reserve. That made it sacred.

I looked up, and they were watching me. Eight men, squatting in a circle, some smoking hand-rolled cigarettes, others picking meat from bone with stained fingers. Their eyes were tired but kind.

One of the younger fighters leaned over and said in broken English, "You like? Is… best part. For friend."

I nodded. "Shukran. Very good."

He grinned and passed me another hunk of meat.

I ate the first bowl with dignity. I let the grease run down my throat without cringing. I swallowed the cartilage. I chewed the fat. My stomach began to hum like a generator on the edge of overload.

They offered seconds.

I touched my chest with my right hand and shook my head. "No. No more. It was perfect."

They didn't take offense. They laughed. One of them handed me a cigarette, lit it for me, and then leaned back on his elbows with the look of a man who'd done something good for someone he respected.

The night air carried the scent of boiled goat and sweat. Somewhere nearby, a donkey brayed. A baby cried. I could hear the soft splash of water at the latrine, maybe a hundred feet away. But in that circle, under that flickering bulb, with AKs resting beside cooking pots and men who had killed and nearly died for us, I felt something strange. Peace.

They asked for nothing. No favors. No extra money. No photos or recognition. Just a seat on the tarp, a bowl of stew, and the chance to show Americans what hospitality meant in their world.

They gave me the best of what they had. And they meant it.

That night, I went back to our compound and tried not to vomit.

But I never forgot what they gave me.

And I never threw it away.

Chapter 14: Close Enough to Kill

It was a dry day in eastern Afghanistan. A convoy operation.

Special Forces HMMWVs kicked up rooster tails across the hard-packed desert. Our ODA commander was on the horn with battalion headquarters. A Predator drone was up front, scanning the route like the eye of God—watching, tracking, confirming. No ambushes. Not today. Not if the feed stayed clean.

We were down two men.

Big Mark had taken a round through the wrist the week before. Solid guy. Sharpshooter. Medevac'd to Landstuhl, then stateside. We missed him.

Another teammate had just lost his wife to cancer. He tried to stay. Tried to work through it.

Our commander sent him home.

"There'll be plenty more war later." It was the right call.

Still broke the guy in half.

That's the part they don't tell you—

You bleed in this job even when the bullets miss you.

———

Intel said we had a high-value courier in a beat-up Toyota near a compound. The Predator tracked him for days. The battalion was hungry.

We moved tactically. The commander pulled into a depression—parked low, out of sight. I memorized his position. No mistakes.

My vehicle was designated assault. Big Mike was driving. I was manning the MK19.

Flat desert. Cracked brush. A crooked line of trees near the compound walls.

Then we saw it.

A rusted steel gate.

And a lone figure inside.

———

He wore white. Long tunic. Beard. Scarf. He stepped out like he didn't care we were there. Too casual.

Then—without warning—he broke into a sprint.

Straight toward the depression.

Toward our commander.

No uncertainty. No pause.

I grabbed my M4. Estimated 150 meters. Adjusted for pace. Looked through the optic.

My cheek welded to the stock.

Pop-pop-pop-pop-pop.

Five rounds. Fast. Controlled.

Two tore through his pants leg. Three kicked up dust near his heels.

He stopped cold. Arms raised. Frozen.

Then he looked down—at the holes in his clothes.

Like he hadn't realized how close death had come.

That's when Big Mike cracked over the headset.

"Drew, he's unarmed, man! No need to kill him! What the fuck are you doing?"

He wasn't wrong.

But neither was I.

I didn't see a civilian. I saw a sprinting silhouette closing in on our commander with too much speed and no context.

If he had a vest? A trigger?

It would've been over.

We cleared the compound.

No weapons. No radios. No Taliban.

Just villagers. Tired-eyed men with AKs worn smooth—not to fight us, but to protect their families from Taliban bleed-over.

Goats in the shade. Bread on stones. Smoke in the air. Children watching from windows.

The man in white had panicked.

Maybe he was trying to warn someone.

Maybe he was just in the wrong place, doing the wrong thing at the worst possible time.

But he was unarmed.

And I had almost killed him.

―――

The intel was wrong. But no one was careless. The intel officer had pressure on him—from the battalion, from higher. We all did. The truth is we were operating under a system that rewarded aggression. "Capture or kill" turned into just "kill." We weren't chasing justice. We were chasing certainty. And in war, certainty is always a lie.

―――

That night, I couldn't shake the image.

The holes in his pants. The way he stared down at them.

Like he'd seen God pass by and leave a calling card in the fabric.

If I'd pulled just a few inches higher…

He wouldn't have walked away.

But he did.

And for once, that mattered.

―――

Maybe he went home and held his kids tighter that night.

Maybe he cursed our names.

Maybe he whispered thanks to the sky.

I don't know.

But I do know this:

God kissed him on the ass that day.

And I didn't have to live with the guilt of killing a man who never raised a weapon.

Big Mike never brought it up again.

He understood. Maybe not in the moment, but later.

There was just a look between us—one of those quiet exchanges only men who've stared into the same fire can share.

He was calm when I wasn't.

Level when I was on edge.

He was the kind of man who could drive the lead vehicle, read the terrain, check on his Afghan Soldiers, and still chuckle when the mission got loud.

On 23 October 2012, Big Mike died of wounds received from a small arms fire in Wardak Province, Afghanistan.

He'd been promoted to Chief Warrant Officer 2, serving as an Assistant Detachment Commander.

Leading from the front—like he always did.

The news came down like a dull blade.

No scream. No ceremony.

Just silence that echoed like a gunshot inside my chest.

A Green Beret through and through—professional, humble, proud of the flag on his shoulder.

A genuine all-American.

I still hear his voice sometimes.

"Drew, he's unarmed, man. No need to kill him."

———

Years later, when I heard he'd been killed, I remembered that look.

And what he taught me—without ever meaning to:

You can be a killer and still be a good man.

You can do your job and still show restraint.

You can protect your brothers without pulling the trigger.

He was one of the good ones.

And so was the man I didn't even kill.

Chapter 15: The Clinic Chronicles

We called it an aid station, then an Unconventional Warfare hospital, but it was really a cement box. No running water. No sterile trays. No hospital hum of machines or fluorescent lights. Just a handful of stretchers, a stack of rolled Kerlix gauze bandages, and a few battered steel and plastic cases full of meds, tape, and the tools of a battlefield medic. That was our clinic in Afghanistan—just two medics, a stethoscope each, and the war.

And war brought patients.

Some were Soldiers. Some were civilians. Some were somewhere in between. We treated them all.

One afternoon, a local Afghan fighter limped into the aid station, grimacing with every step. His leg was swollen, red, and shiny—the classic angry bulge of an abscess high on his inner thigh. It was the kind of infection that couldn't wait. No antibiotics alone. No magic pill. This was "cold steel" medicine.

I numbed him as best I could—1% lidocaine, injected deep into the angry tissue. But with anaerobic bacteria and acidic pus, local anesthetic rarely works the way it should. I knew the pharmacology. I knew the failure rate. But I also knew he had no better options. He recoiled hard when the scalpel touched his skin.

I tried to distract him. Small talk. Reassurance.

Didn't work. He finally had to grit his teeth and took the pain.

The next day, he came back for repacking. I reached for my instruments—his breath caught in his throat. I offered him pain meds. Still no. Even a handful of Afghanis in cash didn't sway him. I was losing my chance to do it right.

Then I remembered a skin magazine tucked in a drawer. Not a dermatology medical journal—one of magazines for men. I held up a centerfold to distract him.

He winced.

Covered his eyes.

My translator chuckled awkwardly, then leaned in close. "Sir... he does not like women." I stared at him.

"He likes men."

I didn't miss a beat.

Flipped to the back ads—naked and muscle-bound men posing like gladiators. Standing proud with full erections. I held it up, and the patient smiled. He was absorbed. Oblivious. I irrigated and repacked the wound while he flipped pages like a man reading the Quran.

Was it orthodox? No.

Was it effective? Absolutely.

He healed clean.

I've used everything in that room to save a life—IVs, antibiotics, tourniquets, scalpels, humor, even soft porn. That's what medicine looks like in war. Creative. Immediate. Necessary.

―――――

Other stories blurred together. A 101st Airborne kid slammed his toe between an ATV and a wall. Dislocated. Purple and ballooned. I didn't have a manual. I just taped a loop of 550 cord to his toe, anchored it to the litter, and yanked. Hard. It popped back with a sickening click. I wrapped it, taped it, and told him he could walk by morning. And he did.

We had rules. Eventually. "No more surgical procedures in the field" said the battalion surgeon. One too many toenail removals that ended in infection and medevac. Medics like to cut. But sometimes, the best medicine is restraint. Antibiotics in the field, before scalpels. Always.

I made my mistakes. I missed a sinus infection once—thought it was dental. I learned. I never forgot. That's the beauty of solo medicine in combat. Every case is a test. You better pass.

I treated a child once—a toddler with sudden deafness. His mother carried him wrapped in a shawl. I checked his ears. Solid black wax—impacted. I mixed warm water with hydrogen peroxide and irrigated until a chunk the size of a pee rolled out into the plastic kidney basin. I continued with the other ear. Same round, black ball of wax.

The boy blinked. Then giggled. He could hear. His mother cried. I smiled and let them think I was a miracle worker.

A senior NCO came in once asking for pain meds. Lower back pain. He was fishing for narcotics—I didn't know better then. I pushed 5 mg of Valium intravenously. He went out cold. Snoring. I panicked. Reversed him with Flumazenil, just like we were taught. He came around instantly, wide awake but safe. I learned to go slower after that. It was a reminder: sometimes, the patient isn't the only one at risk.

I practiced on Afghans. Every day. Not out of cruelty—but necessity. Cricothyrotomies, chest tubes, external jugular IVs, packing gunshots, sutures. Every Afghan body I treated was another lesson that improved my skills. I learned everything I needed to keep Americans alive. Their trust was implicit. Their pain was endured. And I never forgot what it cost them.

I listened to hundreds of lungs. Checked hundreds of throats. Learned the feel of normal so well that the abnormal screamed out at me. No attending physician. No shadowing. Just me, a copy of the Special Operations Forces Medical Handbook, and the weight of every decision.

I treated heat casualties the right way—not just fluids, but cooling. Wet sheets with airflow. Spray-bottles of water. Concrete floors. I treated my own interpreter that way once—on the edge of heat stroke. Years later, he found me on Facebook. Sent me a long message. Said he thought he was going to die that day. That he would never see his mother again. That I had saved his life.

I told him it was simple medicine.

But he still tried to convince me that I had performed a miracle.

Because just maybe… it was.

This chapter isn't about heroics.

It's about the practice of presence. The daily rhythm of healing in a place built for killing.

Special Forces medics didn't win medals for these types of stories.

But we saved lives.

And every Afghan who walked out of my clinic, was one less body on a battlefield.

Sometimes, the job wasn't trauma.

Sometimes, it was humanity.

And every once in a while, in the middle of the blood and dust and screaming…

I got to be a doctor.

Even if only for a moment.

Moral Injury isn't just what you've done.

It's what you've learned to live without.

And for an SF medic, the hardest thing to live without… is the ability to save them all

Chapter 16: The Morning After

The sun was already up by the time I sat down on the edge of my cot.

But it didn't feel like morning.

It felt like after.

After the mission.

After the adrenaline.

After the noise.

The silence wasn't peace.

It was penance.

The air was still.

No talking. No shouting. Just the low hum of the generator outside and the muffled clatter of boots moving past on gravel.

My rifle leaned against the wall, still dusty from the valley.

The dust was always the last thing to leave—clinging to gear, to skin, to memory.

I peeled off my shirt and dropped it next to my vest.

The sweat had dried.

The smell of death hadn't.

I washed my hands in a plastic basin. Not because they were dirty—but because they still felt like they were holding him.

The detainee.

The one we took last night.

The one who wasn't the enemy.

The one whose name was close—but not close enough.

I dried my hands slowly. Then sat.

Stared at the wall.

Waited for something inside me to settle.

It didn't.

There's a kind of fatigue that doesn't touch your muscles.

It creeps deeper—behind your eyes, under your ribs, where the guilt waits.

Where the justifications curl up beside your convictions and start whispering questions you can't answer.

"We did everything right," I said inside my head.

No one answered.

Our commander came by, leaned in the doorway, and at first, said nothing.

He didn't need to.

He'd been there too.

He knew the look.

The way you couldn't quite make eye contact.

The way your fingers tapped the side of your thigh for no reason.

"You good?" he finally asked.

I nodded.

He didn't believe it.

But he left anyway.

Because there's no fix for this.

No medevac.

No morphine.

No field manual.

I sat for a while longer. Then I cleaned my rifle.

Not because it needed it.

Because I needed it.

The ritual.

The discipline.

The illusion of control.

I thought about the man we took.

Not the part where we zip-tied his wrists.

Not the part where we marched him to the gun truck or placed a hood over his head.

But the part where he looked at me and said nothing—because he didn't know what to say to someone who'd just turned his world upside down.

I tried not to picture his daughter.

Tried not to imagine the room we kicked open.

The blanket on the floor.

The spilled tea.

The child's scream, crying and silence afterwards.

Tried not to think of what she'd remember about Americans.

That's the cost.

It's not in body count.

Not in ammunition spent.

But in stories you'll never hear.

And dreams you'll never stop having.

I wanted to call my wife.

Just to hear her say my name.

Just to remember that there was still a world outside of this.

One that didn't smell like diesel and dust and moral compromise.

But there was no call.

No voice.

Just the generator. The gravel. The guilt.

And the weight of a morning that would never feel like enough.

Chapter 17: The Last Warning (Part I)

They rolled out quietly—two dusty, battle-worn Special Forces HMMWVs. No armor. No flash. Just strength, trust, and repetition. The kind of convoy that looked like every other.

But nothing in war is ever the same.

And nothing that night would be forgotten.

MSG Chuck Anderson, Team Sergeant.

SFC Pete Tycz, Senior Medic—the man who always found the bleed.

They had just finished a mission near the Pakistan border. Harsh terrain. Fluid loyalties. The kind of ground where maps fade, and history fights back. They were headed to Kandahar. Just a short hop. Refit. Reload. Reset.

We waved them out with tired hands. Nods. No fanfare. Just that quiet, familiar gesture between brothers—because you never know when it's the last.

The MC-130H Combat Talon II waited for them on an old Soviet strip near Bande Sardeh Dam. Just dirt and memory carved into high ground. No moon. Thin air. Fewer promises.

Chuck drove the cargo HMMWV with a trailer in tow. Pete followed in the gun truck. No trailer—just steel, a .50 cal, and the weight of months of war behind him.

The bird looked like a sanctuary. To Chad, it shimmered through NVGs like something holy. A few hours of flight. Back to Kandahar. A real bed. Hot chow. Just enough time to breathe.

As they loaded, Chuck gave final instructions. Pete had forgotten to clear the .50 cal.

"Want me to unload it?" Chuck shook his head.

"No. Just switch seats when we land." Two brothers. Two seats.

Two choices.

Then she came.

Staff Sgt. Anissa Shero. Air Force crew chief. Young, calm, steady. No theatrics. Just professionalism.

She walked the length of the bird. Checked Chuck's tie-downs. Stepped up to his window.

"It's gonna be a rough one. Strap in tight." He did.

She moved back to Pete. Said the same thing.

We don't know if he heard her. Or if he had time.

The ramp closed. Engines roared. Prop wash kicked dust into the sky.

They accelerated.

They lifted.

They cleared the edge of the runway.

Then silence.

No mayday.

No flare.

No call.

The aircraft broke apart in the air.

The tail section—where Pete sat—was torn free. Swallowed by fire and gravity.

The nose slammed into the earth seconds later. Steel and aluminum folded like cardboard. Cratered the Afghan landscape.

Chuck came to in the dark. Everything was burning. His hands were scorched. His chest shook. A teammate beside him—still strapped in, unmoving.

He looked left.

The fuselage was gone. Just air and wreckage.

He looked up.

Through a hole in the roof, he saw stars.

"Fuck. We crashed."

His voice cracked. But it was real.

He unbuckled. Reached for his Leatherman. Dropped it. Fumbled for it in the dark. Found it under the seat. Cut the belt. Dragged his teammate to the jagged opening and pulled them both onto the dirt.

Then turned back.

Looking for Pete.

But there was nothing left.

Pete didn't make it off the bird.

Neither did the tail crew.

But Chuck was alive.

And so were six others.

Burned. Bleeding. Breathing.

They moved together. Crawled into a ravine—200 meters from the wreck. No weapons. No radios. Just ash and instinct.

Chuck went back. Heard voices from the cockpit. Survivors.

He helped them out. One of the pilots was huge—250 pounds, easy. Flames behind them. Ordnance cooking off. Rounds popping. The night sky pulsing orange.

Chuck brought them together. Survivors in the dark.

Then flashlights.

Movement.

Chuck crouched. Knife in hand.

A figure came close. He lunged.

It wasn't the enemy.

It was Al Akers. B-team Operations Sergeant.

There to bring them home.

They weren't alone.

When the dust settled, Pete was gone.

Seven survived.

But what Chuck carried off that mountain couldn't be treated with medication or gauze.

Somewhere between the fire and the free-fall, he became something else.

Not just a survivor.

But a man who'd seen too much—and still chose to keep going.

Chapter 18: The Weight That Remains (Part II)

Morning rose like smoke.

Ash still hung in the air. The crater left by the MC-130H glowed faintly; its edges crumbled inward like the ribs of something that had once been alive. The wreckage had stopped burning, but it hissed in places. Steel twisted like bone. The smell—jet fuel, scorched nylon, melted aluminum—clung to everything.

Chuck stood at the edge of it all.

Still in his DCUs from the night before. Left hand wrapped in bandages. Burns minor, they said. Called him lucky.

But the real damage didn't show on the skin.

It settled deeper in the marrow.

Silent. Permanent.

He walked the perimeter alone. No cameras. No reporters.

there wasn't even a dog tag left to collect. Just the memory of unbuckling his seatbelt and realizing the entire rear of the aircraft was gone. Just the knowledge that Pete had been back there. That their crew chief had been standing between them.

When the dawn crested the hills, Chuck didn't speak.

Just nodded when they asked if he was okay.

That was enough.

He didn't talk about it after.

Not to his ODA. Not to the command.

Not even to the guys who fought beside him every day since.

But something in his eyes changed.

The gears still turned. The boots still moved. But something inside had rewired.

He didn't slow down. He sped up.

Took missions no one wanted.

Volunteered for every rotation.

Never said no.

Because if he wasn't out there—he wasn't anywhere. Not even home was a place of sanctuary. His guilt of surviving and the seat he chose, ate at him.

Air Force Staff Sergeant (SSgt) Crew Chief.

She was the voice that moved through the aircraft before the ramp closed.

Young. Calm. Steady.

She walked the length of that bird, eyes scanning every man, and gave them a simple warning:

"It's gonna be a rough one. Strap in tight."

She didn't shout. She didn't dramatize.

She just did her job—with the kind of composure that saves lives.

Chuck heard her. So did the man he pulled out.

Pete… we'll never know.

Her name was Anissa.

She didn't make it off the bird.

But her presence did.

No medal.

No headlines.

Just the quiet legacy of a professional who gave a warning that bought another man one more heartbeat.

Sometimes that's all it takes.

―――

At Pete's funeral, the protestors came.

Signs. Slogans. Rage.

They lined the road outside the chapel.

But so did we.

The Brotherhood showed up on Harleys—Green Beret Riders, North Carolina chapter.

Leather cuts. Chrome exhaust. American flags snapping in the wind. They parked shoulder to shoulder between the chapel and the mob.

No yelling.

No violence.

Just presence.

Just respect.

Inside, Pete's five daughters sat in white dresses:

Felicia (10), Faith (7), Tiffany (5), Samantha (3), Elizabeth (1).

They didn't understand why people shouted across the street.

They only knew their dad wasn't coming home.

Julie sat in the pew. Quiet. Crying behind sunglasses. Rage in her clenched jaw for the picket line.

Chuck was there, too.

But not fully.

Part of him had never left that airstrip.

He kept deploying.

Kept climbing the ranks.

Earned his Silver Star two-years later in a firefight, that no news channel reported on.

But that crash… it stayed.

Years later, a new generation of 18D medics opened their trauma bags and found something new:

A seatbelt cutter.

No directive.

No memo.

Just there.

That was Chuck's legacy.

Quiet. Unsung.

But it saved lives.

He never told the story for attention.

He told it so no one else would lose a brother that way.

That's moral injury.

Not what you did.

What you couldn't stop.

What you never forget.

What you survived, while others died.

Pete left behind his family.

Anissa left behind a daughter.

Chuck left behind the part of himself that once believed survival was enough.

And yet, for every seatbelt cutter that saved a life—Chuck never forgave himself for the one he couldn't reach.

And me?

I left Special Forces without ever fixing him.

I carry that, too.

This chapter is for them.

For Pete's five daughters, who grew up without a father.

For Tami, his wife, who kept going anyway.

For the crew chief, who did her job to the end—and for the daughter who will never know her mother.

For Chuck, who survived with nothing but scars.

For every man and woman on that plane.

And for the ones who never made it back.

Because the real war isn't the crash.

It's what comes after.

The silence.

The memories.

The weight.

And for those of us still walking—

We carry each other.

Always.

Chapter 19: Dreams of Home

This chapter is for all the wives.

And for the children who never knew why their fathers came home changed.

The night after the mission, I sat on my nylon cot.

The fluorescent lights above me flickered with a soft hum—steady, low like something barely hanging on. Outside, a generator grumbled. Boots moved across gravel. The war kept breathing, but in here, everything was still.

My hands rested on my thighs, stained with dust, oil, and something darker. My gloves were off. My rifle leaned against the wall beside me like a sleeping dog.

No movement. No radio calls.

Just the unbearable silence of surviving.

I hadn't spoken since we landed.

Not really.

Not about what we'd done.

Not about who we'd taken.

Not about what we'd seen in his eyes.

They called it a success.

They always do.

But success doesn't follow you home.

———

I closed my eyes.

And that's when the dream found me.

———

I was walking a wooded trail. Familiar. Pine needles underfoot. The air was thick with damp earth, tree bark, and a hint of perfume.

She was ahead of me, just around the bend.

Not calling. Just waiting.

Like she always had.

I rounded the corner and saw her.

Light summer dress. Barefoot. Wind in her hair. Her smile cracked open something in my chest I couldn't name.

She didn't speak.

She didn't need to.

Just seeing her was enough.

———

I stepped forward to reach for her.

And then—

He was there.

Not her.

Not the forest.

Just the man who'd taken her.

The man who replaced me when I was gone.

I shook the vision away.

Then he was replaced with another man.

Bound. Kneeling. Eyes locked with mine.

He didn't speak.

Just stared.

Asking a question I couldn't answer.

———

The forest turned to metal.

The scent became gun oil.

My boots were stuck in dried blood.

And my hands— Wet.
Smelling of iron.

———

I gasped awake.

Still in the tent.

Still alone.

But the ache in my chest stayed.

———

I wanted to punch something until my knuckles split.

Wanted to hear her voice again. Just once. Just to remember how it sounded when someone said my name without fear.

But there was no phone.

No going home.

Not yet.

Not for a long time.

I leaned back against my ruck and let my mind drift—not because I wanted to sleep, but because it was the only place I could still find her.

In my dreams, I was whole.

In my dreams, I wasn't the man who dragged another through the dirt after ending his family line. I wasn't the one who stayed silent during the debrief because the truth didn't fit the narrative.

In my dreams, I was just hers.

I remembered the smell of her shampoo. The way her fingers traced the edge of my jaw. The way she curled into me when the world was quiet.

I was lying in bed with her, laughing about nothing. Planning futures we'd never get to have.

Then, the dream would change.

Men I couldn't save.

Moans, I pretended not to hear.

Weight of my vest.

Heat of rotor wash.

Blood soaked through my uniform.

Her hand would slip from mine.

Her face would blur.

The dust would rise.

And I'd wake up again.

———

This chapter is for the ones waiting back home.

Because they saw the version that came back.

Not the one that got left behind.

———

They wondered why I stared at nothing for hours.

Why I wouldn't talk.

Why I flinched when the fire cracked.

Why did the music get turned down?

Why I checked the doors.

Why I seemed somewhere else.

Because I was.

I still am.

———

That's moral injury.

Not just guilt.

Not just numbness.

But the quiet grief for a version of yourself you know won't return.

I didn't stop loving her.

I just didn't know how to bring her into the world I now lived in.

So, I dream.

Because in the dream, I can still feel her arms.

In the dream, I can still be the man she remembers.

In the dream, I can be more than what the war left behind.

That dream is my sanctuary.

My reminder.

My escape.

And sometimes—after the dirt, the blood, the silence—it's the only place I still feel human.

Chapter 20: The Mistaken Family

Some scars don't bleed.

They ask questions you can't answer.

The CH-47E Chinook carved through the night, its twin rotors beating the air into submission. Inside, ten Green Berets rode shoulder-to-shoulder. Faces still. Weapons across armored chests. Muzzles down. Eyes forward.

Captain Evan Kincaid sat mid-row. Calm. Calculating. His knees bounced—not from nerves, but preparation.

Next to him, Staff Sgt. Torres adjusted the strap on his NVGs. Jaw tight. Chewing on something unsaid.

Across from them, the team's senior medic, Mitchell "Doc" Rios, did a final gear check. No wasted motion. Just the rhythm of experience.

They weren't new to this.

The target was high priority—flagged by national-level assets. A known facilitator. Moved fighters and cash across borders. Not a shooter. A ghost. Until now.

The plan was simple on paper: drop in, isolate, extract. Intel said three, maybe four men. The rural compound tucked into a finger valley where the rocks sloped like broken ribs, and every path felt like an ambush.

As the Chinook flared to land, dust rose in sheets. The ramp dropped. The team poured out—weapons up, formation locked.

The smell hit them immediately.

Kerosene. Burned trash. Human waste. Afghanistan.

Kincaid directed the ODA. Moving low and fast toward the village perimeter. NVGs painted the landscape in ghost green.

Up ahead: a flickering fire.

Three silhouettes.

Two men.

One smaller figure.

They fanned out. Took positions. Laser dots hovered. No chatter. Just breath. Just the weight of what was coming.

"Execute," Kincaid said.

Suppressors snapped.

Bodies dropped.

One man reached for a rifle—too slow. The second dove for cover—never made it.

The smaller figure ran.

Not a child.

Barely a man.

Early twenties. Black vest. AK slung. But in that moment—unarmed.

Torres tackled him. Drove him into the dirt.

He kicked. Fought. Eyes wide. Not trained. Just terrified.

Rios moved in. Rifle at low ready.

"Clear," Kincaid called. "Secure. Search."

Flex cuffs. Rough hands. Dragged to the center of the compound.

The young man's chest heaved. Blood and dirt streaked his face—not his own.

"What's your name?" Rios asked.

Nothing.

The interpreter tried. Pashto. Dari.

Still nothing. Just vacant eyes. Like the world had cracked and swallowed him.

Torres looked down.

"He's not the HVT," he said.

Kincaid frowned. "What?"

"The old man said—before he bled out—the real target left two days ago."

Rios stood still.

Looking at the man.

He wasn't a fighter.

Not yet.

But now?

Maybe.

They'd killed his father. His brother.

Wrong house. Wrong bloodline. Wrong war.

———

Back at the HLZ, the Chinook returned.

Ramp opened. Blades cutting through the chill of night.

They loaded the detainee without words.

Just another body. Just another mistake.

Kincaid stared out the back. The valley faded. No reprimands. No apologies.

The operation was labeled "clean."

Rios didn't speak.

He just sat. Hands on knees. Boots dusty.

But inside, he felt it.

They hadn't won.

They'd handed the enemy a story.

They'd built a fighter with their silence.

And there was no debrief for that.

Moral Injury

Moral injury isn't always pulling a trigger.

Sometimes, it's what happens after.

When you see a man's face and know you chained him to a mistake he didn't make.

Rios shrugged it off. Packaged it away. Placed it in the depths of his mind.

But that face—that dust-covered, wide-eyed silence—would come back.

In the stillness.

In the dark.

The war gives you orders.

But it never tells you what to do with the pieces afterward.

And you never really learn where those pieces go.

Chapter 21: The Making of a Ghost

Seven years had passed since the Americans came in the night.

Since they killed his father.

His brother.

Dragged him off in flex cuffs like a dog.

Since boots crushed the fire.

Since rotors kicked dust into his mouth.

Since the eyes behind those night vision lenses never saw him— Just a body to bind.
Just a war to win.

His name had once been Rahman.

Now they called him Shab Rooh—The Night Ghost.

———

He didn't wear sandals anymore.

Didn't feed goats on a hillside.

Now, he moved in silence.

Carried an M4A1 stripped from a dead ANA soldier.

He'd learned English in prison. Learned radio calls from listening to stolen comms. Learned their cadence. Their doctrine.

He could walk into a compound and disappear before anyone smelled smoke.

The village he once called home was gone—leveled in an airstrike two winters ago.

The Americans said it was a Taliban stronghold.

It had been.

After they made it one.

———

Rahman had never fired a rifle until they zip-tied his wrists for a crime he didn't commit.

He had never hated the flag until the boots walked past his brother's body without looking down.

They made him.

And now he made others.

———

The ridge was quiet tonight.

He crouched in the rocks, watching through borrowed NVGs—passed down fighter to fighter. Taken in an ambush. Scavenged from the dead.

Below, a convoy crept through the valley.

American Special Forces.

He knew the type. He'd studied their routes. Their habits. Their discipline. Their arrogance. And their cruelty.

They liked to move low.

Riverbeds. Shadows. Believing the terrain protected them.

He had once believed they were gods.

Now he knew better.

Now, he hunted them.

Beside him, a teenage boy loaded an RPG. Hands shaking. First mission. Still half a child.

"Not yet," Rahman whispered.

The trucks passed below.

Five HMMWVs. Each bristling with firepower.

7.62. 5.56. .50 caliber. 40mm. 84mm. 60mm.

He knew them all.

He'd seen them kill.

He'd buried their damage.

And he let them go.

Not because he couldn't.

But because tonight wasn't about death.

It was about control.

———

Back at the safe-house, Rahman knelt before his fighters.

They called him commander, but he never raised his voice.

He unrolled a torn map.

Drew arcs with charcoal.

Taught them about wind.

Noise discipline.

The art of restraint.

One boy—maybe sixteen—asked why they hadn't fired.

Rahman looked at him.

"Because war isn't just about killing," he said. "It's about knowing when not to."

The room went still.

Somewhere in Rahman's chest, a splinter of the boy he used to be still burned.

The one who screamed when his father bled into the dirt.

The one shoved into a helicopter.

The one forgotten.

That boy still asked questions in the dark.

Still saw the gloved American hand that pushed him down—calm, professional, unseeing.

That boy hadn't been born a killer.

He was forged.

Moral Injury (From the Other Side)

The enemy is never just the enemy.

He's someone's brother.

Someone's son.

Someone who might've built instead of destroyed.

Until war whispered otherwise.

Until a rifle spoke louder than mercy.

Until restraint was left behind.

What we do in war doesn't end when the mission ends.

It ripples.

It echoes.

It creates ghosts.

And sometimes, if you listen closely—

They're not just haunting us.

They're haunting themselves.

Chapter 22: The Hunt for Truth

The mission was clean.

Satellite confirmation. Intel stack from two agencies. Target verified. Coordinates memorized.

But we knew better.

We'd been in-country too long seen too much, to believe in clean missions.

This was Afghanistan.

And the truth always came dirty.

The CH-47F dropped us into a high mountain basin just after midnight. The air was razor-thin and sharp. Snow traced the ridgelines. Moonlight bounced off the rock like a bone under the skin.

Inside the bird, no one spoke. Just gear checks. Quiet nods. The door gunners manned their Miniguns—M134s. Six-barrel, belt-fed 7.62mm dealers of death.

They scanned the blackness, itching to fire.

But there was nothing to see.

Just night.

Just fate, moving closer.

We were after a man. Mid-level facilitator. Not a shooter but accused of feeding GPS grids and troop movements to the other side.

Americans died.

That was enough.

We didn't know if it was true.

Only that his name was on the list.

Our boots hit the dirt with a hiss of hydraulics and a roar of dust. The bird lifted and vanished. We moved out.

Eight-man team. Split team operations. NVGs down. Hearts steady.

Big Mark had point with Hector. Luke and George covered the rear.

The terrain was rough. Incline steep. Every breath burned.

We reached the compound in under an hour.

Stone walls. A heavy wooden door. No guards. No visible weapons.

Just one light inside.

We breached quiet. No flash. No noise.

Just entry.

Rifles up. Corners cleared.

A man stood in the center. Barefoot. Unarmed.

Not surprised. Not afraid.

Just waiting.

He didn't resist.

Didn't speak.

Just knelt. Hands raised.

———

I wanted to see a monster.

Someone who'd traded coordinates for blood.

But I saw a man in his late thirties.

Tired. Thin. Eyes dulled by too many winters.

He said something in Dari.

The interpreter translated:

"If you came for me, take me. But the others here… they are just my family."

———

We swept the house.

No weapons.

No radios.

No resistance.

Just a woman in the back—his sister.

Two elderly parents.

A toddler asleep beneath a blanket.

Hector stared at the child like it had claws.

———

Big Mark and Big Mike lifted the man to his feet.

He didn't flinch.

Didn't ask why.

Didn't ask where.

———

On the walk back to the HLZ, he stumbled.

Jim caught his elbow.

The man looked up and said, in English:

"I tried to help both sides. But there is no middle anymore." Nobody responded.
Because there wasn't.

———

On the bird, I sat across from him.

Our knees almost touched.

My rifle muzzle rested on the floor.

His wrists were zip-tied.

He didn't look like a terrorist.

He looked like a man hunted by both sides.

———

Back at Bagram, he was processed.

Intelligence teams. Language specialists. The full machine.

I never saw him again.

Two weeks later, we got word: wrong man.

Same village. Same family name. Bad intel.

He'd been neutral.

Maybe even helpful.

He was just in the way.

———

No apology.

No correction.

Just a new target package.

Another name.

Another face.

———

That night, I sat alone.

I looked at my hands.

They were clean.

No blood.

No bruises.

Just clean.

But I didn't feel clean.

———

That's moral injury.

Not the kill.

Not the mission.

The knowing.

That you did everything right.

And it still wasn't enough.

Chapter 23: A Line in the Dust

We swung the militia companies into extended lines just after sunrise. It looked like a war film.

Nearly a hundred Afghan fighters staggered and spread wide—some crouched low behind dirt mounds, others prone in the open. Scarves tight around sunburned faces. Dust-covered rifles clutched like lifelines.

Each company fanned out like spokes on a wheel, with our ODA positioned dead center—the hub of the chaos.

We'd responded to rocket fire before. But this time… something felt off.

George checked his sidearm and nodded. Nothing said. Nothing needed.

He was calm in that way only men who've buried friends and finished missions can be.

The MK-19 had an accidental discharge earlier. An overeager Private climbed into the GMV and stood behind the crew-served weapon. He racked the handles; unaware it was already loaded. When the ejected round hit the floor, he panicked and fed another into the chamber. He pulled the triggers, thinking he needed to cycle the system.

The 40mm HEDP launched into a dry creek bed behind us. It struck soft sand and exploded. Nobody hurt—but it could've been bad.

I didn't blame him. He was reacting. Trying to protect us the only way he knew how.

The failure was mine.

I hadn't briefed him.

His NCO jumped in immediately.

Dropped him for pushups right there in the dirt.

Not to shame. To correct.

It wasn't punishment.

It was protection.

A good NCO knows when discipline isn't about forms—it's about forming the man. Quiet correction in front of the right people, handled with calm authority.

That's leadership.

We cleared the area inch by inch.

Two rockets still smoldered near the ridge—aluminum tubes balanced on stones. Scorched dirt beneath them. Fuse wires curling out like snakes.

Our engineers moved like surgeons. Quiet. Focused. Mapping ignition trails. Measuring arc and angle. Documenting the scene with the precision of crime scene techs.

Snipers held overwatch. Steady. Motionless. One covered our six, exhaling slower than the wind.

The rockets were crude—107mm, Soviet or Chinese surplus. Aluminum tubes. Homemade launchers and triggers. Some used fuses. Others used alarm clocks. Old technology, but still deadly.

The crew that launched them was gone.

But the signature was familiar.

We recognized the setup. The spacing. The arc.

An enemy squad or 2-3 men. Same crew who had done this before. Probably, locals paid in poppy. Or foreign fighters slipping across the border—trained just enough to kill and vanish before ISR could get eyes on them.

An Afghan commander walked beside me. Rifle slung. Maybe thirty-five looked fifty. Rope hands. Deep eyes.

He pointed toward the defile.

"We have seen them before," he said.

"You think they'll come back?" I asked.

He shrugged. "If not today… then tomorrow. They never stop."

I looked down the line.

Our Afghan fighters waited. Some smoked. Some fiddled with their rifles. Others watched the horizon like they expected it to open and swallow them.

Maybe it would.

These weren't just militia.

They had families behind them.

Ghosts beside them.

And they were ours.

———

We were responsible for their lives. That didn't end when the shooting stopped.

If one of them died, we found the family. We made it right.

It's not out of policy.

Out of respect.

That was Green Beret ethics.

Some of us built real bonds with these men. Not through shared words—but through shared danger.

They knew who stood beside them when it counted.

And that mattered.

———

There was a Green Beret—different ODA, different battalion—kneeling beside his Afghan sergeant after an ambush. The man was dying. Shot through the chest.

He held him until he was gone.

Spoke words he likely didn't understand.

When he got back to the firebase, he didn't eat. Didn't speak.

He wrote a letter.

Had it translated.

Delivered. With aid. With presence. With dignity.

That's what doing the right thing looks like.

Out here, every act of dignity was a shot fired against chaos.

The rockets didn't hit anyone that morning.

But they reminded us of something deeper:

This war wasn't just about firepower.

It was about people.

On both sides of the wire.

Whether they wore a Green Beret or a tattered scarf—if they stood beside us, we led them.

We trained them.

We carried them when we had to.

And when we couldn't bring them home— We remembered those they left behind.
We made sure someone showed up.

With respect.

With compensation.

With humanity.

That was the line we drew in the dust.

And we held it.

Chapter 24: Smelling Like Roses in Orgun-E

When we first got to Orgun-E, the camp wasn't set up.

No showers. No lights. No plumbing. Just hard dirt, wind, and the smell of diesel and sweat-soaked into every uniform. Only one main building with crumbling walls. Covered windows and a plywood door. A piece of 550 cord was tied to a liter water bottle threaded through a hole in the doorframe—its weight ensured the door closed.

We were still trying to bond with our local militia and interpreters—not too close, but not too cold either. We had to live with them, but we were also the officers, the Americans, the ones behind the wire.

So, you adapt.

Before we left Bragg, I'd asked around—what should I bring for creature comforts? Jim, one of the seasoned team medics, gave it to me straight:

"Get a battery-powered camp shower. Takes four D-batteries and a bucket. It'll change your life." He wasn't lying.

We had water. That wasn't the problem.

We'd dragged a water buffalo halfway across Afghanistan. The water wasn't for drinking; it was for washing. A local water truck kept it topped off.

But for hot water? We got creative.

We hired a villager to run homemade drum heaters—wood-fed, chimney-rigged beasts that could scald your skin. He and the Afghan cook's son kept the fires burning from sunrise into the night. The trick was dropping in a small bucket of cold water to cool it just enough not to melt your skin.

We bought truckloads of dried wood, hauled in from as far as a hundred miles away. Then hand-cut by the villager and the cook's son.

Seven drums. Always running.

Scoop out a bucket of hot water. Walk it to the pallet-and-burlap stall. Drop in the pump.

Boom. One five-gallon shower—straight to the soul.

Pure heaven.

Especially after wearing the same DCUs for a week, pores clogged with dust, sweat, and gun oil.

Around that time, one of my translators handed me a gift—a white Afghan robe, hand-stitched by his wife. The embroidery was delicate: blue and green threads woven into geometric patterns common to her tribe. It had taken her weeks. A gesture of immense respect in their culture.

I was floored. Humbled. In Pashtun tradition, such a gift wasn't casual—it was a statement of trust, even friendship.

But he also had a request. He wanted more freedom to interpret rather than translate. "Too many words," he explained. "It's better if I tell you what he means—not every single thing he says." He wasn't wrong. In the early months, many of our interpreters spoke only broken English. Misunderstandings were common—and dangerous. But now, some were fluent. Reliable. Trusted even in key leader engagements and tribal negotiations.

Still, I couldn't accept the robe as a one-way gift. It needed to be a trade—respect for respect. I told him I would send for something for his wife, from the United States.

He agreed.

And in that exchange, we both gained something that mattered more than translation—mutual understanding.

During a rare satellite call home, I told my wife. She offered to send a care package for the woman—small luxuries, something personal.

I agreed.

Then forgot.

Weeks later, mail arrived.

Packages were gold—jerky, socks, candy, letters, maybe a paperback.

Mine had the usual treasure… and something unexpected:

Two floral-scented soaps and a bottle of rose-scented lotion.

At first, I was confused.

Then I figured Julie must've sent them for me— as hygiene supplies.

So, I brought them back to my bunk. Plywood bed frame. Two-by fours. Photos of home tacked to a plywood shelf. No curtains. No carpet. But a shrine of the life I missed.

I stashed the soap and lotion with my hygiene kit and didn't think twice.

They were sealed and lay there, gathering dust.

Waiting for me; like a woman for her man.

A few nights later, after a long patrol, I needed a real scrub-down—one of those reset-the-soul showers.

I filled a bucket with hot water and cooled it down.

Then I walked through the dust in pitch darkness. Shower shoes were just a pair of Teva sandals.

The night air was crisp. A soft breeze blew, and across the wire came the low murmur of our Afghan counterparts.

I carried a small hand towel—that was it. No toweling off in the dark.

At the screened stall, I stripped down and stepped into the mud left behind by the last few Soldiers.

My eyes adjusted. I found the wood pallet and stepped up.

I placed the bucket down and dropped in the little electric pump.

I wet myself lightly to conserve the hot water, then lathered up.

Face first, then downward—saving the most pungent areas for last.

That's when I noticed it. The soap.

Strong.

Floral. Sweet. Like walking through the perfume aisle of a department store.

But out there, under the stars, in a blacked-out camp, it felt amazing.

I turned the pump back on and rinsed with warm water.

Soap suds pooled on the pallet and spilled into the Afghan dirt.

I let the water run until the bucket went dry.

Still dripping wet, I remembered something I'd once heard, body lotion traps moisture in the skin.

So, I smeared it on—face, arms, neck—anywhere the sun had touched.

By then, I didn't notice the scent.

Just the feeling of clean skin.

Until I walked back into the team house.

The scent hit them instantly.

Heads turned.

Someone muttered, "What the hell…?"

I walked in glowing—like I'd just stepped out of a flower shop. "Got a hot date, Doc?"

"You borrow soap from the terp's wife?"

"Damn, you smell like a funeral parlor!" I shrugged.
"Hey. My wife sent it. I'm gonna use it." And
I meant it.
Julie had four kids at home. Holding it all together.

If she sent something—even rose lotion—I was going to honor that.

What I didn't know…. It wasn't for me.

Weeks later, during another call home, Julie asked:

"Did you ever give that soap and lotion to the interpreter's wife?"

I froze. "…Wait. That was for her?"

"Of course it was."

I laughed. Told her the story.

She laughed too—after a pause.

"Well, at least you enjoyed it."

Later, I grabbed the unused soap and the lotion. Wiped them down. Made them look new. Handed them to the interpreter. Told him the story.

He laughed so hard he almost cried.

Gave everything to his wife, with pride.

I never touched the second bar again.

That's life behind the wire.

Sometimes, you build a UW hospital out of a goat shed.

Sometimes, you treat trauma in the dirt.

And sometimes you walk into a Special Forces hut smelling like roses…

Because your wife loves you enough to send something beautiful into war.

And you're just dumb enough to think it's for you.

Chapter 25: The Morality of the Hunt

The Afghan sun rose like a blade—golden, merciless, cutting through the dust that clung to everything. A stillness hung over the terrain, but it wasn't peace. It was the breath held before something irreversible.

Inside the SF compound, the base stirred awake. Coffee brewed. Weapons cleaned. Radio batteries swapped out. Routine.

But Mark and I weren't staying.

We rolled out early. Just the two of us. Quiet. Intentional.

A tan Toyota truck—civilian specs. Nothing screamed "military." That was the point. Clean. Untraceable. No markings. No armor.

No convoy.

No air support.

No QRF.

Only the ODA knew where we were going.

We were hunting.

Intel said a mid-level Taliban facilitator was in the area. Respected. Known. But this time, he wasn't delivering weapons or fighters.

He was searching for medicine.

That detail lodged in my throat like shrapnel.

Checked the commo ruck, water, MREs, fuel, ammunition.

We mounted up, closed the doors and lowered the windows.

Mark drove. I watched the horizon.

My M4 rested across my lap, its flash suppressor angled through the open window. Dust sucked in around the barrel. Didn't matter. I wanted it ready. My thumb hovered over the selector switch.

We crept past mud-brick homes. Children played in the dirt—too used to war to care about two men in a truck.

The world felt thin. Brittle. Like everything might snap.

We kept climbing.

Into the hills.

Where we could see without being seen.

We waited.

No chatter.

Radio silent.

The quiet of the hillside made listening easy.

We sat there for a few hours. Patient, calm, eyes scanning.

Then—dust appeared on the road below.

A white Toyota sedan. Kicking up dirt in its wake.

Alone. Moving at a high rate of speed. Not for comfort—for purpose.

Mark tracked it through binoculars.

No visible weapons, four men inside, dust caked, windows up.

But the pattern was there.

The energy of someone avoiding pursuit.

The sedan entered town and disappeared behind buildings and narrow streets.

Ten minutes later, it was back.

"That's him," Mark said.

We didn't buckle up, just adjusted our body posture.

―――――

Mark drove hard. Dirt. Rock. Wheels bounced over terrain, not meant for trucks.

No permission required.

No coordination needed.

We just chased.

We hit the gravel road hard. Looked up and saw the vanishing dust from the white sedan.

Mark pressed down on the accelerator pedal. The engine screamed and the automatic transmission down shifted, slammed into gear.

The speedometer hit ninety miles per hour.

The odometer scrolled slowly…… Ten miles.

Well beyond the wire and into hostile territory.

We finally overtook them. Dust and rocks spraying from all four tires.

Then Mark yanked the wheel—side-drifted into their path.

We stopped in a cloud of dust.

The sedan skidded.

Stopped.

I was out before the truck settled. Rifle up. Heart steady.

Mark flanked right. Stood just outside my direct line of sight. Pistol low. Eyes cold.

Four men sat inside.

Well-dressed. Beards trimmed. No weapons in sight. Hands up.

I signaled them out of the car. The driver remained seated.

Our translator stepped from the back seat.

Young. Loyal. Sharp.

He looked at them.

Eyes wide.

Then spoke in Pashto.

I waited.

"I know them," he said. "They are good people." My rifle didn't lower.
"They're getting medicine. For his child. The boy is sick."

I looked at the man in the driver's seat.

He didn't look scared.

He looked exhausted.

Like a father who'd driven through fire to save his son.

I thought of my daughters.

Of what I'd do.

Of what I wouldn't stop to consider.

But I wanted to kill them.

God, I wanted to kill them so bad.

They were Taliban.

Or had been.

Or would be again?

I'd buried too many friends to keep offering grace to men who walked that line.

Mark looked at me.

"What do you think?" One nod.

That's all it would take.

Two rounds to the chest. One to the head.

Clean. Legal.

No one would ask questions.

No one would lose sleep—except maybe me.

Was Mark testing me?

Was he asking for loyalty—or conscience?

I didn't nod.

I didn't lower my rifle.

―――

I told our young translator:

"Tell them to go." The men bowed.

Grateful. Relieved. Maybe both.

They climbed back into the sedan.

Drove into the dust.

Medicine in hand.

Child waiting.

―――

We stood in silence.

Dust settling.

Sun climbing.

Mark exhaled.

"You just made our translator a king."

Out here, being listened to—being trusted—was power. It wasn't just respect. It was protection.

He was right.

The man vouched.

We listened.

That meant everything.

We'd played the long game.

We let them go.

But inside, I still saw my finger on the trigger.

Still pictured four bodies slumped in silence.

Still heard the rifle echo that never came.

That's the true cost of the hunt:

Not just the decision you made— But whether it was right or wrong. And living with it either way.

Years later, I still see their faces.

Still wonder if I spared a father… Or let a killer go free.
No award covers that moment.

No after-action captures the weight.

No chaplain prepares you for what mercy costs.

Because the real burden isn't the rifle.

It's what you didn't kill—and why you didn't kill it.

Or what you did kill… when you didn't have to.

That's the morality of the hunt:

Not just the decision you made— but whether it was ethical and justified.
Regardless, you own it for your lifetime.

Chapter 26: The Things You See in the Dark

The drive back to our forward operating base was quiet.

The kind of quiet that follows a clean mission—no gunfire, no casualties, no questions that gnaw at your conscience. We'd made the right call. Or at least, we hadn't made the wrong one.

That was enough.

The Toyota truck rolled steadily over the dirt road, headlights cutting through the dust. No NVGs. No IR strobes. Just us—two Americans dressed like locals in a dusty civilian truck that looked like a thousand others.

We blended in. That was the point.

Dust clung to everything—our rifles, our skin, even the sweat in the creases of our hands had turned to grit. But we didn't care. We were tired, and the silence between us wasn't awkward.

It was earned.

Mark drove, one hand on the wheel, the other resting loosely on his thigh. His pistol was tucked in tight beside him, untouched. I sat with my M4 across my lap, muzzle on the windowsill, staring into the dark fields as we passed.

Here and there, a flicker of movement and light—shadows behind a wall, a donkey braying from somewhere in the trees.

Villagers. Fathers. Families.

Maybe not.

But not tonight.

Tonight, no one wanted to die.

———

The outer gate appeared up ahead. Two Afghan militia guards stood beside the Hesco barriers. Scarves wrapped tight around their faces, AKs slung low across their backs. One was smoking a cigarette so cheap you could smell it from twenty feet away.

They waved us through without looking up.

classic.

———

We entered the staggered barrier lane—a zigzag pattern of HESCOs meant to stop a VBIED from making a straight run. Our headlights bounced off the sandbags and wire, cutting long shadows.

I leaned back, felt the weight of my armor press into my spine, and exhaled.

Almost there.

———

Then our headlights swept right.

And there they were.

———

Two Afghan militia guards were just outside the main gate.

One bent forward, pants around his ankles.

The other behind him, mid-thrust.

Both caught in the glare of our lights like deer frozen in the absurd.

The standing one looked straight at us… and smiled.

And waved.

———

For a second, I thought maybe I was hallucinating. Sleep deprivation does that. Maybe I was just seeing shadows. Maybe it was a joke.

Then I looked over.

Mark was already grinning.

"You probably saw what you think you saw," he said, laughing. "Don't dwell on it… or it's gonna haunt you forever."

———

I chuckled, more from disbelief than humor.

This was Afghanistan.

This was Special Forces.

———

We rolled through the steel gates and into the FOB. Quiet again. Familiar. Our world, wrapped in concrete and steel and unspoken codes of behavior.

But out there?

Out there, it was theirs.

———

And that was one of the first things you learned in this war:

You don't get to judge.

Not if you want to survive.

Not if you want to get the mission done.

We weren't here to police morality.

We weren't here to fix their culture.

We were here to fight.

To live.

To go home.

What they did in the shadows was their business—so long as it didn't interfere with ours.

Still, I knew some of those men would end up in my clinic one day. Skin infections. Heat exhaustion. Or worse; gunshot wounds, blast injuries.

And a small part of me hoped—really hoped—I wouldn't remember which ones.

Because some things?

Some things are simply better left in the dark.

Chapter 27: The Standoff

We rolled out heavy that morning.

This wasn't a "hearts and minds" mission. It wasn't a medical capacity building (MEDCAP), or a key leader engagement. This was combat operations.

Company-level mission—five ODAs, support elements, and over twenty vehicles in the convoy. The trucks were like Scorpions, purpose-built and packed to the teeth. The kind of vehicles that told people we're not here to ask twice.

Each gun truck was armed like a mobile fortress:

- •A swing-arm M240B, belt-fed 7.62mm, barrel glinting in the sun, ready to lay down suppressive fire from the truck commander's side.

- •A .50 cal or MK19 automatic grenade launcher on top—linked and ready.

- •Squad Automatic Weapons (SAWs) mounted in the rear corner of the bed or behind the turret gunner.

- •M4s beside every man or strapped across his chest.

- •AT-4s racked beside the turret—just in case we needed to punch through a wall or a vehicle.

Each vehicle had a rhythm. Each gunner has a muscle memory. We weren't uniform—but we were unified. That's what made it work.

The enemy called us Scorpions.

They heard it over radio intercepts—descriptions of convoys that moved fast, struck hard, and disappeared. They said we stung from every direction. That when one truck got hit, the rest erupted like a firestorm.

The name stuck.

I was in the turret, manning the MK19.

The MK19 is a beast.

40mm, belt-fed, air-cooled.

It fires high-explosive grenades at 325 rounds per minute.

Maximum effective range to kill point targets, within a 5-meter circle, is 1500 meters.

Every trigger squeeze sends a high arc of chaos out to 2,200 meters.

Each round explodes on impact, shattering everything in a 15-meter radius

Effective. Ruthless. Unforgiving.

You feel like a god behind that gun.

But gods don't get second chances.

Dave was our truck commander—our 18F. One of the sharpest men I've known. He rode like he fought—calm, calculating, with a cigar wedged between his teeth. Sometimes lit. Sometimes not. Just something to bite down on when the world got too loud.

His right hand rested on the butt of an M240B beside him—muzzle skyward, safety on. That gun was the surgeon's scalpel. Mine was Thor's hammer.

We were in the trail end of the formation. Pushing wide, toward the far-right of the objective.

It was a classic SF operation:

Cordon. Search. Finish.

———

Then we saw them.

Two white Toyota Hilux trucks.

Classic Afghan militia—rear beds stacked with men and mismatched gear. AKs, RPGs, chest rigs of Chinese knockoff webbing. No attempt to hide. No attempt to look casual.

They pulled up alongside us, waving like it was a social call.

Our translator climbed up into the wind and listened. They claimed they knew OGA Mike and that they used to work for him. The money dried up, and now they needed a new benefactor.

They said they had a village nearby. Said they could help us. Said it was just up ahead.

Too much information.

Too fast.

I didn't like it.

But I trusted Dave.

And Dave said, "Let's hear them out."

So, we followed.

We dropped into the valley.

Switchbacks were so tight the trucks creaked with every turn. Rock walls on both sides. Blind corners. High ground.

I was scanning every ridgeline. MK19 off the T&E, disconnected and ready to free-gun. The safety off. My thumbs rested on the butterfly triggers.

I wasn't going to get caught staring.

If this went sideways, I was going to level the valley.

Then the terrain opened up—and there it was.

A town.

Out of nowhere. Built from stone and sand. Windows dark. Doors closed.

No kids. No women. No livestock.

No movement, just silence.

A single road cut through the center. One way in. One way out.

We followed the Afghan trucks into the valley. Followed behind the dust of the two vehicles. Entered the huge open steel gates, that marked the entrance.

Drove down deserted streets. Deathly silent. Every door and window locked tight. It felt like we were driving through an ambush alley.

My automatic grenade launcher wouldn't be effective in these tight alleys.

And then we turned the final corner, and the streets opened up to a huge town square. A massive courtyard of stone, ancient lumber, a well and every door and window, still closed.

Dispersed everywhere were at least three hundred fighters.

Uniformed. Armed. Ready.

Black tunics and pants. Matching gear. AKs, PKMs, RPGs. Some leaned against the walls. Others stared. Eyes locked on us.

My hand tightened around the MK19 grips, thumbs resting on the butterfly triggers.

If I squeezed, the first round would arc. Land. Detonate.

The second, third, fourth, and fifth would follow.

Then all hell would break loose.

But I didn't.

Dave stepped out of the passenger seat and stood up calmly, cigar clenched, eyes scanning the kill box.

The warlord stepped forward like a man greeting old friends.

"Come," he said through the translator.

"Tea." Tea?
In a kill zone?

They wanted to stall us. Disarm us.

Maybe capture us.

Maybe worse.

I kept the MK19 leveled at chest height—low enough to be subtle, high enough to wipe a street clean in seconds.

My heart didn't race.

My hands didn't shake.

I felt something… slower.

Something hollow and certain.

This is going to hurt.

I imagined the rounds—hundreds of them—tearing into my chest, my throat, my arms.

If they started firing, I would be the first to die.

And in a strange way, it felt almost poetic, romantic.

A stupid way to die.

But not a coward's death.

Dave leaned into our translator.

Calm. Precise.

"Tell them we'll be back. We have to check-in. We don't make decisions without confirmation." They nodded.
A performance. We nodded back.

Another performance.

Then, we reversed.

Slow.

No sudden moves.

Three hundred pairs of eyes and weapons followed our exit.

As we turned the front of the truck around, I slowly rotated the turret to cover the rear.

Calm, focused, ready.

No one in our gun truck spoke for a long time.

We continued the mission, scanning the landscape, driving towards the objective.

Eventually, we rejoined the rest of the company. Took our spot on the outer cordon. Radioed our status.

But something had changed.

Not just the tension.

Not just the risk.

Us.

We'd come face to face with annihilation—and we'd walked away.

Not because we couldn't fight.

But because we chose not to.

That's what nobody teaches you.

The hardest decision in combat isn't when to pull the trigger.

It's when not to.

―――

I think about that day often.

About the MK19 in my hands.

About that defining moment…… When I almost gave in.

About Dave—silent, calm, drawing a straight line through chaos with an even voice. Never showing fear, nervousness, or panic. Trusting me in the turret. Confident in my skills to back him up.

―――

Some of those fighters? They'd still be there years later.

They'd fight other Americans. They'd shoot down Chinooks. They'd kill Navy SEALs. Lone Survivor wasn't the only story from those hills.

But that day?

That day, we lived.

That's the burden of restraint.

The war won't record the shot you didn't take—no citation for the man you chose not to kill, no headlines for the Americans who lived because you held your fire.

No one will speak of the firefight you won by waiting, not reacting.

But your soul remembers.

Not with words.

With silence.

With weight.

Chapter 28: The Commander's Plaything

It started with a sound.

A low rumble, then a crash—a sickening metallic grind that echoed off the ridgeline and rolled across the valley like a death knell.

Then the radio crackled:

"Afghan commander's vehicle. The truck rolled off the road. Survivors inbound."

No time for questions. No time for feelings.

Tonight, the unconventional warfare hospital would go hot.

By the time they reached us, the sun had dipped behind the mountains. The compound was dark. The medics moved like ghosts—quiet, fast, focused.

The first casualty was the commander.

Barely conscious. Lips tinged blue. Skin cool and clammy. Breathing shallow and rapid. Face slack. Eyes open but drifting.

"Pelvic fracture," I muttered.

You didn't need a CT to see it. The signs were all there—legs splayed awkwardly, blood-soaked clothes, skin graying by the minute.

Next came one of his bodyguards.

Both arms were broken. Legs crushed. But conscious. His teeth clenched so tight they clicked.

Then… the boy.

He hovered near the edge of the litter, refusing to sit.

Twelve, maybe thirteen. Thin. Wide-eyed. A bruise on his neck. No visible injuries otherwise.

He didn't need help.

Not medically.

The translator followed behind him, eyes flat.

"The boy was with him," he said.

He didn't need to say more.

I knew.

Everyone in the room knew.

He hadn't been a passenger.

He'd been the distraction.

He'd been beneath the commander when the truck rolled.

And the only reason he was alive… was because the man using him as a plaything had cushioned the impact with his body.

———

I swallowed the bile rising in my throat.

Didn't have time for outrage.

Didn't have room for emotion.

The war didn't care what you thought.

The patient was in front of you.

And he was bleeding out.

———

"Jim," I called, keeping my voice steady,

"Start a trauma sweep on the bodyguard. I've got the commander."
Gloves snapped tight.
Hands moved on instinct.

Massive hemorrhage. Airway. Respiration. Circulation. Head injury. Hypothermia.

MARCH—burned into my bones.

BP low. Respiratory rate shallow. Distended abdomen.

His pelvis was wrecked.

We had MAST trousers and one pelvic stabilizer. Only one. I wasn't going to use it on this man and be short when I needed it to save an American. Once Gear left the UW hospital, we rarely saw it again.
And resupply took time we didn't have.

———

So, I applied a field-expedient pelvic binder—white sheet, cravats, and pressure. Stabilized him the best I could. Started a line. Warm fluids. No more than 500ccs. Too much, and he'd bleed faster.

I'd seen it happen.

I wouldn't make the same mistake.

Jim worked beside me. Tourniquets applied. Fractures splinted. Morphine dosed and logged.

We were a machine now—hands passing over broken flesh. No second guessing. Trained, practiced, professional.

Then, I reached for the catheter. Prepped the site. Cleaned from the tip down. Gripped the rubber and began to insert it.

Two inches in, he moaned.

Too much pain.

Even for a pelvic fracture.

A memory surfaced—ER rotation in NYC. Trauma case. Multi-system injury.

"Always conduct a digital rectal exam. High-riding prostate means torn urethra. Push a catheter, and you'll make it worse." Another echo—from SOCM school:

"Do no more harm."

Damn…

I'd skipped the rectal exam.

Didn't want to put a finger inside that man.

Not after what he did to that boy.

Not with his sweat still lingering in the air.

But this was war.

And war doesn't give you choices—it gives you moments.

I forced myself to check.

Sure enough—high-riding.

Transected urethra.

If I'd forced the catheter, I'd have destroyed his bladder.

I withdrew the bloody tip.

"Catheter's a no-go," I said to Jim.

"We stabilize and move. Bird's inbound?"

"Ten mikes."

I looked down at him. He would live.

Fluids slowed. His bladder would fill. Surgeons would have to tap it—a long needle and syringe.

I dulled his pain with 10mg of morphine. It would wear off before he hit the Spanish hospital.

Flight medics weren't trained to give narcotics back then. Even if I handed off some morphine, it would go unused. They didn't have the tools or training to inject the glass syrette.

Another thought: did he deserve to live?

Probably not.

But medicine wasn't justice.

It was saving the body in front of you, even when the soul inside was rotten.

The boy stood near the door.

Still watching.

Still shaking.

I wanted to say something.

Anything.

But there were no words.

Only psychological and physical trauma.

Only this moment.

Only the knowledge that my hands had just saved a man who had used this child, like a piece of furniture.

Because that's what medics do.

You treat the wound, not the man.

You save him.

And then you walk away.

And later—

When the gloves come off, and the gear is stacked— You wonder if you saved the right one.

Chapter 29: The Cost of Mercy

The commander survived the flight.

His bodyguard did not.

He died somewhere in the air—somewhere between the ragged Afghan hills and the aluminum-walled trauma bay at Kandahar. Not fast. Not quietly. According to the flight medic, he was awake for most of it.

Both arms were broken.

Both legs shattered.

Jaw slack. Eyes open. In pain. And then… he wasn't.

That's how it goes.

By the time dawn spilled over the ridgeline, the compound felt… still.

Not quite. Not empty.

Just still.

Like the dust itself had paused out of respect.

I sat outside the clinic, palms on my knees, staring toward the mountains. My sleeves were still damp with sweat, and my wrists were stained faintly red at the seams of the gloves, I hadn't fully removed.

I wasn't tired.

I wasn't angry.

I just felt like a man carrying two bodies—one who lived and one who didn't.

Jim sat down beside me without a word.

Familiar, so was the silence that followed.

"Hell of a night," he said finally.

That was his way.

Never filled the air unless it needed filling.

Didn't try to patch the wound. Just sat beside it.

Jim was technically junior to me—on paper. But I learned from him more than I ever admitted. He would go on to spend 30 years in SF. Highest Warrant rank you could reach. A man built for the edge of the map.

Loyal. Quiet. Steady.

One of the good ones.

I nodded.

Said nothing. Just grunted.

We sat like that for a long time.

Two men who had worked past the limit.

Trousers and boots caked with blood.

Breath still catching from the weight of everything we had just done.

The smell of bleach still clung to my forearms. Sweat and antiseptic. Latex and iron.

We had done everything right.

We'd followed protocol. MARCH PAWS (Pain, Antibiotics, Wounds, Splinting).

We'd done it all: Tourniquets. Decompressions. Field splints. Needle sticks. Fluids measured to the drop. Narcotics logged to the milligram.

Two patients.

One bird.

One lived. One didn't.

That's medicine in war. It isn't fair. It isn't dramatic. It's just final.

Jim looked out over the gravel and said the thing I was already thinking.

"Would you have tried as hard… if they had been bad guys?" Not an accusation.
Not judgment.

Just a question.

A wound, really.

I didn't answer right away.

Because there is no good answer.

That question cuts where you don't expect to bleed.

It's not about politics or prejudice. It's about moral injury—that quiet, corrosive erosion that comes not from failing… but from wondering if you wanted to.

In my mind, I saw it all again.

The boy.

The commander.

The blood pooling under the litter.

The smell of diesel fuel mixed with arterial spray.

The catheter with its tip soaked in red.

The tremor in the commander's leg as I tied off the pelvic splint.

My own gloved hands moving like machines, headlamps bouncing off torn flesh and blood-soaked dressings.

And I remembered something from years ago—trauma rotation, civilian ER.

An older Green Beret physician assistant. Vietnam era. Elbows deep in a gang member's GSW, muttering to no one in particular:

"You don't get to choose who you save. You just save whoever's in front of you."

Back then, it sounded cold.

Now, I understood.

"It doesn't matter who they are," I said quietly.

"It only matters that we don't judge them and try and save everyone."

That wasn't detachment.

That was survival.

Because once you start deciding who deserves care… You're not a medic anymore.
You're something else.

The moral weight doesn't arrive like a bomb.

It seeps in.

Through the gloves. Through the gear.

Through the moments that don't break you—but bend something inside that never quite straightens again.

One life was gone.

One life saved.

The mission moves on.

But the ledger never closes.

We always prioritized American Soldiers. It wasn't written. But it was known.

You don't put the guy who tried to kill your team on the bird before your teammate.

The doctrine says worst-case first.

Reality says your brother comes home.

But sometimes, there's no brother.

Just strangers.

Just a broken Afghan fighter and a commander who used a boy, like he was a rubber toy.

And in those moments… You treat them anyway.
Because that's the difference between being a medic and being an executioner.

That's the cost of compassion.

You give everything to save a man you don't respect.

And you carry the weight when it's not enough.

There's a lesson buried in that night.

Sometimes, you save the wrong man.

Sometimes, the one who dies deserves better.

And you'll never know.

But you do it anyway.

Because that's what Green Berets do.

Because that's what medics do.

Because it's the only way you survive the night with your soul intact.

———

Jim and I eventually stood. Packed up our gear. Cleaned the blood from the floor and from the litters.

Refilled the medical kits.

Restocked the shelves.

Set up for the next casualty, we knew would eventually come through our doors.

We didn't say much else.

But the silence between us said everything:

We didn't save everyone.

But we didn't become something we'd regret.

And in this war?

Sometimes… that's enough.

Chapter 30: The Deadly Chaos

Night fell fast and without mercy.

The air at the forward base was thick with grit—dust hanging like smoke, the horizon lit only by the occasional burst of gunfire. Helicopters roared overhead, their rotors slicing through the darkness like blades. The sounds weren't just loud. They were alive. They owned the night.

Outside the UW hospital, I stood waiting.

Pistol on my hip. Gloves ready. My headlamp already on. Trauma sheers stowed. Stethoscope dangling around my neck. Tongue depressors in my pocket.

Tonight, someone would die.

The call came minutes earlier—mass casualty inbound. Two vehicles. Ambush aftermath.

Inside the unconventional warfare hospital, Jim had already cleared space for movement. I double-checked the chest tube tray: scalpel, curved hemostats, chest tube, suction, gauze, and Heimlich valve. Lidocaine was preloaded. Tourniquets, wound packing, airway gear, decompression needles—all prepped.

We were ready.

But readiness doesn't change what comes through the gate.

The wounded Americans had been evacuated by helicopter, directly from the blast site. They were already undergoing surgery.

The first vehicle skidded to a stop, was waved through, and rolled toward us. In mass casualty events, everyone worked—non-medics crouched behind litters and took pulses.

The covered area behind the UW hospital was marked for the dead.

You never stack the dead with the living.

Never load them on a helicopter with the wounded.

It was callous. But necessary.

Two Afghan fighters jumped out from the cab of the Hilux. AK-47s at the ready, pointed at the trucks bed. They dropped the tailgate.

The first casualty was dragged out.

They were enemy combatants.

Mid-30s. Unconscious. Gunshot wound to the chest.

Two Americans unloaded the second one.

An old man. Seventy, maybe older. Blood soaked his tunic. His face was bruised and swollen—but his eyes were wide. Terrified. Searching. He didn't scream. He didn't plead. He just stared.

A third was carried out—gurgling with every breath. Barely alive.

"Private! Get over here!" A young medic froze.

Nineteen. Face pale as chalk. His aid bag was still zipped up. Gloves were still in his pocket.

"Medic!" an SFC bellowed.

"Move your ass!" Nothing.
Jim moved first.

"Give me the needle," he said, calm and low.

The kid fumbled through his kit. Pulled out a spinal needle—wrong size, no prep, no lidocaine. Useless for needle decompression.

Jim didn't react. Someone else handed him a decompression needle and a preloaded syringe from their kit.

He dropped to one knee and peeled back the patient's shirt. The chest was a wreck—broken ribs, paradoxical movement, bubbling blood, and air hissing from open wounds.

Flail chest. Bilateral pneumothorax. The man was suffocating from the inside out.

The first needle went in.

Too shallow. No release.

Jim tossed it aside.

"Lidocaine and scalpel," he barked.

They were handed to him in silence.

He injected the local anesthetic into the fifth intercostal space at the mid-axillary line. Not too high. Not guesswork.

Precise.

The scalpel parted the skin.

Jim inserted a finger, gently dissected for adhesions, then guided the curved hemostats through the tract—spreading muscle and fascia with practiced hands.

Then, the chest tube. 28 French. Lubed. Loaded.

He advanced it carefully.

At the pop, they knew he was in.

"Valve!"

A medic snapped the Heimlich valve into his hand. He attached it. Nothing.

Jim grabbed the handheld suction, connected it to the inline port, and pulled.

Hard.

First came air.

Then blood.

Then—the breath.

The old man's chest rose.

His eyes widened. His body shuddered.

He was back.

Jim sutured the tube in place and repeated the procedure on the other side. A second tube. Another flutter of breath.

The man stabilized.

10 milligrams of IM morphine. Jim stood to move to the next casualty.

The Green Berets were already in motion. Cross-trained, competent, saving lives.

One began applying bulky dressings to the man's chest.

"Bag him," Jim said. "Ventilate with the small oxygen bottle. His chest is too unstable to breathe unassisted." Still, the young medic stood frozen.

His squad leader erupted.

"Private! Bag the patient—or Get the Hell Out!" Finally, the kid moved.

Clumsy. Hesitant.

But he squeezed the rubber bag, and the man received oxygen.

Jim stripped off his gloves and replaced them.

"He's stable enough for evac. Prep the litter. Keep the tubes anchored. Don't let them get pulled."

He looked at the kid—pale, wide-eyed, hands still trembling.

No yelling. No public humiliation.

Just one sentence:

"Next time, you'll move faster." That night, we saved lives.

Not because the wounded were good people.

Not because they deserved it.

But because that's what medics do.

You don't ask what side they're on.

You don't judge.

You cut. You decompress. You suction. You save.

And sometimes, when the night is long, and the blood won't stop, the only thing separating you from chaos— is men like us.

Steady and calm.

Flawless in our craft.

Driven to save lives and protect the defenseless.

Care for the wounded and then move to the next broken body.

The primary goal of mass casualty incidents (MCI) is to provide the highest level of care to the greatest number of patients, while maximizing survival rates.

Sometimes you pass over a wounded man who may not survive.

Sometimes you spend too long on someone who dies.

Then theres the ones who you leave to die. Not because you're callous, because you're efficient.

And you'll never know if you made the right choices.

Some live, some die, and you carry those outcomes.

That's moral injury, not PTSD.

Not the chaos of trauma. Not the sight of broken bodies.

Just the weight of your decisions. The memories of the dead. The ones you couldn't save.

The ones you didn't get to in time…… the ones who should have lived.

Chapter 31: Don't Cry for Me but for the Widows

The sky tore itself open.

Two F-15E Strike Eagles screamed overhead, trailing afterburners like comets made of fire and fury. Their engines shook the valley, the ground vibrating beneath our boots as they banked hard south toward a target we'd never see.

Up there, they were dropping hell from 30,000 feet.

Down here, in the heat and the dust, we were earning it one bullet at a time.

The radio squawked in my ear, voice clipped, urgent:

"Troops in contact. Heavy resistance. They're still picking up weapons. Secure the site."

I moved forward, boots slamming into packed earth, rifle pressed tight to my chest. The sun hung high and mercilessly, baking the valley until the air shimmered like a mirage. The smell hit me—sweat, blood, gunpowder, and something else.

Burnt meat.

The sickly-sweet scent of cooked flesh.

The battlefield was chaos.

Bodies lay in twisted positions, arms splayed, torsos riddled. But some still moved. Some still fought. Even in death, they reached.

A man crawled through the dust—thick beard matted with blood, his right arm shattered. But his left hand crept forward toward a rifle.

He wasn't dragging himself to safety.

He was dragging himself to kill one of us.

I exhaled. Slow.

Centered the red dot.

Squeezed.

The round punched through his forehead with a wet pop—a sound I'd never forget. His body seized once. Then stilled.

No screams.

No pleas.

Just silence.

Technically, we weren't supposed to use hollow points. Geneva said no.

But we were Special Forces.

We did what had to be done.

And we didn't need permission.

Let some politician in D.C. Write a policy from behind a mahogany desk. Out here, we were the policy.

To my left, George fired a short burst—three rounds across another man's chest. The fighter had just gotten his hand on a rifle.

Too late.

He dropped like a stone.

Somewhere, a widow would cry for him.

Do they mourn like we do? I wondered.

But the thought didn't last long. No time for ghosts in the middle of a firefight.

Another figure stumbled out from behind a crumbling wall.

Young. Eighteen? Maybe less.

Blood poured through his fingers, staining the front of his tunic. He looked at me—eyes wide, dark, panicked. Then he twitched. His hand moved toward a pistol tucked into his waistband.

I hesitated.

Just for a second.

Luke didn't.

Two to the chest. One to the head. The third round snapped his skull back, and he dropped in a cloud of red dust.

I nodded.

"Thanks, Brother."

The fighting didn't stop.

Wounded men crawled through the dirt. Others dragged them to cover. Rifles clattered. Boots thudded. Somewhere, someone screamed in Arabic. Somewhere else, someone laughed—high, shrill, unhinged.

They kept coming.

Not organized. Not smart.

Just stubborn. Desperate.

They picked up weapons, and we put them down. One after another.

It wasn't war.

It was execution by momentum.

And it had to be done.

Because hesitation didn't just get you killed.

It got your brothers killed.

And that was worse.

We kept shooting.

Controlled pairs. Center mass. I took headshots only when I had to.

The recoil felt normal. The noise didn't even register. Just a rhythm. Like breathing.

But every time I pulled the trigger, it added something to the weight I carried.

And that weight doesn't come off with your gear.

Later, the ghosts would come.

They always do.

Not in battle. Not in the chaos.

But in the quiet.

When you're cleaning your rifle.

Or folding laundry.

Or watching your daughter sleep.

Maybe when you're camping back home.

That's when the faces come back.

That's when the boy with the pistol in his waistband looks at you like he didn't mean it.

And you remember how close you came to believing him.

But I don't cry.

Not for them.

Not for myself.

Not anymore.

The gunfire faded. The smell didn't. It clung to me like oil.

I stepped over a body, boots slipping on blood-slick stone. I looked down. Eyes open. Mouth ajar. A man, now meat.

There would be a widow.

There would be children.

But there would also be one less ambush waiting on our next route.

Do they cry like we do?

I didn't know.

Didn't want to know.

Because if I knew that—

If I really believed they felt what we felt— Then, I
might not be able to do what had to be done.
Luke patted my shoulder.

We moved forward, rifles still up. Another enemy crawled. Another twitch. Another shot.

Dust. Blood. Smoke.

And the weight of another name I'd never know.

Don't cry for me, I thought.

But maybe… cry for the widows.

Because we don't get to cry.

We just keep walking forward.

And they're the ones who bury what's left of us.

Chapter 32: The Triangle of War

Forward Operating Base (FOB) Orgun-E—once known as Camp Harriman—evolved from a small Special Forces outpost into a major operational hub for U.S. Army Green Berets. The name may have changed, but to those of who lived and bled there, it will always be Camp Harriman.

The air inside the wire was no better than outside.

Dust mixed with diesel, burnt trash, and sweat.

It clung to your skin, your rifle, your lungs—made everything taste like rust and regret.

From the raised guard position near the main gate, I scanned the perimeter behind my Oakleys. The sky above was a punishing blue. Not a cloud in sight. Just heat. Relentless, blinding heat that blurred the mountains and baked the ground until it cracked.

Beyond the wire, jagged ridgelines stood like serrated knives under the sun. The Hindu Kush didn't care who ruled the valley. Soviet. American. Taliban. Warlord.

The land had outlasted them all.

Our firebase sat in a natural bowl at the mouth of three valleys—an old Soviet layout repurposed for Special Forces use.

A triangle of war.

Each point of that triangle belonged to a separate Afghan militia company. Each one was loyal to a different warlord. Each man was armed, proud, and waiting for a reason to fight.

Keeping the peace inside the wire was a full-time job—and one mistake away from bloodshed.

This was more than a forward operating base (FOB). It was a powder keg.

At the triangle's corners, we had our gun trucks staged.

Three Humvees, one in reserve. Mine mounted the MK-19—belt-fed, 40mm grenades that could turn a crowd into red mist in seconds. The others had .50 cals. All were parked low in shallow pits we'd carved with a village bulldozer. Enough to hide them from direct fire but still give us a line of sight if we needed to support all three militia companies.

It was a tactical nest.

Controlled chaos.

Regular Army filled the gaps between our corners. SAW gunners posted.

Machine guns. Sandbags. Steel.

A wall of American firepower that kept the Afghan fighters honest.

Inside our base, every entrance meant something.

The north gate belonged to one company. The south to another.

Every section of the wire was tribal territory.

Every inch of gravel came with memory—blood, loss, and grudges older than America's presence in the valley.

I wiped the sweat from my brow and let the heat rise off me like steam.

Afghanistan was a land of extremes:

Scorching days. Freezing nights.

Unforgiving weather. Unforgiving men.

George walked up beside me.

Broad-shouldered. Quiet. Eyes always moving.

"You see the dogs last night?" he asked.

"Yeah," I muttered. "Tripped the flares again. Almost put rounds downrange."

He nodded and kicked at the dirt.

"Just another thing you gotta kill out here."

He wasn't wrong.

The dogs were feral. Scavengers. Drawn to our trash pits. They prowled at night, eyes glowing like ghosts. You didn't hesitate. You fired. Not out of cruelty. Out of habit. Out of survival.

Out here, mercy costs lives.

The sound of engines shattered the quiet.

Two Toyota Hilux trucks screeched to a halt in a cloud of dust. Steel welded to the sides. Windows shot out long ago. Diesel exhaust filled the air.

Armed men spilled out. Yelling in Pashto. Weapons low, but hands twitching.

George and I exchanged a look.

This was bad.

The gate guards—fighters from a rival company—were already postured. AKs raised. Eyes narrow. Fingers on triggers.

It was seconds from going hot.

We moved fast.

Boots pounding the dirt, weapons holstered but close. George and I walked into the chaos, like Moses into the Red Sea.

They parted—not because we ordered them to, but because of who we were.

Both operators. Equal rank. Equal respect.

I was the commander.

So, I spoke.

I drew my Beretta, held it low, and visible.

"Stop," I barked in Pashto.

"Not here. Not now."

The noise died. But the tension?

It was thick. A razor pulled taut between egos.

One of the Afghan commanders stepped forward.

Weathered. Scarred. Makarov on his hip. Pride in his spine.

"They insult us," he growled.

"They won't let us pass." I
turned to the guards.
"Why?"

"They're not from our village," one of them said.

They don't enter without permission." It was about face. Not protocol.

Pride. Territory.

Not one of them cared about rules on a whiteboard in a TOC.

They cared about what the other man's eyes said about his worth.

I nodded slowly.

"You followed the rule. That's good," I said to the guards.

"And you didn't force your way," I said to the commander.

Then I made the call.

"One man enters. As a guest. With honor." Long pause.

Then a nod.

One man stepped forward. The rest stayed back.

Rifles lowered.

Tension broke.

Another war averted for now.

George exhaled.

"You really have a death wish." I holstered my pistol.

"Nah. Just doing my job."

That should've been it.

But in Afghanistan, peace has an expiration date.

Later that afternoon, when the heat felt like it was boiling your spine and the dust turned to paste on your skin, it started again.

Another insult. Another stare. Another rifle raised.

I ran again—straight into the center.

This time, the weapon didn't drop.

An Afghan fighter leveled an AK at my chest.

Twenty feet away.

His eyes were wild. His jaw tight.

I didn't blink. Didn't raise my weapon.

Because I was the commander.

And if I showed fear, we'd lose the entire FOB.

Then I felt it.

Boots jogging behind me.

Rhythmic. Controlled.

Ten Soldiers from the 82nd Airborne appeared like a Storm front. Full kit. Kevlars tight. Eyes forward. Rifles at the ready. They didn't say a word.

Just formed a wall behind me.

Ten young Americans.

Black. White. Latino.

No difference. No individuality.

Just one unified machine of violence and restraint.

It was beautiful.

The militia fighters froze.

Some dropped their weapons.

Others backed away slowly.

Then came the man who saved the day.

Big, broad-shouldered senior NCO. Midwest-built. Arms like tree trunks.

He didn't slow his pace.

Grabbed both instigators. Slammed them to the ground.

"Get your shit," he growled.

"You're out."

We didn't tolerate undisciplined fighters.

Not inside our wire.

Later, I thought about that moment.

Not the weapon in my face.

Not the Afghan's pride.

But the wave of Soldiers behind me—how they moved, how they didn't flinch, how they made my heart swell with pride even as it cracked.

Those were my little brothers.

Some of them wouldn't make it home.

And I learned, in that moment, to feel nothing.

To add another layer to the armor.

Another tally to the ledger.

That's how you survive in the triangle of war:

De-escalate first.

Be ready to kill if you must.

But always—lead with dignity.

Chapter 33: The Quiet Debrief

The worst part wasn't the trauma.

It wasn't the blood.

It wasn't the shattered ribs or the chest wall that moved like a bellows.

It wasn't the screaming or the suction.

It wasn't even the look a man gives you when he knows you're the only thing between him and death.

The worst part was what came after.

Because once the litter was gone… once the blades faded into the distance…

You didn't get five minutes.

You didn't get to sit with it.

You grabbed your aid bag and started over.

Repack. Restock. Rebuild.

I always did it in silence.

The others would head back to the team house. Decompress. Debrief. Maybe sleep.

Not me.

That was the burden of being a medic. Everyone else walked away.

You stayed.

I opened that bag like it was sacred because it was.

It had saved lives. And it had failed to save others.

And that night—it had let me down.

I'd fumbled for a chest tube. Dug through the wrong pouch. Reached for tape that wasn't there.

Nobody died—not that time. But the moment hung in me like a missed shot.

So, I fixed it.

I built a new pouch. Chest tube only. Packed with intention, muscle memory, and hate for that hollow second of panic.

I laid it out like a chef-prepared for war.

- Lidocaine 2%, 5cc syringes
- 18- and 27-gauge needles
- Scalpel blades—#10 or #11, seated tight
- Curved hemostats, large and small
- Chest tubes, Heimlich valves, occlusive dressings
- 4x4 gauze. Four-inch tape.
- Curved suture needles—0 proline or silk
- Everything in its place. Every time.

I didn't do it because I was disciplined.

I did it because I never wanted to feel that cold again—that reach into a pocket and come up empty.

That's what kills people.

So, I got faster.

Smarter.

Cleaner.

One night, I was outside the aid station under a white headlamp, refitting the kit. My hands were moving on their own. Wiping clamps. Checking expiration dates. Replacing opened bandages. Checking wrappers on others.

A PFC walked by on his way to the guard tower.

He stopped. Watched me work.

"You always clean it yourself?" he asked.

"Absolutely."

He stood there a second longer, watching the rhythm.

"Looks like a ritual."

I didn't answer. Just gave a quiet snort. That was enough.

"Thanks, Doc," he said. And walked away.

He didn't know what he was looking at.

But he knew it meant something.

That bag stayed with me for years.

The same one I carried through Afghanistan. Same zippers. Same frayed straps. Smelled like diesel, sweat, iodine, and memory.

It sat beside us in the gun trucks. Rode on the floor of birds. Pressed against my body armor during foot patrols, always within reach when I slept.

It was part of me.

And I never let anyone else touch it.

After the war, I brought it home.

Stored it in my shed. Told myself it was for training. Maybe to teach someone. Maybe I wasn't ready to let go.

Then, one afternoon, years later, I opened it again.

The seams were shot. The fabric felt stiff in my hands. The zipper stuck halfway and refused to budge.

And I realized something.

I didn't need it anymore.

Not because the memories were gone.

But because they weren't.

They were still with me—most dreams. Every quiet moment when my hands stopped moving and my mind didn't.

That bag hadn't carried my war.

I had.

So, I walked outside.

Opened the trash lid.

And dropped it in.

No reflections. No salutes. No goodbyes.

Just a moment of silence between me and a bag that once held life and death in equal weight.

There's no ribbon for restocking your trauma kit.

No medal for prepping supplies at 2 am.

No commendation for remembering the pressure of a dying man's hand after the rotor wash fades.

But that's part of the job. Maybe the most important part.

Prepare. Refit. Be ready for the next one.

Because the next hole in a man's chest might show up before the sun does.

And you don't get to be tired.

You get to be the ODA medic.

Chapter 34: The Boy with the Grenade

The world had collapsed into chaos.

Smoke burned the back of my throat. Rifle fire cracked across the valley—short bursts, controlled pairs, clean, disciplined. Shouts blurred into the roar of helicopter blades and the low thrum of adrenaline. Wounded were already being carried toward the medevac bird, boots bogged down in soft Afghan earth.

Then I saw them.

Two men—one from Utah, one from Bragg—moving with purpose. Between them, they carried an old wooden door. On it lay a boy. Maybe fifteen. Maybe younger.

Just a body now. Shaking. Blood was venting from five holes in his back and chest, heat and fear rising into the night like steam off a fresh kill.

His hands were flex-cuffed. His eyes wide. His mouth opened and closed without sound.

They said he'd had a grenade.

Said he was reaching for the pin.

But the pin was still in.

Maybe he panicked. Maybe he didn't know what he was doing. Maybe he was trying to surrender and nobody had time to see it.

Five shots. Entry wounds in the back. Green-tip rounds—tungsten core, steel-jacketed. They shattered ribs and exited through his chest. Likely more than one shooter. In that chaos, no one wanted to be the guy who didn't fire. Easier to explain an overreaction than a dead teammate.

I wasn't judging.

We'd all done things we'd bury if we could. Things that sleep in the dark until the day your grandson climbs in your lap, and you feel the shame crawl up your throat like smoke from a war you never left.

Inside the bird, the rotors devoured the world. Gunfire faded. But the weight didn't.

The Crew Chief hovered nearby, hand on his weapon, eyes fixed on the boy like he was still wired to blow.

Across from me, the doctor—a lieutenant colonel brave enough to fly out with us—grabbed my shirt with a shaking hand.

"You have to uncuff him, Sergeant. If you don't, he's going to die."
I paused.
He was still a detainee. Technically. Rules said no medical treatment without proper security.

But I'd already made my decision.

I reached across my chest, drew the Cold Steel push knife from its sheath above my heart, and sliced the cuffs.

The boy sagged against the aluminum floor. The Crew Chief didn't lower his weapon.

But I lowered myself.

Blood soaked my gloves before I even made the cut.

I angled the scalpel down, slid it directly over the rib, and felt the resistance give way.

The pleural cavity erupted.

A geyser of dark blood poured out.

I guided the chest tube in. A 28 French. Pre-lubed. Inserted blindly but by feel.

The Heimlich valve hissed: Heimlich valve – a one-way device that allows air and fluid to escape from the chest, preventing a collapsed lung from worsening.

Then— a gasp.

The boy's chest rose. He sucked in a breath. Ragged. Wet. Alive.

The doctor's voice cracked.

"Damn… you did it."

Half a smile broke through his shock.

"Now get the other side before we land. I'll take it from there."

I didn't tell him I'd done this before. On goats in training. On victims in New York. On Afghan fighters in valleys with no names.

I just nodded.

And cut again.

I sutured fast. Heavy monofilament. Loop and tie. Cross-stitch to keep the tube anchored. Left three inches of slack at the top so it wouldn't rip loose when we hit the ground. It wasn't pretty. It wasn't clean.

But it would hold.

There was no suction. No sterile field. Just blood, grit, and the knowledge that the next breath might be his last.

The theory was simple:

Let the trapped air and blood escape.

Let the lung reinflate.

Let the heart shift back to the centerline before tension collapses the mediastinum.

If I saw tracheal deviation or distended neck veins, it was already too late.

Not this time.

Not yet.

I slowed down on the second side. More time now.

Same technique—cut over the rib, not under it. Avoided the neurovascular bundle between the bones. That's where the life is.

Ranger medics were still being taught needle decompression back then—14-gauge angiocath, second intercostal space, midclavicular line. Worked sometimes. Temporarily.

I didn't bother with temporary.

I went for the tube.

We used to follow the doctrine:

Three-sided occlusive dressings. Wounded side down. Air out, not in.

In theory, great.

In blood, sweat, and wind? Worthless.

Nothing stuck.

Not in a helicopter.

Not in fear.

So, I carried plastic. Thick sheeting. Anything.

I'd slap it over the hole and cinch it down with ACE wraps—six-inch elastic bandages, stretched tight, anchored to the torso like armor. Tubes left hanging out the sides like tails, hissing or draining or doing whatever kept them breathing.

That was medicine at the edge of the map.

The boy made it to surgery.

I didn't follow.

The doctor stayed with him—his hands stained, his face softening.

Sidebar: The MARCH Algorithm

MARCH is the battlefield trauma care sequence used by Special Forces medics:

M – Massive Hemorrhage: Control life-threatening bleeding first.

A – Airway: Ensure the patient has a clear airway.

R – Respiration: Treat chest injuries (like tension pneumothorax) and support breathing.

C – Circulation: Maintain perfusion, manage shock.

H – Head/Hypothermia: Prevent brain injury and protect from exposure.

This boy had bypassed the "M" step—he was still bleeding but not exsanguinating. The fight was at "R": respiration. If his chest couldn't rise, nothing else would matter.

Chapter 35: The Price of Survival

The flight back was quiet. Just rotors and memory.

The doctor sat across from me, staring at the boy like he was his own son. He said nothing. Just kept his eyes on the rising and falling chest of a kid we weren't supposed to care about.

But we did.

We were Special Forces and surgeons. We were Soldiers and medics. And in that moment, none of us gave a damn about what he had or hadn't done.

He was alive.

That was enough.

When we landed, I stepped onto solid ground. The sun hit my face, warm and real. For a second, I closed my eyes and let myself believe I'd done something right.

The doctor jogged beside the litter. Drops of blood fell through the green nylon, trailing behind him like a memory.

He never looked back.

He didn't need to.

The FST men were already moving. No panic. No shouting. Just work.

He would get a medal for what he did that day.

I wouldn't.

Didn't matter.

That wasn't why I was there.

Years later, I visited him.

Same man. Still sharp. Lean. Respected. He'd built a quiet empire—a surgical practice up north. Residents. PAs. White coats who looked at him like he carried fire in his hands.

He greeted me like family. No rank. No ego. Just a hug and a smile that said, I remember.

We sat in his backyard, drinking coffee in the shade. Talked medicine. Talked life. Didn't mention the boy.

We didn't need to.

He was still the same man I met in Afghanistan.

And I was still the medic who had once watched a teenage boy with a grenade survive the worst day of his life.

Not because he deserved it.

But because we did what we were trained to do.

Quietly. Relentlessly.

Because that's the job.

That's the standard.

Chapter 36: The One Who Froze

The bird was already airborne. Chinook blades hammered overhead like a heartbeat too fast to control. I was kneeling beside the boy, shot five times. Dying, but not dead.

Blood covered my gloves. My arms. My pants. The cuffs were already off. The chest tube was in. The Heimlich valve hissed as his lungs took over. The doctor crouched next to me, still catching his breath, half-disbelieving what he'd just seen.

And that's when I noticed him.

A Private First Class. A young Ranger medic. His squad had been on the Chinook when our Team Leader confiscated it to provide medical evacuation for our men.

Young. Clean. Field-dirty. Fresh eyes—still trying to understand what war really meant.

He had been in the back of the Chinook the entire time. His squad leader had tried to push him into the trauma scene. They'd been on their way back to Kandahar. Just a shower run. No words were exchanged.

He was frozen.

Arms stiff. Eyes locked on the blood spilling across the floor. He wasn't shaking. He wasn't blinking. He wasn't breathing.

He was just... locked.

His jaw was clenched, but his eyes had gone somewhere else somewhere far from that bird.

His squad leader had shouted at him once— "Help the medic!"—but the kid didn't move.

He couldn't.

And I didn't blame him.

The Crew Chief didn't say a word. The doctor didn't even notice.

But I did. Because I've seen that face before. That stare. That internal break. The exact moment your brain splits: one part wants to run, the other knows it's already too late.

So, I let him be.

I finished the procedure. Stabilized the boy. Handed him off to the FST when we landed. The wheels hit gravel, and the mission moved on.

The private walked off behind me. I had placed my M4 down during the chest tube procedure, and he handed it to me.

His hands trembled. Just slightly.

His eyes were wide.

Trying to stay strong.

He handed it to me as he got back on the Chinook to fly off to the showers.

I moved on.

But that Private didn't.

Freeze.

It's not a weakness. It's biology.

It's the brain's final stall before overload.

Fight. Flight.

Or freeze.

Years later, I saw his face again.

Not in uniform. Not on the line.

In a newspaper article. Then, on a podcast.

He told a story—our story—but it had changed.

In this version, he was the one who saved the boy.

The one who uncuffed him.

The one who placed the chest tube.

The one who stepped up.

Said he crawled toward the casualty under the glow of a red-lensed headlamp. Talked tough. Claimed a doctor and an SF medic had stood frozen.

"All they had was outdated gear from the Vietnam era. National Guard. Not trained for the terrors of war." He named no names.

But I recognized every detail—because they were mine.

I sat with it for a long time.

Dr. McAllister—Bob—saw it too.

We pulled up the surgical notes. His original after-action report. The letter of commendation he'd written for me. We compared the timeline. Found the article on Wikipedia. Found the holes.

The boy had been the youngest detainee in Guantanamo Bay. Transferred. Released. Went back to Canada. Sued the government. Won.

The gaps were clear. Hours of the story were missing—especially when the boy was under surgery at the FST.

Bob, now a respected orthopedic surgeon, was still direct.

"That wasn't his story to tell," he said.

"I was there. I want to set the record straight." He was calm. Professional. But angry.
"This isn't about medals. It's about what we let the world believe."
But I told him no.
Because I'd seen what that day did to that young man.

I had watched his face freeze like a photo burned into memory.

And I knew—deep down—that the stories he told weren't for applause.

They were for survival.

Maybe he needed to believe it.

Maybe every retelling, every podcast, every panel was less about ego and more about building a wall around what really happened:

He froze.

That he couldn't move.

That someone else did the saving.

And I knew if we stripped that wall away too fast, too brutally… He might not survive what was underneath.
He wasn't just battling PTSD.

He was suffering from moral injury.

Note:

In 2003, wounded detainees were considered dual-status patients—casualties and threats. Per protocol, restraints remained until formally cleared by security or med command. But sometimes, protocol gets trumped by humanity.

Then there's the quiet battlefield no one talks about.

Not the firefight.

Not the trauma.

But the moment when you could destroy another man's identity—and choose not to.

That's moral injury.

And that's where I stayed.

Because some men die in silence.

And some rewrite silence to survive.

Let him have the podcast.

I've got the memory. The truth.

And that's enough.

Chapter 37: The Consequences

The aftermath always came quietly.

It didn't announce itself. It didn't crash through doors like an RPG or roar overhead like a Chinook.

It settled.

Slow.

Heavy.

Like dust.

Like grief.

I sat alone in the mud hut we called home.

Walls made of plywood, sandbags stacked high, mosquito netting hanging limp in the heat. The air inside was stale—sweat, foot powder, dirty clothes. I stared at the brown wall in front of me, one hand drumming a dull rhythm into the edge of my cot.

No music. No light.

Just silence.

And weight.

Out there, we were gods with scalpels and rifles.

We saved lives with one hand and ended them with the other.

Out there, you didn't think about the consequences.

You moved.

You acted.

You did what had to be done.

But in here?

Here, the questions had nowhere else to go.

I could still see their faces.

The wounded enemy—bleeding out on our stretchers. The way their eyes clung to us as we worked. Fear in the whites of their eyes. Trust, even. Like they knew we were supposed to hate them… but we didn't.

Not in that moment.

I'd used the best American medical equipment to save the life of a man who might've killed a U.S. Soldier the week before.

Chest tubes. Morphine. Pelvic binders. Decompression needles.

For him.

Not for justice.

For humanity.

And that's what gnawed at me.

Not what we did.

But what we might have undone.

What if the man I saved stood across from a young American kid next year?

What if the bullet I kept out of his thigh ended up killing someone else later?

That's the cost you don't read about in field manuals.

That's the wound they don't issue medals for.

It wasn't the blood that haunted me.

It wasn't the dying.

It was gray.

The space between what's right… and what's necessary.

How many had we saved? How many had we killed?
And how many were still waiting out there—just beyond the ridge, another mission, another ambush, another long, broken radio call asking for a medevac we knew would come too late?

The war had stopped shocking me. That
scared me the most.

Once you stop recoiling at death…

Once you stop wondering who they were…

Once you stop asking if it matters…

That's when you realize you've become exactly what the uniform warned you not to be.

But even then, I knew one thing:

If I stopped caring altogether…

If I stopped feeling that weight…

If I stopped holding the line between care and cruelty…

Then, it wouldn't just be the enemy who lost their soul.

It would be me.

So, I sat in the silence.

Not to rest.

Not to recover.

But to remember.

Because in this war, you don't just carry ammo and morphine.

You carry the weight of decisions that will follow you home.

That night, I didn't sleep.

But I didn't pray either. I just lay there…
awake… asking the only question that still
made sense:
If we keep surviving… at, what point do we stop coming home whole?

Chapter 38: Not Here. Not Now.

The firebase was dust, stone, and tension—held together by sandbags, sweat, and the thin wire between restraint and rage.

Razor wire curled around the perimeter like a rusted snake. The guard towers stood like tired giants. At night, the only light came from chem sticks and stars. By day, the sun baked everything it touched—tents, plywood, patience. The wind blew fine powder through every seam in the canvas and into every corner of the shacks we called home.

about a hundred yards from our team house, an infantry platoon had set up their own little city—young guys, squared away, clean-cut. Good Soldiers. Their lieutenant was textbook: college grad, type-A, polished, always moving. He ran his platoon by the book. Still green. Still trusted the book.

Then came the IED.

It hit in town. Premature detonation. Lucky break—it had been meant for us. Some of our guys missed it by minutes. No casualties. But the bomber didn't get away.

They brought him back—alive.

Black clothes. Scraggly beard. Skin like stretched leather. Long, knotted hair. Thin. Filthy. Defiant.

He didn't appear scared. Didn't beg. He wore hate-like armor.

They dumped him in the center of the compound. On his knees. Flex-cuffed. A hood over his head.

He swayed slightly as he breathed, head tilted like a predator in a cage.

Years later, I'd see that same fire in the eyes of American kids during the riots back home. Same rage. Same disconnection. Different cause—same emptiness.

Big Mark yanked the hood off and barked something in broken Pashto. The bomber didn't react. Just stared.

As Mark turned to walk away, the prisoner spat.

It landed between his shoulder blades.

I was moving before I knew it.

Six-foot-one. 210 pounds. Full of adrenaline and something darker. My boots hit the gravel hard. My heart was pounding too loud to hear footsteps. I didn't shout. I didn't slow down.

The bomber saw me coming. He didn't move. He wanted me to break.

I did.

I grabbed his filthy knot of hair and yanked his head back. His eyes finally widened. I drew my M9 and shoved the barrel into his mouth—steel grinding against teeth.

His lips peeled back over the slide. His jaw clamped down. He tasted the weapon. He tasted his own fear.

Safety off. Round in the chamber. Finger hovering.

A sneeze. A twitch. One bad breath, and I'd paint the rocks red.

I wasn't thinking about the rules of engagement.

I wasn't thinking about the Geneva Convention.

I wasn't thinking about anything except, this ends now.

Then I heard it.

Not the crying.

A quiet sound nearby. A PFC. Just a kid. Tears in his eyes.

He'd seen gunfire. He'd seen combat. But he'd never seen this—a man inches from executing a prisoner over spit and fury.

Then the voice came—clear, sharp, familiar.

"Drew! Stand down!"

Our Captain. Team Leader. Charging across the compound like he already knew what I was about to do. His voice cracked through the haze.

I blinked.

The trance broke.

I pulled the pistol out of the bomber's mouth. Wiped the bile and spittle off on the prisoner's own shirt. Holstered it.

He was trembling now.

I turned.

The captain grabbed my arm—firm, calm. No lecture. Just his hand on my shoulder and four words in my ear:

"Not here. Not now."

He told me half the infantry platoon had seen it. That their Lt had been standing right there.

"You're lucky," he said.

"We can't afford to lose a Green Beret right now."

He wasn't wrong.

But it wasn't luck.

It was grace.

And it came from a man who cared more about me than the paperwork that would've buried me. By the next day, I'd buried the incident in the back of my mind.
Compartmentalized it. Like we always did. Move on. Keep moving.

That afternoon, I was restocking med gear outside the aid station when OGA Mike walked over.

Big. Quiet. Moved like a shadow.

He didn't say hello. Didn't ease into it.

"Lieutenant tried to report what you did." I stopped stacking gauze. "Was gonna send it up," he said.

"Abuse of a prisoner."

That would've been it. Game over.

Mike stared out at the wire.

"I took care of it." I looked at him.

"Walked into his tent. Had a nice little chat. Told him if that message left his laptop, his career was over." He smiled. Not as a threat.

As a promise.

He didn't outrank that officer. But he had something better: influence.

And influence moves wars.

He looked at me and said it again.

"Not here. Not now."

Then he walked away.

I've thought about it a thousand times since.

What the lesson was.

Don't abuse prisoners? Obvious.

Control your temper? Always.

But maybe it was more than that.

Maybe it was this:

Even the best of us is one bad breath away from losing everything.

One trigger-pull from becoming the thing we swore to fight.

One split-second from crossing the line that can't be uncrossed.

That bomber didn't deserve mercy.

But I didn't deserve the mercy I was given either.

And yet, I got it. Twice.

From my Team Leader.

And from a man in plain clothes who reminded me of what mattered—without ever raising his voice.

Maybe they saw something in me that I couldn't see that day.

Maybe they knew I could still be saved.

And maybe that was the lesson.

Chapter 39: Rotor Wash and Razor Wire

We had just loaded three casualties onto the bird—Afghan militia fighters. Bloodied but alive. It wasn't the first time. It had become routine. Muscle memory.

One patient per stretcher. Shoulders high. Carried from our little goat-shed hospital, without fanfare, without panic. Just tired boots, steady hands, and the sound of gravel crunching underweight.

We moved through the rock wall we'd built—five feet high, dry-stacked stone cut by hand. The Afghans had built it for us. A month's labor, paid in greenbacks and sacks of rice.

Past the wall, a dirt path curved toward the outer perimeter—where a shack of plywood and sandbags sat near the airfield. Inside, the Regular Army pulled security. Tired eyes watching the wire, never blinking. Always waiting for something to crawl out of the dark.

The last gate was a triple-stacked concertina wire. Two rolls deep. Iron posts, hammered in by hand. Single-strand barbed wire cradled the sides like a man's hands around a woman's hips. Our seal against the outside world.

Beyond that—the landing pad.

A hundred yards long, fifty wide. Two feet thick with gravel. We'd built it ourselves—American hands, besides Afghan hands. Same sweat. Same fatigue. With shovels, a tractor, and stubbornness, it became our lifeline. Birds came here when they couldn't make it to Bagram, when they were too wounded. Too low on fuel. Too full of stories that needed to end somewhere.

That gravel held memories.

Some beautiful.

Some were covered in blood.

The night was black. No moon. No stars. Just two helicopters sitting on the pad—blades spinning, dust rolling, ready to lift.

One medevac. One gunship.

We loaded the patients. Quiet. Efficient. No goodbyes. No prayers.

Just straps pulled tight. IV bags hung high, a thumbs-up to the crew chief.

The first bird lifted—smooth. Controlled. Perfect.

Then the second one… didn't.

The rotor wash came hard.

It didn't just kick up dust—it unleashed it. A solid wall of brown talcum powder roared across the pad like a sandstorm from a broken world. It punched the breath out of my lungs. My eyes vanished. My ears stopped working gravel bit into my face like shrapnel. I backed off—slow at first, then stumbling. Boots sliding in the loose rock, hands up, blind.

And then I realized—

I was outside the wire.

Wrong side.

No cover.

Just me, barbed wire, and a helicopter I couldn't see or hear anymore. Somewhere in the black. Moving. Losing control.

The wind shifted again. Harder. Angled.

The bird was too close.

I felt it before I saw it—a landing gear wheel clipped my shoulder. Not enough to crush me, just enough to hurl me off my feet.

Threw me into the concertina beside me.

Metal teeth tore my uniform. Sliced through cloth. Caught skin. I went down hard—straight into the coils.

Tangled. Trapped.

No screaming. No panic.

Just one clean thought:

"This is gonna hurt." And then another:

"I hope my brain gets cut first."

That's how close I was. That's what death looked like: barbed wire and spinning steel. No gunfire. No explosion. Just a flying machine turned animal. Blind. Angry. Out of its cage.

But it didn't happen.

The bird lifted. Miraculously. Shuddering. Rising like a broken phoenix.

Rotors slicing the sky. Engines howling.

It cleared the wire by inches, dipped once, and then surged upward into the dark. Its tail wagged like a wounded animal. Out of control, barely flying, but airborne.

It thundered over the tents of a nearby 101st platoon.

The Blackhawk crash-landed between them. Kicked up dust like a detonation. Slammed the earth. But no one died.

No one was there.

Green Berets swarmed toward the tents in pitch black. Hands moved by instinct and feel. Not shouting. Just checking. We knew what we thought we'd find.

I dropped to one knee and wrapped my bloodied hands around the remains of a tent.

I felt a large, heavy, unyielding shape.

A body.

My breath stopped. My chest locked.

No.

Just a full duffel bag. Packed tight with clothing and gear.

Across the tent row, Jim felt the same thing. Stiff bag. Same shape. Same thought. Same cold fear.

We didn't speak.

We didn't have to.

We have the same medical minds. Same quiet compassion. We both braced to feel bone and skin. Instead—canvas and nylon.

Sometimes, what you don't find is the only thing keeping you upright.

And that's when I realized not a single man was inside those tents.

They were all on gate duty that night.

Every one of them.

Five empty tents.

The next morning, still bloody and scratched; I stood near the wire.

I looked out over the scorched gravel where the helicopter hit. It was still there. Sitting like a wounded animal. UH-60 Blackhawk. The rear tail rested on shredded canvas, with the wheel had sheared off. The windshield cracked like a spiderweb.

The sun rose behind the jagged Afghan mountains.

The crew had been picked up later that night. Flown back to the CASH. They didn't even sit down. No thank-you. No closure. They just wanted out. No one blamed them.

They had no intention of sleeping at our camp.

Not where death and destruction had reigned.

I couldn't shake it:

I had been given something I didn't deserve.

Another chance.

Maybe it was luck. Maybe it was God.

I don't claim to know.

But I never forgot it.

Some of the crew from that night will probably suffer from PTSD.

Fear.

Flight trauma.

The memory of spinning blades and black sky, control slipping away.

One incident.

One vivid fear loop. Triggered every time they stepped onto a bird again.

That's PTSD—a body that won't stop reacting to a past that's over.

But for me?

I didn't fear what happened.

I carried what almost happened.

I had survived another incident of Moral Injury.

The war left holes everywhere.

Some you could see.

Some you couldn't.

We talk about the bullets. The bodies. The blasts.

But some wounds come from what almost happened.

From the deaths that nearly were.

That night, I didn't lose a teammate.

I didn't fire a shot.

But I almost died.

And that almost stayed with me longer than some of the deaths.

Because it forced me to see how close we all were to vanishing without a sound.

Just another name. Another stain on the wire. Another tent filled with silence.

So, I concentrated harder.

Checked my gear twice.

Moved slower in the dark.

And I treated every helicopter like a wild animal—beautiful, powerful, and completely unpredictable.

We still loaded the wounded.

Still walked the gravel.

Still trusted the night.

But I never forgot what that rotor wash could do.

And I never forgot what grace felt like—

Especially when I had come that close to becoming a red mist, sprayed over concertina wire, that someone else would've had to clean up.

I still loved getting close to helicopters.

Still pumped up when boarding one.

Still pined for them in the middle of the night, somewhere deep in the Afghan mountains, waiting for Exfil.

Still stepped off the back ramp and grabbed a fast rope.

Still jumped out with an SF-10A parachute.

Still treated casualties on their aluminum floors.

But I remembered and I learned.

Because Green Berets adapt.

They overcome obstacles encased in fear.

They continue the mission.

And they teach others about lessons learned.

They get back up when they're slammed to the ground.

They wipe off the blood, dust and sweat.

And they move on.

Chapter 40: Five Empty Tents

They lifted clean off the gravel. Dust swirled. Torque held. No unusual vibration. The gunship climbed first—standard staggered liftoff.

They were second in line. Chalk 2. Tail clearance, forward transition, hover just above the pad—ten feet AGL.

"Looks good," said Chief Warrant Officer Alyssa Drake over the ICS. Calm. Composed. Her right hand on the cyclic, boots braced. Left hand wrapped around the collective.

Her copilot, CW2 Brennan, kept eyes on the gauges. "Main rotor torque's holding. Rpm stable. Pedal feels a little loose."

"Roger. Adjust trim. Left yaw's dirty," she said.

Below them, the gravel pad disappeared into a roiling wall of dust. Full brownout. No ground visual. Just rotor wash and turbulence curling off the blades like heat off the gravel

"Confirming instruments. Pitch stable," Brennan said.

"Maintain hover. We're light," Alyssa replied.

Then it started.

The aircraft began to drift. No visual cues. No horizon. Just the collective in her hand and the tremble of air trying to throw them.

Inside the cockpit of Dustoff 66, the MFDs glowed against their faces like ghost-light.

"Hold her steady," Brennan said. "You're drifting right."

"I see it. The pedal's down—right yaw compensation's soft." The right wheel kissed something.

It wasn't a full landing. Just a bump. A contact point. Enough to act as a pivot.

Her body did what training had hardwired. But in the back of her mind—just for a second—she wondered if this was the one they wouldn't walk away from.

Alyssa adjusted, but the aircraft rolled right.

"Contact right gear!" the crew chief shouted.

The dynamic rollover was starting.

Alyssa pulled—not forward, not lateral—just up.

Straight up.

The bird jerked into the air. Tail swinging, nose down, rotors clawing for lift.

The right main gear had caught on barbed wire strung between concertina coils lining the edge of the pad. No one had seen it through the dust.

"Tail's in the wire!" the crew chief shouted.

"I've got it—climbing!" Alyssa called out, both feet pressing into the pedals, cyclic locked to her chest.

For a second, nothing but drag.

Then—a jolt.

Then—lift.

The bird surged upward like it had been kicked.

Below them, barbed wire twisted loose, flinging back into the dirt. A tent corner collapsed. Plywood was ripped of the guard shack.

"Clear of the wire!" Brennan shouted.

"We're light," Alyssa confirmed. "Get us down. No lateral movement."

"Thirty yards ahead. Hard-pack. No soft soil."

Alyssa eased down, no dramatics. Just a slow, steady descent.

Tail first. Nose flared.

They touched down.

Hard.

"Blades winding down," Brennan said.

"Hydraulic light just cleared," Alyssa muttered.

"Power off. Transmitting mayday to Harriman. Stand by for recovery."

The rotors spun for nearly a minute, winding down like a storm fading.

No one moved.

Alyssa's hands stayed on the controls. Brennan stared straight ahead.

Then, over ICS:

"We still have our crew," she said.

Brennan nodded. "Somehow."

The flight medic, Specialist Felix Ortiz, braced in the rear.

A casualty on each litter. One moaned. The others stayed still, but breathing. No new injuries.

Ortiz unclipped from his seat and crouched low. He stared at his hands. They were shaking.

Later, a QRF bird landed. Alyssa climbed down last. Her helmet stayed on. The chin strap buckled. Her eyes swept the pad like it might jump up again.

They rode back to the Cash in silence.

No one wanted to sleep near the crash site.

No one spoke until morning.

Ortiz vomited before breakfast.

The crew chief didn't return to flight status for a month.

The crew chief never talked about that day. But for months, he shivered when the wind hit the bird wrong. Just a twitch. But it was always there.

Alyssa sat on her bunk for almost two hours, just staring at her hands.

She didn't sleep that night. Couldn't. Every time she closed her eyes, the wire came back. The rotor screams. That tilt. That awful tilt.

The Army called it a brownout-induced landing anomaly.

No deaths.

No medals.

No reprimands.

Just another near-death story that never made the report.

Later, she walked the perimeter of the pad. Her copilot walked beside her.

Then she whispered to Brennan:

"You ever think about what it would've felt like?"

"What?"

"If that tail rotor hit a man." He didn't answer.
She didn't need him to.

"Don't ever tell me that didn't happen."

**Sidebar: What This Was and Wasn't*

Helicopter crashes imprint in seconds. The crew doesn't forget the tilt, the metal scream, the sudden claw for lift.

This was not moral injury.

This was fear—thwarted by skill, enveloped in luck.

No one pinned medals on the crew. No one called them heroes.

But every one of them had looked death in the eye and said, "Not yet."

The silent aftermath of surviving what could've killed everyone on board would haunt them.

Some would suffer intrusive thoughts, flashbacks, and vivid recollections—reliving the trauma through memories and nightmares.

Others would lean into avoidance: steering clear of anything that reminded them of the crash—people, places, even certain sounds.

Untreated, the damage would turn inward: guilt, shame, numbness. Difficulty focusing. Sleep that wouldn't come.

Over time, many would develop symptoms of hyperarousal: heightened alertness, irritability, insomnia, exaggerated startle responses.

Statistically, one-third of the crew would recover within a year.

Another third would develop chronic PTSD—symptoms persisting for ten years or more.

Chapter 41: The Weight of Leadership

The smell hit first.

Acrid, bitter smoke rising from the half-cut barrels of human waste, flames licking hungrily at filth soaked in diesel. The black plume curled skyward, folding into the dusty morning air already thick with exhaust, burned cordite, and sweat that had nowhere to go.

The sun was barely up, and it was already punishing. A dry, blinding light that glinted off the razor wire and cast long, jagged shadows across the compound floor. The FOB felt alive—grinding, breathing, never resting. The steel ribs of a machine built on exhaustion and necessity.

Jim and I stood side by side, sleeves rolled, pant legs dusty, boots caked in ash and shit. One gloved hand on the burn barrel handle, the other gripping a steel stir-stick we'd fashioned from rebar and scrap. It wasn't glamorous.

But this was leadership.

"You see that?" Jim muttered, nodding toward the edge of the wire.

I didn't need to look. I already knew.

A line of junior enlisted Soldiers—E-2s, E-3s, maybe one or two Corporals—moved towards their tents with M4s slung loose across tired shoulders. Their uniforms were sweat-faded, salt-crusted, dust streaked. Most were barely shaving age. No wives. No kids. Just long watches and long silences.

They lived in two-man tents, pulled security all night, and rotated through tower duty in six-hour blocks.

And here we were—two Green Berets—burning their shit.

That's what they saw.

And that's why it mattered.

———

Jim stirred the barrel. Flames jumped as he tilted the drum, and the thick sludge hissed like it was alive. The stench made your eyes water. But neither of us turned away. This wasn't our first burn detail.

"They're watching," I said quietly.

"No doubt," Jim nodded. "Let them."

Because if they saw us take the worst jobs seriously, they'd know this wasn't about rank.

If they saw us shoulder the mess, they'd follow orders not because we gave them—but because we earned them.

That's what leadership looks like.

You show up. You do the work. You never act too important to grab a shovel or stir a barrel full of raw human waste.

———

Jim wiped the sweat from his forehead, the edge of his Bonnie hat fluttering in the wind.

"Ever seen Platoon?" he asked.

I smirked.

"Yeah. Of course." He chuckled.

"Exactly like that… except we're not high."

I didn't answer. I'd smoked a little weed before the Army. Years ago. But not here. Not in the war. Not with young men counting on me to be sharper, faster, and calmer than they were.

Out here, there was no room for escape.

No margin for error.

No drugs. No drink. No off-switch.

Just discipline and the knowledge that you were their last line of safety.

A platoon sergeant approached. A Senior NCO built like a cinder block. Face lined with hard miles. He nodded respectfully; eyes narrowed against the sun.

"Sergeant," he said. "I got men for this. You don't have to do it." I met Jim's eyes. He gave a small shake of his head.
"We know," I replied. "But these are our little brothers."

"You look out for your own."

The platoon sergeant nodded once—slow and deliberate.

That kind of understanding doesn't come from orders.

It comes from shared sacrifice.

We worked out a rotation.

One day a week, his guys would rest.

Jim and I would burn the barrels.

A small thing.

But small things add up.

Out here, they add up to trust.

Later that day, I sat by the wire and watched one of those kids eating cold MRE meatloaf straight from the pouch. He glanced over at me. I saw the way he nodded. Just once.

Respect isn't declared.

It's earned.

Leadership in Special Forces wasn't about salutes.

It wasn't about screaming across the FOB.

It was about setting an example.

It was about the man you were when no one was supposed to be watching.

Influencing others to accomplish the mission.

Providing your men with purpose, direction and motivation.

I often thought about their families back home.

Mothers who never saw their sons clean-shaven again.

Fathers who couldn't understand why their kid hadn't called.

Girlfriends who sent letters that never got answered.

Most of these boys didn't have anyone waiting.

But they had us, and their command had entrusted these boys to our Special Forces FOB.

That mattered and meant something.

Leadership isn't about glory.

It's about being the first one to pick up the slack.

The last one to eat.

The guy who burns the shit so the 19-year-old can get one more hour of sleep before a patrol that might end in a firefight.

Nothing in war is free.

Every ounce of comfort, every second of safety, every decent meal—it costs something.

And out here?

The price is paid by the men who show up early, leave last, and never act like the job is beneath them.

Jim and I finished our task in silence.

Diesel hissed. Fire snapped. Smoke curled into the morning sky.

The sun rose higher. The day rolled on. The war waited.

But for a moment, it felt right.

We didn't just lead them.

We honored them.

And that's what you keep.

Chapter 42: In the Dust

The M68 was my close-quarter combat optic. I wiped at my sight. The red dot still burned on the lens. I could see the scratch marks on the rail of my rifle. Marked for the ACOG, if needed. I set up my rifle like that—dialed to the mission at hand.

The desert wind came first—dry, sharp, tasting of copper and sand.

It stung my face and drove grit behind my Oakleys. Dust coated everything: the skin around my eyes, the seal of my gloves, the filter of my breath. The air was so dry it hurt to inhale, like trying to breathe through crushed stone.

We moved in a diamond formation across a wide plateau, kicking up small cyclones of dirt with each step. Above us, the sun hung low but violent, burning through the windstorm like a torch behind the smoke.

The silence wasn't peace.

It was camouflage.

"Cover!" someone shouted.

We dropped fast—shoulders to dirt, rifles snapping up, eyes searching for threats inside a wall of dust that moved like smoke.

Visibility was garbage. No more than twenty meters. Then ten. Then none at all.

My heart pounded, but my hands were steady.

"Stay focused," I whispered to myself.

Then the explosion hit.

Far off—but close enough to feel in the soles of your boots.

Not small and not random.

It wasn't meant for us, but for another ODA.

My chest tightened, I gripped my pistol grip. I couldn't see anything. I looked through my red-dot sight. Useless in this weather.

We jogged towards a ridgeline. The wind made everything feel underwater—sound warped, sight blurred. My boots crunched on the rock, the fine dust now coating the inside of my mouth.

I was positioned at the bottom point of our diamond formation.

I caught myself glancing behind us.

Not expecting to see the enemy.

Checking not from discipline, not out of fear…… but out of shame.

Why? Because it wasn't us.

I should've felt relief, but instead I felt guilt.

The blast had been massive. Bigger than anything I'd felt before. I could already picture it—Humvee split in half, bodies flung into the air like scarecrows, the medic screaming for his bag, and maybe no one answering.

And here I was alive, upright, and walking.

Another boom in the distance.

Farther off, but same direction.

A secondary.

They'd rigged it. Waited for recovery, or backup, or both.

"Another IED," someone whispered.

We froze, instinct locking us down. No movement. Just breath, thoughts, and the fine sting of dust in our eyes.

"You're a coward," my subconscious screamed.

Because deep down, you're glad it wasn't you.

And I was.

That's the truth I can barely admit.

The QRF call came through the radio.

82nd Airborne. ETA unknown. No update on casualties.

Please don't let it be the medic.

I tightened the straps of my aid bag. I could feel every ounce of it pulling at my shoulders—packed for trauma, loaded to save. Every tool where it belonged. I had double-checked every supply.

And still… it wasn't me who needed it.

I scanned the men around me—my brothers. They moved like they always did; slow, alert, trained. Calm in the storm, with no fear in their eyes.

But I knew they felt it, too.

We were in the wrong place at the right time.

The kind of luck that breaks something inside you.

The guilt of being spared, but thankful for it.

My wife flashed into my head—not her face, but her laugh.

Bright and playful.

Out of place here, like a candle in a sandstorm.

I squeezed my grip on my rifle, even tighter.

Not now……. I whispered, stay focused.

We crested the ridge. Nothing. Just heat waves and shadows.

Then, a dark smear across the horizon. Smoke. Just a plume but rising fast.

"It's them," someone muttered.

Too far away to reach them by foot.

Too open we decided, as the dust cleared temporarily.

We waited. Minutes passed like hours. The dust returned and choked the air.

Then, the hum of rotor blades.

The QRF.

They came in fast—two BlackHawks cutting across the sky, swinging low over the valley. I watched them descend near the smoke column.

I prayed they were fast enough.

Prayed their medics were better than they were trained to be.

Prayed one of ours wasn't screaming for help that never came.

I had the tools.

I had the training.

I could've saved them.

But today…I didn't.

———

And that's the part you carry.

Not the explosion.

Not the blood.

Not the body count.

The part where you're spared—and someone else isn't.

———

That night, I sat in the corner of our mud hut and repacked my aid bag.

Tore out every item. Wiped them clean. Reorganized the narcotics. Rechecked the IV kits. Refilled the medications. Inspected the tourniquets.

Because I wasn't going to be caught unready.

Not next time, not if it's one of ours…. Not if it's me.

You don't always carry the blood.

Sometimes, you just carry the fact that you weren't the one bleeding or dying.

That can be heavier than a ruck; that's when when we call it moral injury.

Chapter 43: The Night Riders

The wind cut through the valley like a blade—dry, thin, freezing. It moved low over the rocks and through the passes, whispering past our tires, sliding under uniforms, gnawing into bone. The mountains around us stood like jagged teeth under brittle stars. Snow dusted the ridgelines. Just enough moonlight to see how far we had left to go—and how far from safety we were.

We rolled dark. No headlights. No radio chatter. Just the low growl of engines and the occasional creak of a turret.

Nobody spoke.

There wasn't anything left to say.

I was in the turret, gloves stiff with cold, fingers numb on the grips. The MK19 rested in front of me—belted, loaded, ready. I'd already burned through too many rounds this week to romanticize it. Tonight, it was just weight. Steel. Responsibility.

Dave was the truck commander (TC).

Calm, as always. Watching the terrain ahead through the IR filter.

M240B mounted beside him. His presence was quiet reassurance. The kind that holds a team together.

We crested another incline. Afghan fighters rode in the lead truck. Scarves wrapped tight. Eyes scanning. They weren't Americans.

They were trained by us. Sometimes they bled beside us. That counted for something, but trust ran only so deep.

Some of our men bonded with them. They smoked and laughed. Built temporary bridges. Some lasting bonds.

Me? I kept my distance.

I wasn't judging them. But complete trust is earned, not given.

The cold got worse the higher we went. Even with layers, the wind found every seam in your uniform. I tried to flex my fingers to keep the blood moving. My knees locked. Ankles stiff. I hadn't slept in 72 hours.

And that's when it started.

Micro-sleeps. Head bobbing. Helmet clunking into the turret lip. The CVC absorbed some of it. But eventually, I took it off, thinking the jolt of bare steel would wake me up.

It didn't.

The next time I nodded off, I split my eyebrow. Warm blood ran down my cheek. No adrenaline. Just shame.

I knew better.

But the body doesn't care what you know. After three days without sleep, the brain starts rewiring itself. You lose track of time. Of place. Eyes stay open, but your perception flickers.

Every movement becomes a reaction.

Every shadow becomes a threat.

Every breath feels heavier.

I tried everything—face slaps, cold water, talking to myself. Nothing worked.

I blinked longer. Slower.

And I hated myself for it.

Because when you're in the turret, you don't get to fall asleep. Not on patrol. Not on overwatch. Not when everyone in the truck trusts your eyes more than their own.

That's the job.

Stay awake.

Even when it hurts.

Even when your brain starts playing tricks.

We reached the saddle of the mountains. The valley below was still—silent, dark, watching. We paused for a moment. Took it in. No movement. No gunfire. Just the breath of the mountain.

That moment stuck with me.

Because I realized I didn't remember the last mile.

Didn't remember scanning. Didn't remember crests or curves or turnouts.

I had been there. And not.

We made it through. Another night. Another silent stretch of Afghanistan with nothing but wind and the whir of engines.

But that night taught me something I never forgot:

You can have the best weapons. The best training. The best men.

But if you can't stay awake when it matters?

None of it saves you.

Later, I learned that certain units had started using stimulants. Prescription-grade. To keep men alert during long operations.

We didn't have that.

We just had discipline and perseverance.

And sometimes, even that runs out.

I didn't fall asleep again after that night. Not in the turret.

But the shame of almost doing it? Of nearly failing my team?

That stayed.

Long after, the blood dried.

Long after the mission ended.

Because in war, your worst moment isn't always a firefight.

Sometimes, it's the second your body gives out…

And you're too tired to stop it.

You wake up with a start.

Experience a feeling of terror.

A feeling of letting your ODA down.

And that can sit with you for years.

The what ifs? The almost. The slow absorption of a moral injury.

The shame and embarrassment of failing and falling asleep.

Chapter 44: Stand Down

September 11th, 2002.

Exactly one year since smoke poured from the towers and silence fell across a nation.

We were standing in a place no one back home had ever heard of—Deh Rawood. Just a name on a map most Americans couldn't pronounce. The FOB wasn't finished. HESCOs and barbed wire. A few tan military tents had been pitched in the dust. No towers. Half crumbling mud walls. No steel gates. No luxuries. Just sand, mud and steel.

We'd left Orgun-E a week earlier. OGA funding had dried up. Our militia disbanded. No more puppet strings. No more influence. We consolidated with two other ODAs, trying to hold something together in a place where everything unraveled faster than we could rebuild it.

The land felt different here.

The air was heavier. Less stand off from the mountains. Too much dead ground. The local village, butted up against our compound.

The locals' faces were harder. New tribes. New rules. New eyes were watching us from behind closed windows and doors.

And we'd started disarming them.

A week earlier, we'd confiscated heavy weapons from the local militia commander—Soviet AA guns, RPGs, belt-fed DShKs welded to beat up Hiluxes. It wasn't a security force. It was a private army.

They didn't appreciate the correction.

And we knew payback was coming.

It came just after sunrise.

A long dust cloud rose to the north—then the trucks appeared. At least fifty.

Packed with fighters. Armed and ready.

Within seconds, we flowed from our tents, like water finding low ground. Controlled aggression. Every position occupied. Every optic focused. Safeties whispered off.

No shouting. No panic. Just preparation.

We were a wall of calm, lethal resolve.

We saw the machine guns first. A fighter laid down behind his PKM and pointed it towards us. Then, the rocket tubes. Then, the faces.

They weren't here to talk.

I dropped into prone behind a makeshift berm, M4 on the bipod. Clear field of fire. I already knew who I would kill first. He had the PKM. The second was near the DShK. The third wore black and stood in the bed of a truck.

We were unafraid and ready.

That's what civilians need to understand.

It's not fear that takes hold.

It's clarity.

Every breath slows. Every choice narrows.

Your heart doesn't race.

It aims.

Then the voice cracked over the net.

"No one fires. If anyone opens fire, I will end your career. That's an order."

Our company commander. A Green Beret major. Tabbed like the rest of us.

Some of us lifted our heads from our scopes, like we'd been slapped.

That combat order, didn't sit right—not at first, not on this day.

September 11th.

Twelve months since the towers.

Twelve months of burials.

Twelve months of watching ghosts grow teeth.

And now, here they were. Armed. In formation. Daring us.

We weren't afraid of dying that day.

Some of us welcomed it.

I welded my cheek to the stock, finger beside the trigger, mouth dry, jaw locked.

Just give us a reason, I thought.

Then something happened.

From the left side of the perimeter, a few men moved.

The best of us. Senior NCOs. Gray-bearded Green Berets. Veterans of Panama, Somalia, Desert Storm. Men with hard eyes. Quiet, experienced, and combat tested.

One leaned his rifle against the Hesco baskets.

Then walked forward.

No rifle, just a sidearm and presence.

He moved straight into the kill zone.

Even with so many Green Berets covering him, it took stone-cold courage.

He placed his right hand over his heart and nodded gently to show both respect and sincerity. He spoke the common greeting in Arabic, "Salaam Alaikum." Peace be upon you.

A message not meant to dominate but disarm.

It worked.

The Afghan commander stepped out and met him halfway.

The Green Beret spoke the words "how are you?" in Pashto as, "tsenga yee?"

He added in Dari, "chetoor hasti?"

As they closed the gap, the American's voice reverberated with, "khoob hasti?"

Starting off with a direct question, can be considered impolite when greeting people in Afghanistan. But he had already spoken the Arabic greeting.

Two men. Two leaders. Surrounded by enough firepower to burn the valley down. And they talked.

Slowly, tension eased.

Rifles lowered.

The charge left the air.

He knew not to give the thumbs-up gesture, which is considered rude and has the same connotation as raising one's middle finger.

The "Ok" sign was another one he refrained from. This can symbolize the evil eye or something lewder.

He was familiar with the stroking of one's beard or pounding a fist into one's hand; that may signify revenge.

After a brief discussion in the warlord's native language; they turned around.

Each walking towards their own men.

The Afghan aggressors lowered their weapons. They mounted their vehicles and dispersed by driving away.

Back in the TOC, there was no celebration.

No high-fives and no war stories.

There was just silence. Only the sound of men realizing how close we had come to losing ourselves.

That day taught me what leadership looks like.

Not shouting.

Not posturing.

Not pulling rank.

But walking forward—into danger—with your weapon lowered and your soul steady.

We could've killed them.

And we would've been justified.

But we didn't.

That's not a weakness.

That's strength.

The kind that only a few men know how to carry.

At the time, our commander's order felt wrong.

Not betrayal—but a sharp break in momentum. A pause where instinct wanted action. It took time to process. To understand.

Some Soldiers develop moral injury from moments like that. When the trigger finger is steady, the order says no. When the instincts say act, but the strategy says wait.

But our NCOs that day—and our commanding officer —showed something greater than reflex.

They showed judgment.

Our commander wasn't frozen or afraid. He was on the radio the entire time—coordinating close air support if things went sideways. Talking to battalion headquarters. Watching the board. Reading the terrain.

He saw the bigger picture.

He knew what most of us didn't yet—that the war was shifting. That restraint had power, too. Sometimes, the fight is won by not taking it.

We placed that incident on a shelf.

Instead, we remembered the ones we lost that day, one year earlier.

We all knew that revenge wasn't a moral choice, that mitigates a threat.

Would firing on those trucks have honored them?

Would a retaliatory airstrike, decimating a village be justified?

Would losing one of ours that day have given meaning to their deaths?

I don't know.

But what I do know is this:

No one else had to die on September 11th.

Not this year. Not again.

Chapter 45: The Cheat Card

The blast hit just outside the wall.

Close enough to feel it in your teeth.

ANA Soldier. Thirty, looked forty-five. One of the better ones—always smiling, always ready. I didn't know his name. But I knew his face.

We were moving back from a short patrol when the explosion hit. I felt the concussive wave in my chest before I heard it. We turned. Ducked. Raised rifles and assumed a defensive posture.

Then someone shouted, "one ANA Soldier is down."

Two men dragged him behind a mud wall—his body limp. One boot missing, his foot was still inside. Face was pale. Almost bloodless. The stump was cauterized from the heat, but I knew it wouldn't hold.

I dropped beside him and pulled my gloves on.

His body started to progress into decompensated shock. Blood vessels would relax.

Arterial spray began, timed with his heartbeats.

I slapped a CAT tourniquet, above his knee. Tight, until there was no distal pulse.

A pressure dressing was applied to the stump. It continued to bleed.

I reevaluated the blast injury.

The wound was higher.

Blast injuries don't read clean. The force balloons soft tissue upward, then drops back down, masking the true origin.

I repositioned the tourniquet. Cranked it. Clamped it.

The bleeding stopped.

But he was still unconscious.

Blood sweep. I ran my hands over his entire body, from head to toe. Feeling for the wetness of blood and glancing at my hands for redness.

I secured his airway, checked his breathing. Radial pulse still present.

No obvious head wound. No blood from the ears. No skull deformity. But he wasn't responsive. Breathing turned shallow. Skin paled. Pupils were uneven.

I assumed that he had suffered a traumatic brain injury (TBI) from the blast.

Under fire, I couldn't run the protocol from memory. My mind was already juggling steps.

So, I reached into my right-side trauma pouch and pulled out the laminated reference card.

Head injury protocol. Intracranial pressure (ICP) control: Airway management. Fluid guidance. No Hetastarch.

God bless that card. I remembered that Hetastarch used for volume resuscitation, had the potential for serious adverse side-effects.

Kidney damage, increased bleeding, unfavorable neurological outcomes, and even death.

I elevated his head and adjusted his airway. Prepped Mannitol. Seizure meds ready. I had to keep him alive until the dust settled.

Those team members not providing cover for me, while I worked; started clearing a nearby home. Inside, a family huddled. An old woman covered her face. A child peeked from behind a curtain.

We carried the ANA to a stone shelf used for food prep. The closest thing to a table.

Our 18E called in the 9-line medical evacuation.

One reason we cross-train. It's a poor use of skills and resources for the 18D to get on the radio. He was the expert in providing medical care and monitoring the patient.

I checked his vital signs. His blood pressure dropped. I had stopped the massive hemorrhage in time, so I knew it wasn't from blood loss—he still had a radial pulse.

His respiratory rate ticked upward and then I heard it.

A deep and wet rattle inside his chest.

I hadn't picked it up on the "R" stage of MARCH.

He'd suffered a blast lung injury.

When the explosion happened, his lungs too the brunt of overpressure. Capillaries ruptured and gas exchange collapsed. Turned the injury into a pneumothorax.

I rechecked the chest—no clear signs. But his trachea was shifting. Breathing worsened.

I reached for a needle decompression, 14-gauge, 3.25 inches long. I found the second intercostal space, 2-3 fingers below the middle of his clavicle. Pushed the needle over the top of the rib, until I heard a "pop."

Air hissed out and the lung pressure equalized.

I left the plastic catheter in and removed the needle.

He stabilized. Barely.

Then he started to seize.

I drew Lorazepam and administered Im. Called for help. One of our guys knelt beside him and held his arms down as he convulsed.

The ANA were crowded in the doorway. Scared. Not of the firefight—but of losing him. Of watching us work.

They'd seen how other medics sometimes treated them—fast, rough, indifferent.

One of them knelt beside men and whispered, "Doctor."

I wasn't one, but to them I was more than a medic. I was an American who carried medicine in a world that carried death.

Apaches rolled overhead. Green smoke popped and a UH-60 BlackHawk circled us…. Then dropped down.

The 82nd Airborne QRF swept the ridges with armored vehicles. No resistance. Just the wind and silence.

They cleared the valley quickly, methodically.

We wrapped the casualty in a Skedco litter and secured his neck.

The plastic wings were laced closed round his body. Then we loaded him into the medevac helicopter. He was gone in minutes.

I stayed kneeling on the stone slab, blood on my sleeves, the cheat card still in my hand.

I'd saved him.

But what if I hadn't?

What if I'd missed the pneumothorax?

What if I had left the tourniquet too low?

What if I hadn't had that card?

Those questions and doubt can eat into into your mind.

That's when moral injury creeps in.

The doubt. The recalculation. The guilt for what almost happened.

That's what it means to be a medic.

You carry the living and the almost dead.

You ruminate about the version of you that almost got it wrong—the one that still whispers in the back of your mind, even when you did everything right.

Chapter 46: Smoke and Silence

It was the cook.

He made the best chai in the compound. Always handed it to you with both hands. A kind family man, working long hours to serve the Americans.

He'd been inside the Afghan-side kitchen when the fuel line caught. A flash fire—no warning. Just flame and screaming. By the time we got to him, he was crumpled in the dirt, face down, motionless. Smoke still rolled from the doorway. Someone had thrown water—too late.

I flipped him over. His face was scorched. Lips blistered. Nares black. The hair in his nose was curled and burnt away. No soot around the mouth, but his chest rose in short, shallow lifts. Burns covered both forearms and the left side of his face. What got me most—he wasn't coughing.

He was unconscious and not moving. That changed everything. I knew he was on a timed clock.

Another Green Beret assisted, moving him to the aid station. It was really a plywood box in the corner of the FOB—barely a roof, a cot, two tables, and my gear. I cut away the cloth, assessed for burns, and checked the cap refill. My biggest concern wasn't what I could see; it was what I couldn't.

Airway.

There's one thing you learn early: a burn patient who is unconscious and not coughing, has an inhalation injury until proven otherwise.

We cleared the table and propped his head. Oxygen was running from a portable tank. I watched his chest rise, then looked at his lips. They were already starting to swell.

I grabbed my laryngoscope and 6.5 ET tube. Lubed. Tested the cuff. Set out the BVM. I imagined the airway—glottic landmarks red and tight. Soot on the cords. This airway was going to close rapidly.

Intubation now—or a cricothyrotomy later.

I snapped the laryngoscope blade open. Gripped it with my left hand. Inserted the tube in. Cuff inflated. ET secured.

I connected the BVM port to the port on the endotracheal tube. Connected an oxygen tube to the back of the bag. I squeezed and forced air into his lungs. I asked another Soldier to help. He dropped to his knees beside me without a word.

The patient's oxygen saturation climbed. Color improved. Not great, but better.

Then, the waiting started.

We had no burn center. No Role III. No ICU. We called for a medevac.

Nothing.

All aircraft were allocated—to combat operations. Priority to wounded Soldiers.

He was a civilian and we weren't getting any help.

The ODA Commander tried. He got on the radio, then the satellite phone. He made calls. Reiterated the urgency of our situation.

Still nothing…. We were on our own.

I kept him alive for a few hours. Continued to monitor his breath sounds. I watched his chest rise. Maintained his airway. Adjusted pressure. Prepped suction in case he threw up. He was stable. Fragile, but stable.

The ODA commander poked his head into our clinic. His jaw was tight. He glanced at the man on the table, then at me.

"There's a Hilux truck," he said. "Local hospital is the only option."

He didn't look at me when he said it. He couldn't.

That's the moral complexity when you're in charge of decisions, about life and death—when there are no good options.

BVM bag in my right hand, squeezing 10-12 per minute.

I looked down at the cook.

He was still unconscious. Still intubated. But alive.

I wrapped his wrists together. Secured the tube and sent him with two fighters and a note.

He died that night.

No oxygen. No airway maintenance. No nursing. No power.

The next morning, I found myself scrubbing down the inside of the kitchen.

I cleared the char, replaced the fuel lines and hung a fire extinguisher beside the stove. The same one we joked about never needing.

The kitchen was repaired, but the silence remained.

I replayed the scene in my head.

What did I miss, what if I had kept him longer, should I have fought harder to transport him?

No answers. Just the noise inside my head.

Later, there would be guilt, even when you did everything right.

That's moral injury.

Not from failure, just the brutal arithmetic of war. And knowing that somewhere, a mother still makes bread in a fire-blackened room—because the man who fed the others never came home to eat again.

Chapter 47: Through Quiet Valleys

The sun had barely crested the mountains when we rolled out of the compound. One ODA, a string of jingle trucks behind us, and a huge Afghan water truck that somehow lumbered impossibly over the ridgelines. A dozen Afghan fighters were crammed into the back of Hiluxes and beat-up gun trucks. It was already hot—the kind of heat that sinks into your bones and stays there.

We were headed out for what would become a twelve-hour convoy—through dry riverbeds, steep switchbacks, and terrain that looked like the moon one minute and an oasis the next. Mud-walled compounds clung to the hillsides like sunbaked scars. Paths carved by centuries of footsteps. It all felt ancient.

The jingle trucks struggled to keep up as we climbed higher. We winched them more than once. One man would hop out, secure the towline, wave them forward, and then sprint back to the cab. Nobody complained. That was just the job.

The militia fighters stayed mostly quiet. A few smoked. Most stared into the horizon. Teenagers with thousand-yard stares.

The mountains were jagged and godless. We twisted through valleys etched by runoff and war. Every now and then, there was movement along a ridge—men walking, AKs tucked under robes. You could always tell by the way they carried the weight. One shoulder was slightly lower. Their silhouette gave them away.

We called in every sighting, but no engagements.

The valley opened into a wide, meandering river, glinting in the sun like something sacred.

On one side, barefoot boys played in the shallows—laughing, chasing each other, splashing water and mud. Their clothes clung to their waists, little more than oversized rags or wrapped scarves. But their joy was bright, loud, and pure.

Downstream, the young girls knelt by the riverbank. Smaller. Focused. They scrubbed laundry on flat stones, dipping and wringing with rhythm. Their Afghan dresses bloomed in the current—bright colors of saffron, indigo, green, and red. The water caught their sleeves like silk flags.

Beyond them, across the river, mud-brick homes clung to the slope. Their walls were smooth and sun-cracked, doors open to the breeze. Faded rugs hung from windows. Some houses had corrals with goats or sheep milling inside hand-stacked stone fences. Small paths wound between the homes like veins.

A narrow dirt road followed the river's edge. It curved lazily with the water, framed by sycamores and dust. The whole scene looked like a postcard from a time before the war.

Afghan men walked the dirt road slowly. Eyes sharp. Movements deliberate. Robes long and neutral. Their pakols shaded faces worn by sun and memory. Each one had a rifle hidden somewhere—under a tunic, behind a bundle. We knew it. They knew we knew.

But none of us raised a weapon.

Maybe they were just protecting their families. The last time they saw military vehicles; it was the Soviets. They still remembered the sound of tank tracks and gunships. Then came the Taliban, with their laws and fear.

All they wanted now was a simple life, safety, family, and order.

Everything was clean. Neat. Dignified. No trash in sight. No chaos.

Just a village pretending to live in peace.

Our HMMWVs rolled slowly through the road's bend. The lead vehicle's turret panned slowly—mounted gun tracking every ridge. Extra gas cans were strapped to the rear of our vehicles. Some of our gun-truck Soldiers, manned the 5.56mm Squad Automatic Weapon (SAW), mounted in the rear.

We watched, they watched, and no words were spoken.

Just a long mutual understanding.

In one gun truck, an Afghan warlord with a narrow face tapped the mount and pointed.

He spoke fast, sharp.

The translator hesitated.

"He says... he killed five Russians there." The warlord grinned. Continued.

"Slit their throats in their sleep," the translator added. "Desecrated the bodies."

Laughter followed—not loud. Just low and warm. Like they were remembering something fond.

The warlord smelled like old chai and rot. His teeth were stained red. His eyes were hollow but content. He smiled at me.

I didn't smile back.

The story hung in the air like smoke. Like blood drying on stone. There was no way to feel clean after that.

And still—I said nothing. We had hours left to ride together.

Later, the hills opened wide. A lake appeared—still water, abandoned dam machinery rusted on the far side like steel bones. Power lines, devoid of wire stretched across nothing. The land felt forgotten. Like a dream you only half-remembered.

It looked like a resort that time had forgotten.

We stopped and circled into a defensive posture.

Half the ODA pulled security. The rest of us stripped off sweat-soaked DCUs. Body armor dropped in clumps. Shirts off. Tevas on.

We walked into the water.

It felt like forgiveness.

Cool, soft, no current. The kind of water that made you forget about the war for a few minutes.

We swam. We floated. We grinned.

Some leaned back in the shallows, arms folded behind their heads, eyes on clouds.

The militia fighters stayed near the trucks. A few watched. A few squatted and smoked. Some smiled.

I lay on the rocks after, sun-drying my skin.

And for ten minutes, I remembered what peace felt like.

Then came the return.

DCUs back on. Sweat reactivated. Armor refastened. Holsters adjusted. Turrets remounted.

The second half of the ODA got to enjoy their swim time.

An hour total and the convoy continued to roll forward.

We passed poppy fields—thin stalks rising, colors bright.

Early summer 2002. First real harvest since the Taliban fell.

Not our mission.

Not yet.

But we knew. This was the new war. Drugs. Corruption. Money.

Same story, different latitude.

Vietnam, Colombia and now Afghanistan.

The war always follows combatants' home.

We were surrounded by beauty—children playing, water glistening, hills painted with homes.

But under it all was something else: the knowledge that every man here was prepared to kill. That every kindness came with history. That every laugh echoed from blood.

The men on the road? They weren't enemies. Not yet.

But they weren't at peace, either.

And neither were we.

What haunted us wasn't a firefight.

It was the quiet calm. The normalcy.

And knowing what would come next.

Moral Injury; not pulling a trigger; but passing through someone else's life with steel and suspicion. Knowing they'll remember you long after you're gone. Even if you never fired a shot.

That night we would ride again.

But for now, the sun was high, the trucks hummed on, and no one had bled.

At the end of this tour, not all of us would make it home, alive.

Chapter 48: The Specialist

He wasn't one of us—not by MOS.

No Special Forces tab. Just a qualified paratrooper. An E-4 Specialist. A mechanic.

But out there on the vehicle patrols, he was part of the team.

He had a round belly and short arms, and nobody ever saw him pass a PT test clean. But he could rebuild a Humvee transmission in the dark, bare-handed, with half the right parts and a bad attitude. He was always under the trucks, welding mounts, rewiring switches, and replacing belts. All while the rest of us were eating.

He'd sleep on a creeper under a vehicle and wake up with a wrench in his hand.

He didn't take any crap, and we didn't give him any. He was a real asset to have on our vehicle patrols. When something broke out in the middle of nowhere, it wasn't the tabbed guys who fixed it—it was him.

One day, he stumbled back from the maintenance shed with his hand over his face.

"I think I just lost my eye," he said calmly, like it was a joke.

I saw the blood. The tear pattern. The shine.

He wasn't joking.

Metal shavings. Pressure-fitted bracket he'd been hammering came loose and snapped a shard straight into his right cornea. Caught a mix of metal, grease, and grit. Direct puncture.

We got him into the aid station fast.

He sat on the table, breathing heavily but not panicked. His voice was tight. "Can you see anything?" he asked. "Like… is it gone?"

I flushed the eye with sterile saline. Over and over. I opened a single-use vial of Proparacaine. A few drops into the eye to numb it. He grunted. Said nothing. It ran red. Then pink. Then mostly clear.

His nares flared. His knuckles were white.

I snapped on my gloves. Unwrapped the fluorescein strip. Dipped it in saline. Touched it to the inside of the lower lid. Waited.

I clicked on the UV light under magnification.

The green glow lit up the tear in his cornea like a roadmap. Linear puncture. Jagged edge. No full rupture—but deep enough that he couldn't keep the eye open. A small sliver of metal was deeply embedded.

"I'm gonna try once to remove it," I said.

He nodded.

I used a sterile loop and a small-tipped swab. One attempt. No success.

"Alright," I said. "That's it. You need surgery."

His face fell. "You mean now?"

"Now."

He didn't cry. But he blinked a lot.

I prepped the bandages. Applied sterile eye pads over both eyes.

"Why both?" he asked.

"If the good eye moves, the bad one moves too. You don't want that."

He sat there. Blind. Alone in a war zone. Holding onto my arm.

"Don't let go," he said.

I didn't. I guided him with my hand on his shoulder, telling him when to step up when to duck under the rotor wash. The whole way, he never let go.

I walked him to the bird—his hand gripped my sleeve like a child. He stumbled once on the ramp. Apologized.

"It's alright," I said. "I'm your eyes now."

He sat in silence as the blades spun up. No medal. No speech. Just a Specialist flying home from a war nobody would remember he was part of.

―――――

We redeployed 7-months later.

New trucks. New route. New breakages.

No one to fix them at midnight.

The new mechanic didn't know as much. Less experienced. Didn't like to accompany us on vehicle patrols. Didn't know how we liked things rigged. Didn't know that duct tape on a relay wasn't a shortcut—it was a promise.

―――――

Years later, I heard he was medically discharged. Partial vision in one eye. Lives on his parents' farm. No kids. Just a '55 Chevy step-side truck he keeps trying to restore.

He doesn't come to reunions.

He wasn't invited.

But he should've been.

Because that kid with the gut? He gave everything. And we forgot him.

Not because we were cruel.

But because the mission rolled forward—and he didn't.

That's another kind of injury.

Not one you can treat.

Not one that bleeds.

Just the kind that turns a good man into a ghost.

And if you're reading this, brother?

We remember you.

And I'm sorry it took a war and a book to finally say it.

Chapter 49: Four Feet from Home

We heard the blast before we saw the smoke.

IED, maybe a pressure plate. The lead EOD squad was sweeping a route just off a village road—standard clearance. Then, the dog started barking. Then the handler yelled.

Then the earth lifted.

We ran to the site. Dust was still hanging in the air, thick and yellow brown. The EOD handler was kneeling in it, rocking.

The dog was on its side.

Whimpering.

Blood pooled beneath its body, seeping into the sand. One leg—gone. The other mangled. Breathing fast. Mouth open. The handler had pulled off his helmet. His face was wet with snot and tears.

I stopped a few feet away. Didn't move closer.

He looked up at me, voice broken. "Can you save her?" I hesitated.
I was a Special Forces Medical Sergeant. An 18D. I'd decompressed lungs. Clamped arteries. Performed invasive medical procedures. Treated goats in training and conducted lifesaving interventions, under night vision.

But I had never treated a dog.

I stepped forward. Gloves on. I scanned the damage like it was a human. It wasn't. The anatomy was off. Bleeding was everywhere. Bones wrong. The dog's eye followed me.

I started working. Pressure bandage. Two tourniquets, improvised with a bootlace and tension.

She whimpered again.

The handler crouched beside me. His hand was on her neck. He whispered her name—as she could still hear it. Like she might answer.

I asked him to hold pressure.

He did, with trembling hands.

She bled out ten minutes later.

We covered her body with a poncho liner. The handler didn't move, and the mission continued.

We rotated him back to Bagram airfield. He walked like he'd been shot. Carried her collar in his fist the entire ride.

I didn't say much to comfort him. I didn't understand his pain back the.

I thought that she was just a dog.

We'd killed them when they scavenged in our trash pits.

We'd lost teammates, and I thought it was different.

To him, it wasn't.

Years passed and I retired from the army. I bought a house. Moved into a quieter life.

My wife suggested we get a dog. I told her no. Too much mess and too much work.

She always rescued stray animals and eventually brought one home.

The dog was emaciated and shaking with fear. It was a female and wouldn't leave the laundry room for three days.

I fed her. Didn't touch her. Didn't name her.

But she watched me.

After a few weeks, she started sitting by the bed. Then, sleeping beside it.

It wasn't long before she climbed up onto it.

When I had nightmares, she'd nudge me. Just once. Then, lay down again.

My wife brought another one home. Another female. A companion for her this time.

Now, they both sleep at my feet.

They know when I need space, when I need quiet, when I'm angry.

They don't talk or ask questions.

They just stay quiet, roll onto their backs for a stomach rub. I facilitate them.

I think back to that K9 handler.

I think about what I didn't say.

About how I treated his pain like it was smaller than mine.

About how he lost a partner—and I saw a paw instead of a teammate.

Now I get it. She wasn't a dog; she was his Soldier.

And I would've given anything to save his Soldier.

That handler wouldn't suffer from PTSD. He would suffer from the guilt of losing her. The sadness of loss. That's moral injury. A quiet suffering when losing your best friend. Made even worse when they die in your arms.

Chapter 50: Developing an Asset

The Suv rolled to a stop just outside the gate. No markings. Tan. Dust-choked.

Two men stepped out—one in local garb, the other in faded cargo pants and a plain gray shirt. No patches. No rank. But I knew who they were.

CIA. Or, as they preferred—OGA.

The one in civvies flicked a cigarette to the dirt and stepped forward. Blue eyes. Cropped hair. Callused hands.

Mike.

We'd crossed paths before. He was Force Recon before the towers fell. He was one of those guys who didn't need to say he'd been places—you could see it in the way he scanned rooftops mid-sentence.

This wasn't his first war. He had been forward deployed during Desert Storm.

Back in '02, the CIA's support structure was minimal. No medics. Limited infrastructure. Mostly shooters and shadows.

He came looking for someone who could move in the gray. Someone with a steady hand and a trauma bag.

"You ever think about working for us?" he asked.

I thought about it briefly, then I said no.

Not because I wasn't tempted. Because I had a responsibility to my Team.

I wasn't going to leave them short a medic so a guy in a nondescript shirt could make me feel special.

You don't abandon your brothers in a firefight.

And you don't abandon them before one.

Now he was back.

And this time, he brought an asset.

The guy looked like hell. Afghan. Mid-30s. Twitching, sweating, sunken eyes. He was detoxing—bad.

And I could already see what Mike wanted.

He wanted me to hold this guy together just long enough to use him.

We walked him into the aid station— bare cot, med bag on the floor. Mike leaned against the wall, arms crossed.

"Think he's usable?" he asked.

I checked the man's pupils. Tracked his heart rate. Watched him shake.

"He won't hold up in the field," I said.

"But he'll do what you say—for now."

Mike pulled a few small ampules from his pocket. The local markets sold anything you needed. Even intravenous narcotics. I drew up a syringe with enough to take the edge off. He wouldn't be completely comfortable. Just enough to keep him upright.

I crouched beside him.

"You want this?" I asked.

He nodded. Quick. Desperate.

"Then listen. You don't freeze or lie to these men."

I injected the dose slowly. Deliberate. His shoulders softened. The twitching slowed. He looked up like I'd just pulled him out of the ocean.

Mike watched from the corner.

"You're good at this," he said.

I stood.

Adjusted my rifle.

Didn't look at the man.

"I'm not here for him," I said.

"I'm here to keep Americans alive." Mike nodded. Same half-smile. "Same thing."

But it wasn't.

Because I wasn't sure what I'd just enabled.

This wasn't a casualty. It was a weapon we'd just reassembled.

A broken man made useful again—barely—and pointed at something none of us could see.

Outside, a lone Apache buzzed the ridge. Dust kicked up. The man on the cot didn't move.

Which was good.

Because if he froze in the wrong moment…

If the intel was bad…

If he got caught playing both sides—

That sound wouldn't be a warning next time.

It would be the last thing he ever heard.

Chapter 51: The Cow

The heat of the Afghan summer pressed down on the valley, dry and relentless. Off in the distance, Apache gunships barked out warning bursts from their 30mm cannons—lethal punctuation echoing through the mountains. It was late June, and the Fourth of July was coming. After months of eating rice, flatbread, goat stew, MREs, and T-rats, I wanted to do something special for my ODA. Something real. Something American.

Beef.

As the team's 18 Delta, my job didn't stop at trauma medicine. It included food procurement, food preparation, and sanitation. When we utilized a local cook, the medic oversaw all aspects of the Afghan's food handling.

When we initially hired our first cook, he insisted on sleeping in the kitchen. It was a mud brick building with a gas fire and pressure-cooking pots. The Afghans pressure-cooked all the meat—to kill bacteria and parasites. I couldn't eat rice for years after I left Special Forces.

The village market was alive in that way only Afghan bazaars could be—equal parts brutal and beautiful. Flies hovered in a dense cloud around goat and beef displayed on homemade tables. Butchers carved meat with ancient knives, their hands fast and casual. Beef slabs hung on rusty hooks, slick with moisture. The air was heavy with dust, spice, and blood.

My translator stood next to me. He wore traditional Afghan whites with a black vest and a green chest rig loaded with AK mags. His AKM was spotless. He was a survivor of too many wars to count, his eyes holding the hard truth of what happened when ideals clashed with reality.

"You want a cow?" he asked.

I nodded.

We found one tied near a stall—a sturdy black-and-white with big, too-human eyes. She looked up at me. Calm. Curious. Flicked her tail once. Licked my hand.

That shouldn't have mattered.

But it did.

I paid $400. Way more than it was worth. The money wasn't mine. U.S. Government funds. I didn't blink.

Back at the FOB, we tied her under some shade. She tracked me every time I walked by. I tried not to look back, but I always did. Her eyes followed me like she knew.

Growing up poor, I was taught not to get attached to animals. Survival first. If you couldn't feed it, you didn't keep it. I'd slaughtered plenty before. Goats. Pigs. SFQC taught us how—jugular cut, proper drainage, skinning, butchering. I knew what I was doing.

But this one felt different.

I told one of our militias to feed her. She kept tracking me.

A few days before the Fourth, I walked out to her pen and stared. She stared back.

She was just another female I didn't need in my life.

That day, I took her back to the market. The butcher gave me $200. Half of what I paid.

"A fool's trade," my translator muttered. "Tomorrow, she dies anyway. You will buy her meat then." Maybe. But not from my hands.

Then came the miracle.

On July 3rd, a Chinook touched down and offloaded vacuum-sealed ribeye steaks. One hundred of them. Sent by other Green Berets up the chain. They always looked out for us. Never forgot the guys out front. That's how Special Forces takes care of its own. Doesn't matter the Ao.

The local metalworkers had built us two grills from my sketch—a split 44-gallon drum, hinges, welded legs, and steel grating. Afghan ingenuity paired with American craving.

The FST men cooked all day. Real fire. Real steak. It felt good for someone else to look out for us. It felt special, and it mattered.

Morale soared across the entire camp.

As evening settled, the smell of steak hung thick in the air. Soldiers sat around, talking and laughing. But the night wasn't over.

While the rest of the U.S. Soldiers celebrated, a few of us prepped a deception op. Intelligence suggested Al-Qaeda might target us during the festivities. We used that to our advantage—staged groups around fires and created the illusion of distraction.

We slipped out quietly and set up sniper positions. Two-man teams moved to the high ground posted up on observation points. We waited. NVGs up. Safeties off. Watching.

Nothing moved.

Then came the encore.

Our Bravos had acquired several Javelins when the 10th Mountain Division rotated out. They turned in all their ammo, and we grabbed whatever we could. But Javelins—and multiple? Rare as hell. Stateside, you can't even get a live one unless you're in a training unit.

That night, they fired it.

The launch was thunder.

Infrared guidance locked in. The missile arced out toward a wrecked vehicle on the test range—a rusted-out hulk from some long-forgotten fight.

Then—impact.

Sparks. Fire. Metal. A bloom of violence against the night sky.

I'll never forget that night—steak on my breath, enemy unseen, and the strange, electric pride of watching a Javelin erupt in sparks against the Afghan night sky.

War is strange. One day, you spare a cow. The next, you launch a missile worth more than a house in Fayetteville.

Somewhere between those two moments was the truth.

And that night, surrounded by brothers, meat still warm, stars overhead—I let myself believe that maybe, just for a minute, we were human.

I never asked what happened to the cow. But I stopped looking toward the butcher's stall after that.

Chapter 52: The Afghan Commander's Bargain

The Afghan sun showed no mercy.

It pressed down like judgment from above, baking our compound into a kiln of grit and steel. Dust hung in the air and never settled—just shifted with every gust. It coated our boots, our rifles, our teeth. We coughed it up like guilt.

Beside me stood my interpreter—white tunic, black vest, three worn AK mags across his chest. His AKM was spotless, stock folded tight. No prayer beads, no tribal cloth, just function. Just survival.

We weren't going on a mission.

We were going to negotiate.

A few days earlier, we'd sent one of our militia commanders north toward the Chinese border. His orders weren't tactical. They were logistical. Psychological. Morale-based.

He was sent to bring us something rare.

Vodka.

Maybe some Armenian cognac. Maybe a few crates of Soviet-era spirits that still floated down trade routes like ghosts.

In Afghanistan, anything worth having moved in strange directions—especially hope.

We entered the market through a narrow alley of mud walls and old shade. The smells hit first—meat, sweat, cardamom, open sewage. Goat carcasses swung from hooks. Flies hovered in black clouds.

Butchers hacked with cleavers like they were splitting firewood. The sound echoed like distant gunfire.

It was chaos. But it was alive.

He stepped out of the shadows like he'd been waiting for us.

The Afghan commander.

Thick shoulders. Dark blue shalwar kameez. A cracked leather chest rig crossed in an X. Inside it, a worn Makarov. His eyes were granite—flat, unreadable.

"You sent your men north," he said.

"They returned," I answered.

"The vodka is here. Your payment is ready." Then, the pause.

"Perhaps… a trade is better." That was the game.

Always was.

Cash wasn't valued. Leverage was.

He gestured toward a goat tied to a post. Brown. Clean. Eyes wide.

"A fine animal," he said. "Good for a feast."

"We're not here for goats."

He smiled. Didn't press. Didn't need to.

He wanted something else.

"I hear your men are planning a celebration," he said.

"A feast. Perhaps… a race?" The word was out.

Inside our compound, a few of the Civil Affairs guys—SF-tabbed—had cooked up a donkey race. Bareback, ropes for reins. Military helmets for protection. Wagers. Absurdity for the sake of sanity.

"Let me enter a rider," the commander said.

"My own donkey." He wasn't asking.

"If he wins?" I asked.

"A gift," he said. "A case of vodka."

"And if he loses?"

"Then you buy more."

The real deal wasn't the vodka. It was the relationship.

The bargain behind the bargain.

A way to stay inside our wire without raising his rifle.

I extended my hand.

"Agreed."

His grip was dry and firm.

Like holding onto history.

"My man will meet you at the old Soviet tank," he said.

"He'll be waiting."

As we turned back toward the compound, my interpreter chuckled low.

"You look like them," he said.

"But you're not one of them." I adjusted my Oakleys. Smiled.

"No," I said.

"But I'm learning."

The donkey race was ridiculous.

But it was ours.

And sometimes, the smartest thing a Green Beret can do…

Is smile, shake hands, pretend the race matters—and walk away with the goat still tied to the post.

Because sometimes winning a war means losing a deal.

And living with it.

Chapter 53: Ice, Vodka, and Donkey Races

The Afghan soldier rolled up in a battered Hilux, suspension groaning as the truck had lived too long.

Dust followed like a shadow, curling behind him in long brown ribbons. He stepped out lean and tired, the kind of man shaped by years of war—not gym strength, but survival strength.

Strapped beneath his arm: a cracked leather holster, sagging from time. Inside it, a Russian pistol. The grip had been worn to bare metal. Probably looted from a dead Soviet long ago.

I stood among our Afghan counterparts, half-camouflaged by beard, sun, and time. My Oakleys and rifle were the giveaways. The rest? Just another man burned brown by war.

My M4 hung tight. Suppressed. Painted in dust and desert. It wasn't a weapon anymore; it was a limb.

The Afghan fighter stepped forward. His AK slung casually. His men followed—quiet, serious, competent.

"You have something for me?" I asked in Pashto.

He grinned; teeth stained from naswar. Gestured to the truck bed. A tarp peeled back.

Vodka. Armenian cognac. Dusty crates of Soviet beer. Nestled among them were old glass Coca-Cola bottles—the kind that hiss when opened, the kind that tastes like memory.

"Next time… something stronger?" He asked. 'Something from the fields?"

I didn't blink.

"We'll see."

We wouldn't. That was a line we didn't cross. It wasn't our mission, at least not yet.

It was July. The heat pressed like armor. Sweat pooled in our boots. Trash fires from the village drifted through camp in greasy waves.

And somehow—we had ice.

A whole block from the village. Machete-carved. Undrinkable. Loaded with bacteria. Perfect for chilling glass Coke bottles.

We dropped them in a steel tub and packed the ice around them.

That cold Coke might as well have been gold.

After the Fourth, with security quiet, our Civil Affairs senior NCO grinned at the Team Sergeant.

"Top… about those donkey races?" The MSG gave a nod.

That was all it took.

If you've never seen grown men racing half-wild donkeys across a dirt track in a Special Forces FOB, then you've never seen real morale.

Local kids wrangled the animals—biting, kicking, furious. Perfect.

One Civil Affairs guy tried to mount his donkey and got tossed flat on his ass. His gear scattered. His pride took longer to find.

He was a mess. Always high. Valium from the local bazaar. Slurred his speech. Sweaty even in the cold.

His teammate—an 18D like me—had stopped trying to fix him.

He just kept him alive.

Kept him close and covered for him.

That's how it worked sometimes.

We didn't burn each other down.

We just made sure no one fell apart too loudly.

Years later, I remembered a different man.

Iraq. I knew him from my PA class. He was an army captain. Very smart and well liked. He was found dead in his room. He'd missed two days of work when they went looking for him. Another classmate had found him. Partially naked. Down to his spandex underwear. Needle still in his arm. He been dipping into the hospital's narcotic supplies.

The command tried to cover it. Tried to protect the image. It didn't work.

The war eats people in different ways.

But that day?

That day, we laughed.

Dust choked the track. Donkeys screamed. Men cursed. Someone fired celebratory rounds into the sky—because, of course, they did.

For a moment, it felt like something human.

That night, we sat around the grill. Goat meat over crackling wood. Coke bottles sweating cold. Vodka warm. Men warmer.

We weren't just Soldiers.

We were Brothers.

Most of us would make it home.

Some wouldn't.

But that night, we were all still here—watching the last donkey disappear into the dark, laughing like it mattered.

In the middle of nowhere, surrounded by enemies… We found our sanity in cold soda and dumb bets. And in a war where everything else was temporary—that was enough.

Chapter 54: Unconventional Warfare (UW) Hospital

We didn't have a sign—just a red cross painted on a white building.

No flag.

Just a goat shed turned into a place where people didn't die—if we were lucky.

No doors at first. No real walls. Just a dirt floor, a table that once held fertilizer, and a pile of med bags I treated like sacred tools.

Over time, we built it up. Hung ponchos for privacy. Sandbags for cover. A cot to lay the broken on.

And me—the medic with no license and the weight of life and death in my hands most days.

We called it the clinic and then the UW hospital.

It was rarely quiet, and never enough.

The Woman with the Miscarriage:

She arrived on a donkey cart. Wrapped in blankets. Eyes half-open. Silent.

Her husband never spoke—just stared at the ground. The old woman beside him did all the talking. Loud. Pointing to the blood between the young woman's legs like I was supposed to undo what had already been done.

I could smell it.

Sepsis.

She'd miscarried days ago. Maybe more. Now, she was dying.

I told them—through the interpreter—she needed evacuation. Surgery. IV antibiotics we didn't have in volume.

They refused.

"If she dies, she dies here."

So, I cleaned her gently. Gave her morphine. Dressed her modestly.

She smiled at me before they carried her back out.

I never saw her again.

The Man with the Open Jaw:

He walked in on his own.

Hands clutching his face like it might fall off.

It nearly had.

A blast had torn his mandible apart. Some kind of IED or a grenade. His jaw was blood and tissue. He couldn't speak.

I sat him down, numbed what I could, and packed Kerlix into the wound. Then I wrapped an ACE bandage overlaid with Coban, building a facial sling around the back of his neck.

He never made a sound.

The translator stood silently, his hand over his mouth.

We gave the man a letter for a field hospital farther south. He left that hour.

Weeks later, I saw him again.

Same eyes. Same broken face.

He pointed to me. Nodded once, unable to smile and walked away.

The Flail Chest:

A tribal fight. The kind that predated our war by centuries.

They dropped him at our gate—shirt soaked in blood, chest moving like a paper bag in the wind. Flail chest.

Three ribs, at least. Paradoxical motion with every breath.

No lung sounds on the right.

I laid him down. Found the fifth intercostal space, mid-axillary line.

Needle. Decompression.

A hiss. Then, a sigh.

I had no suction. No X-ray. No ICU.

But I had him breathing.

That night, I lay awake in my cot, listening to the wind rattle the ponchos we hung for walls.

No beeping monitors. No nurses.

Just me, God, and a stack of gloves I was running low on.

The Boy with the Eyes:

He wasn't injured.

Not physically.

He came with his father—a village elder. Stood silently behind him, eyes wide, unblinking.

They asked if he could stay with us.

A companion. A helper. A gift.

I said absolutely not!

I said it calmly while something inside me boiled.

Later, one of the older militia men approached and asked why I'd refused such an honor.

I told him, through the translator:

"In America, we don't accept boys as gifts. No man owns another. I'm a healer. Not a buyer of lives." He nodded slowly.

"In America," he said, "you must very be lonely."

The Truth of It:
I wasn't a doctor.

I didn't have a license.

But I had a team to keep alive. And a village trying to survive in the cracks of a forever war.

Some days, I felt like a surgeon.

Some days, I felt like a butcher.

Some days, I felt like a priest.

Because when your Afghan patient has no other options, and your decisions aren't documented. You carry every outcome in your chest for the rest of your life.

I don't remember every face.

But I remember the smells and the weight of decisions, about life and death.

I think back to that little aid station that never had a name—Just blood in the dirt and hands that did their best. And I know that I made a difference.

Chapter 55: Shoulder to Dust

The Blackhawk lifted off into a column of dirt and rotor wash, the pitch of the engine fading into a heavy silence as the crew chief secured the cabin. Mark lay on the helicopter's deck. His uniform was soaked, his shoulder wrapped tight in bandages and pressure dressings that had already bled through.

Jim still knelt beside him, gloves still sticky with blood, IV line taped to the inside of Mark's arm. Coban stretched tight across the gauze. No bubbling at the neck or subcutaneous emphysema Mark's trachea hadn't shifted and his neck veins weren't distended. Breath sounds were equal and clear. The bleeding was slowing, but the muscle had been shredded. The bone was cracked. He couldn't know for sure—not yet.

Mark's eyes fluttered open.

"I wasn't screaming too bad out there, was I?" Jim looked down.

Even now—broken, pale, half-conscious—Mark was worried about appearances. About setting an example.

"These guys really look up to us," he muttered, barely audible. "I didn't want to let them down."

Jim didn't answer. Because the truth was, he didn't know if Mark would ever use his arm again. He'd done what he could—packed it, wrapped it, stabilized it—but nerves don't tell you what they're going to do. Not in the back of a bird, not under NVGs, not when every second of training has been compressed into this moment.

SF medics don't get to say, "I don't know." Not when the patient is still breathing. Not when that patient is looking at you like you're the only thing standing between them and the void. Not when the casualty is one of your own.

So, Jim gave a tight nod.

Let the silence speak.

Because sometimes the lie isn't cruel—it's necessary.

Years later, Jim told me, "Mark is a tough motherfucker…… But we were both bluffing. He was trying to look strong for the Team, and I was trying to make him believe everything would be okay. And I didn't know if that was true or not. But I had to make him believe that I did."

That's what we do.

Not just stop the bleeding.

Not just pack the wound.

But carry the truth alone so someone else doesn't have to.

The lie we tell our wounded, when we're not sure if they'll make it.

That knowledge, the forewarning, the outcome… they sit with you for life. Guilt sometimes creeps in. Those feelings of not doing enough.

The slow tentacles of moral injury, wrap around the mind.

It's usually only a problem if you lose them. You tried your utmost, and they still didn't make it.

But tonight, Mark would survive. He would heal and regain full use of his arm.

Minimal muscle loss.

No PTSD. No moral injury. He was one of the lucky ones.

Chapter 56: Blackout Days

Bagram Airbase, 2003.

Resupply came in waves—pallets of C-130s filled with everything from wet wipes to toilet paper. Somewhere between the forklifts and the fresh produce, a quiet economy emerged. It wasn't a black market. It was survival.

Young Soldiers—mechanics, cooks, fuel handlers—started trading snacks, energy drinks, and gear. Need an extra cot? Ask Rodriguez from supply. Looking for baby wipes after a two-week patrol? Jones from the laundry probably had a stash. A bottle of whiskey? Harder, but not impossible. The supply chain had gaps, and these guys knew how to fill them.

Green Berets didn't just tolerate it—we protected it.

Because those weren't just hustlers.

They were the guys who kept our trucks running when we cracked an axle on a rock shelf. The ones who refilled our fuel bladders after being sucked dry by helicopters. They replaced tires, fixed wiring, and built the showers when no one else did.

They weren't in the spotlight. But they kept the lights on.

We made sure they got what they needed. Helped them set up unofficial shop space. Covered for them when a clipboard-holding officer came sniffing around. The "unauthorized activities" were "logistics calibration drills."

They were in our unit, and we were in their corner. In our war trust wasn't rare, but comfort was, and they gave us both.

One day a month, there were no briefings. No whiteboards. No official memos. But every man in Charlie Company knew when the blackout period had begun—because someone was dragging the coolers behind the weight benches. Then, someone was pouring the first round, and we knew we were off the clock.

We were still in country. Still on the airbase. Still in the war. But for one night, behind the Red Door, we weren't carrying rifles—we were carrying each other.

Coolers full of Crown, Jim Beam, and Johnny Walker. Smuggled in by the embassy staff or cases of beer, disguised in vehicle part crates, carried in like sacred offerings. We lifted. We partied. Not to forget—but to remember what it felt like to laugh.

Green Berets mingled wearing black company T-shirts, short black shorts and either running shoes or military boots.

This was a time when you could put your weapons away. Locked in our rooms, in the same compound as our parties. You didn't leave through the red door unless you were armed. But behind it, in the open courtyard, in our secure compound; we could relax.

One night, the speakers blared 3 Doors Down. Another country music. The plywood bar was more like a table than anything else. Just a place to balance cups or cans on. It didn't matter what rank you wore. We were all equal during blackout days. Some nights, the Air Force and Army NCOs joined us. Not flings—real relationships. Women who deployed beside us. Who laughed like we did, drank like we did, and still made it to formation the next morning without complaint. They didn't need our protection—they'd earned their place beside us.

Those weren't parties. They were decompression rituals. Everyone looked out for each other and made sure we survived the nights just as fiercely as we survived missions. We all knew that the silence after a mission could kill you faster than a bullet. And sometimes, the only thing that keeps you sane is knowing your brothers are right there beside you.

We worked hard, but some of us played even harder. There was always a sober medic on standby. Always someone to patch up a teammate, in need.

Chapter 57: The Neckline

We were half an hour into Exfil and already behind schedule. One wounded, one disoriented, and one ghost-pale Afghan strapped in the bed of the Hilux, his eyes wide with the kind of fear that didn't need translation.

Jim was in the back with him, cutting his clothes away with trauma shears. Blood soaked through the waistband, pooling near his kidneys. No exit wound, which meant internal. That's worse than bad. That's death on a time delay.

I leaned in beside them, pulling out my IV kit. "Peripheral?"

Jim shook his head. "Collapsed veins. Nothing."

I pulled down my NVGs. The green haze made him look like something already dead.

I went for the external jugular.

Some guys flinch at that. Textbook medicine tells you to avoid the neck unless it's sterile, unless you've got an ultrasound unless you've got a degree. We didn't have any of that. What we had was a dying man, no access, and two 18Ds in the dark.

I'd practiced it dozens of times. Sometimes in trauma bays. Sometimes, on real Afghan patients in the FST—if I was lucky enough to get hands-on before the docs took over. I knew the risks. Infection that goes straight to the heart. Thrombosis. Air embolism. It's not a line you throw in for hydration or some hungover GI needing Zofran.

But this guy was cratering. Sweat beading on his forehead. Heart rate through the roof. Blood pressure bottoming out.

"Neckline," I said.

Jim didn't argue. He held the light while I found the vein—barely visible in the low light, but I knew the landmarks: the angle of the jaw, down the sternocleidomastoid, just above the clavicle. I felt for the bounce. It gave.

Needle in. Flash. Thread the catheter. Tape it down as if my life depended on it—because he did.

"Got it." I handed off the bag. "Get that bolus in. Let's see if we can reverse the slide."

Jim didn't waste a second. "You ever done this before on a real casualty?"

"Three times. One in training, one Afghan kid last rotation, one guy in the FST."

"And?"

"The kid lived. The Afghan made it to surgery. The FST doc thanked me. Still had to go burn shit right after, but he told me it saved time." Jim cracked a grin. "Medic life."

I looked down at the Afghan's face. He wasn't calm—he was somewhere between terror and surrender. But he wasn't flailing anymore. The fluid was doing its job for now.

Flashback – Goat Lab

They drilled it into us hard during 18D training:

Respect the goat like it's your brother.

Not because we practiced IVs on dead animals—you can't. Dead goats don't have blood pressure. There's nothing to find, nothing to hit.

But we did work on live anesthetized animals under tight veterinary supervision. We learned how veins shift under shock and how skin changes when perfusion drops, how failure feels.

And how to come back from it.

If you couldn't show restraint and compassion when no one was watching, you didn't belong in this craft. You didn't belong on a team. Period.

That training wasn't about brute force. It was about presence. Precision. Pressure when it mattered.

Because one day, it wouldn't be a goat.

It would be a Soldier.

And there wouldn't be anyone else.

Back in the Fight

The vehicle bounced hard, and the IV fluttered. I reached out, instinctively cupping the line with one gloved hand, steadying it.

"Why the E.J.?" Jim asked. "Why not the IO?"

"IO's good," I said. "Sternal, tibial—hell, Rangers will try to stick them through ceramic plates. We both laughed.

But we don't all carry enough drivers. Sometimes, you're down to one. Sometimes, you save it for a second casualty." He nodded. He understood.

"And sometimes," I added, "you need medication access, not just volume. You push the wrong dose of morphine, and you need to reverse it. No time to get an IV after the fact."

He glanced at the casualty. "You think we'll need to reverse anything?"

"Not this time. But I'm not going to let my tools go rusty. If I don't use this skill here, it's gone the next time I need it."

He nodded again, quietly this time. We both knew the truth: no one teaches this anymore. Not in the official tactical combat casualty care (TCCC or TC3) guidelines. Too risky. Too many unknowns. But that's the difference between textbook trauma care and Special Forces Medical Sergeants in combat.

We don't always follow checklists. But we always solve problems.

Later, after we handed off the casualty, the FST anesthesiologist came out and said, "That line saved us ten minutes." I thanked him. He thanked me.

Then, I walked back to the latrine buildings to burn human waste and stir diesel ash.

That's what being a Special Forces medic is. One minute, you're threading a needle into a dying man's neck. The next, you're holding a stirring stick in a steel drum under the sun.

No glory. No medals. Just knowing you did your part.

And when I finally laid down that night, hands still smelling faintly of iodine and death, I whispered a quiet thanks:

To the goat that gave its life in training.

To the Afghan who let me practice on him months ago.

To my classmates who didn't make it past goat lab.

They made me better. And that night, better was good enough.

Medic Notes on Emergency E.J. Access:

Not first-line access.

High infection risk.

Risk of air embolism, thrombosis, and cannula migration.

It must be secured properly and never left uncapped.

Useful in shock patients, IV drug users with collapsed veins, or critical trauma.

Only to be attempted by experienced medics in extreme settings.

Practice often.

Respect it.

Use it only when nothing else will do.

Chapter 58: The Light Behind the Wall

It was the only light visible during the night.

A single bulb, strung through salvaged wiring, flickering beneath the inner wall of our firebase. It swayed slightly in the wind—just enough to cast dancing shadows against the Hesco barriers and the rough plywood siding of our makeshift aid station.

If you could even call it that.

Inside, there were two cots, a field litter, an IV pole, and a plywood shelf stacked with gauze, syringes, ACE wraps, bottles of Betadine, and whatever else the battalion could spare. The air smelled like iodine, old canvas, and dried sweat—a scent that lived in your nostrils long after you rotated home.

That bulb wasn't just a fixture.

It was a beacon.

We'd rigged it from an old cord, spliced and taped with the kind of urgency only field medicine demands. Every blackout zone needed its own North Star—and this was ours.

Most nights, someone came by—bleeding, sick, broken, or just holding the pieces together long enough to make it through one more.

Beneath the light.

It wasn't always trauma.

Sometimes, it was skin infections from poor hygiene, constant sweat, and the endless friction of plate carriers.

Fungal rashes bloomed under arms and belts.

Fevers came without warning.

I treated pneumonia once—low oxygen saturation, fever, chills, and diminished breath sounds bilaterally. Both lower lobes were congested.

Another time, a support guy came in with a deep, hacking cough that wouldn't quit. No fever. No sputum. Just burn pit lungs that wouldn't heal. I gave him doxycycline. It wouldn't fix the air, but it gave him something to hold onto.

And then there was the night the shrapnel guy arrived.

Afghan civilian. He'd been plowing his field and detonated an old Soviet mine. He was brought in by his teenage son. The blast drove metal into his thigh; dirt and gravel packed the wound like concrete. We had no sedation, so I numbed him as best I could and dug it out beneath the bulb. He didn't cry. Just bit his hand until I was done.

When it was over, he smiled—missing teeth and bad breath. He laid back and closed his eyes.

I let him rest for a few hours.

He had to be gone before the bulb was extinguished at the break of dawn.

Sometimes, it wasn't patients at all.

Sometimes it was a teammate.

A man with too many faces behind his eyes, trying to smoke his way back to sleep.

He just sat in the light.

Like it made the night smaller.

Sometimes it was me.

I'd sit there with a headlamp and a notebook, writing vitals, meds given, how many bags of saline we'd used, how many IVs started, and who needed follow-up. It was the only system we had—handwritten logs sent with the situation report to battalion medical.

If something we logged matched something they had, they'd push it forward the next morning on the next bird: morphine, doxycycline, tourniquets, pressure dressings.

Once, battalion medical sent us a massive box of suture kits and an even bigger box of suture removal sets. We didn't have much use for suturing out here. We figured they had an overstock and needed to clear the shelves.

Seemed like the main goal.

We had a way of relaying difficult calls to our battalion surgeon or physician assistant.

Not with formality.

With honesty.

"Doc, I can't get his migraines under control."

"The patient has a Christmas tree rash on their back."

"She's had pain with urination. After the medication, her urine turned orange."

"His knee swelled up after a foot patrol. There's pain, swelling, and tenderness over the patella. Should I treat with antibiotics?"

You never knew what would show up at the light behind the wall.

Another night, one of our own came in—pale and sweating. He kept wiping his eyes like something was stuck.

Turned out it was a migraine triggered by stress collapse.

I gave him IV fluids, some diphenhydramine, toradol, and ondansetron. Shaded the bulb to decrease the glare, and let the silence do the rest.

He slept under that flickering light for two hours before walking out into the dark.

Not every story ended like that.

We'd been in the country for seven months. The fighting had slowed, but the wounds hadn't.

One night, two young men dragged in a woman with an AK-47 gunshot wound to the chest. Her eyes were open, pupils fixed, mouth slack.

She was already gone.

There was a pause.

The kind of pause where your hands move, but your heart stays still.

The two men were her sons. They begged me to save her. Tears streamed down their faces. Our translator explained what had happened:

Her husband—one of the local warlords—had shot her. Point blank. Then he ran off. Now in hiding.

He'd recently taken a second wife. Younger. Prettier. The older woman hadn't taken it quietly. She challenged him, asserting her place. He'd lavished gifts on the new bride—clothing, jewelry. The first wife, once respected, wore underwear she had mended herself with black thread. Her bra was threadbare. Her body showed a history of childbirth. Her grief was visible. Her dignity—intact but battered.

And he killed her for it.

I called in two junior medics.

It was training night.

I told them: "Show respect. Treat her like she matters. This is about practice—but it's also about dignity."

There was no need to fully expose her. We worked around her undergarments.

I taught them how to place a chest tube. How to secure an airway. How to decompress a chest.

More than that, I taught them how to treat a woman—even one already gone—with reverence.

We kept her for two hours.

When the teaching was done, we removed the tubes, cleaned her skin, and left the wounds visible.

Not for effect.

For truth.

To show we had tried.

That she had mattered.

We wrapped her in a fresh sheet and handed her back to her sons.

They wailed.

But they thanked us.

And for the first time that week, I wished the light above us could reach farther than the walls.

There were nights when the generator hiccupped, and we lost power.

At that moment, the only sound was the wind over the wall, the slow flap of canvas, and the distant churn of a helicopter.

Above us, the night sky cracked open wide.

Stars spilled across the valley like shrapnel frozen mid-flight.

You could see the Milky Way like it was painted—smears of white across black velvet.

All you could hear was silence and the occasional whisper of a teammate shifting in his cot.

Eventually, our engineers installed a proper fixture.

Mounted. Shielded. Safe.

It never shined the same.

Because it wasn't about the wattage.

It was about what we saw when it was barely enough.

The things confessed under dim light.

Their lives were made better with the last doses of antibiotics.

The trust was built without words.

That's what made it sacred.

Not the bulb.

But the fact that it was our light.

The light behind the wall.

Chapter 59: The Bridge They Built

It wasn't made of steel.

No rebar. No concrete. Just wooden planks, dried rope, and hand-sawn beams carried up the ravine by men who barely spoke the same language.

But they built it.

Together.

The bridge crossed a dry creek bed that only filled during spring runoff. Most of the year, it was nothing—just a ditch in the dirt, scarred by wind and time. But during the wet months, it became a wall. It cut the village off from its grazing fields, its access road, and—most importantly—from us.

We couldn't have that.

One of our 18Cs—newly pinned but sharp—looked at the ravine, squinted against the glare, and said confidently, "We can build it in a week."

Nobody believed them.

Not at first.

But no one argued, either.

The Assistant Team Leader—our warrant—and the 18F walked out to the edge of the wash the next morning, hands on hips, watching the two engineers survey the terrain. Tape measure. Clipboard. Notes in pencil on the back of a blank fire plan.

The engineers—Espi and Craig—didn't even look up. They were already in it.

"Talk to me," the warrant said casually.

Craig, the taller one, pointed toward a stack of salvaged limber the village elder had laid out. "Grain's good. No rot. We'll lap the supports at two-thirds height, bind with braided rope, then reinforce the crossbeams with angled deadmen on both sides."

The warrant grinned. "Deadmen? You boys just graduated?"

"Two months out of 18C school, Chief," Espi said. "Robin Sage to Afghanistan."

The 18F leaned in. "What's your plan for anchoring the footers?"

"Hand-dug, widened at the base, gravel-filled," Espi said. "Two verticals into each bank, cross-braced with angle iron from that rusted Soviet radio tower. Sandbags at the base to mitigate undercutting."

The warrant raised an eyebrow. "You came up with that on-site?"

Espi nodded. "We ran a simulated footbridge in Phase Ii. This one's easier. Not as much heat, no humidity, and better slope." The 18F and the warrant exchanged a look.

It wasn't envy.

It was pride.

They'd both started out as engineers—before the intel desk and the warrant bar. What were they hearing now? It was smarter. Cleaner. More refined.

Better than we were when we graduated.

The warrant clapped Espi on the shoulder. "Carry on, Engineer." From that moment on, they left them alone.
They didn't require supervision.

The engineers worked directly with the village elder and a crew of teenage boys—barefoot, sun-darkened, too lean from too many winters. They drew diagrams on paper, used hand signals, laughter, and one battered copy of Field Expedient Engineering for Humanitarian Operations. The elder's sons showed up every morning, swinging hammers that were too heavy for them, lifting beams in pairs like oxen yoked by duty.

One had a club foot. Another limped from an old fracture that had healed wrong. None of them wore gloves. No hard hats. No Osha inspection. Just calloused hands and willingness.

We helped when we could. Cut wood. Hauled rope. Delivered nails and spare tools.

But mostly, we watched.

And learned.

On the sixth day, they finished it. That night, the skies broke.

Rain hammered the valley. The dry creek surged to life, swollen and fast—churning brown with mud and momentum.

The western bank was steeper, so the engineers had offset the central support and angled the downstream bracing to reduce shear.

And the bridge held.

The next morning, we watched from our OP as a young girl—maybe seven—crossed it barefoot, carrying a tin of goat's milk in one hand and a smile.

She waved at us.

Didn't say a word.

Didn't need to.

It wasn't just a way across the creek.

It was a way across the distance between us and them.

We'd spent weeks clearing compounds, blowing IEDs, calling in airstrikes that left nothing but craters and ghosts.

But that bridge?

That was the only thing we built that stayed.

The next week, the rains returned.

So did the girl.

This time, she was followed by her little brother. Smaller. Wobblier. He nearly slipped, but she reached back without a word and caught him.

They crossed together.

Safe.

Of all the blood and fire, the trauma, the brothers we couldn't save—

I remember her.

One barefoot child walking across something no bomb could erase.

That's what Green Berets do.

We don't just break.

We build.

And long after we were gone… the bridge remained.

So did the girl.

Chapter 60: Parachutes in the Dark

Orgun-E Drop Zone | March 2002

The C-130 was blacked out as it made its final pass over Orgun-E.

No running lights. No cockpit glow. Just the low thunder of props grinding the valley air. A floating shadow over a war.

Inside that bird: five pallets. Food. Water. Calories. The only thing keeping a 60-man outpost operational in a region where roads didn't exist and convoys were suicide.

Big Mark and our Team Sergeant—also named Mark—stood at the OP with NVGs and IR chem lights taped to their vests. Calm. Focused. Watching.

"Three seconds," Big Mark muttered into his headset.

They'd marked the drop zone with IR chem lights taped to stacked rocks—visible only through night vision. Primitive but effective.

Then came the thump-thump-thump of pallets shoving down the ramp.

One. Two. Three. Four. Five.

The canopies opened like broken flowers.

No steerable systems. No GPS. No JPADS. Just wind, silk, gravity, and men who knew how to read them.

The parachutes caught the air and drifted hard east—wind off the mountains pushing them just enough to complicate the math.

Three landed perfectly inside the wire.

But two of the pallets floated out.

Past the perimeter. Over the trench. Outside the wire and into the desert.

Hector adjusted comms and patched into the aircraft. "Two outside," he confirmed.

"Copy," said Dave. "We're rolling?"

Big Mark nodded. "Mount up."

We took four ATVs, engines low idle, crawling into the dark. No headlights. No chatter.

This wasn't about action. This was about accountability. You don't leave resupply exposed. Not in Afghanistan. Not in 2002.

We found them both within a klick—one on its side in a ditch, the other flattened a thorn bush but sitting upright.

Bottled water. Boxes of MREs. And the motherlode: T-Rations.

We posted Afghan fighters beside each bundle. Squad-sized elements, rifles across their knees. They'd watch the cargo until sunrise.

Back inside the wire, we did an inventory:

Bottled water: 120 cases

MREs: Mostly Chili Mac and Beef Stew

T-Rats: heavy, ugly, and exactly what we needed

T-Rats weren't gourmet. They were boil-to-serve, aluminum-tray hot meals. Feed-a-fire-squad type food. The kind of rations you could dish out in a bucket and call it dinner.

Our Afghan cook was quick to learn. We showed him how much water to boil, heat trays, and serve hot. No seasoning. No complaints. Just calories.

In the field, calories are combat power.

We didn't bring every tool or comfort.

But we brought discipline.

No drinking from local sources. No raw produce.

Fruit and vegetables were soaked in light bleach solution, then rinsed with bottled water and peeled if needed. That wasn't luxury. That was survival.

You don't win by being high-speed.

You win by not getting dysentery.

We had plenty of ammo—an entire bunker full of it.

But ammo doesn't hydrate you.

Ammo doesn't keep a young kid from the 101st from collapsing after two days in the sun.

When the Regular Army arrived—two Chinooks at a time—they brought minimal gear. Just their A-bags. When they rotated back, their B-bags would meet them at Kandahar or Bagram.

Until then?

We fed them.

We watered them.

We kept them going.

The drop wasn't flashy.

It wasn't dangerous.

It wasn't complicated.

But it kept a forward firebase running.

Weeks later, when a helicopter went down, and we walked through the wreckage—sifting through flattened tents—we found their duffels. Still zipped. Still packed.

They never got to unpack them.

But they never went hungry either.

ODA Rule #43:

You don't win wars by starving your men.

Moral lesson?

You can have the best shooters, best gear, and best comms.

But if you can't eat, you can't fight.

If you can't hydrate, you can't move.

If you can't sustain, you can't stay.

And if you can't stay—you don't win. We were the first ones to successfully run this kind of aerial resupply in Afghanistan.

No guides. No doctrine.

Just a C-130, five pallets, and two guys named Mark.

And somehow, it worked.

Because in Special Forces, you improvise early—

So, others don't have to later.

Side Note: JPADS (Joint Precision Airdrop System)

JPADS, the steerable, GPS-guided parachute system, wasn't operationally fielded until around 2006. In 2002, Special Forces relied on low-altitude, low-cost resupply drops using disposable parachutes and visual signals. These early drops were the foundation for what would later become a precision logistics platform.

Side Note: T-Rations (T-Rats)

T-Rations, or "T-Rats," were pre-cooked, semi-perishable tray packs designed to feed groups in the field. Unlike MREs, which are single-serving and ready-to-eat, T-rats require boiling and group service. They were often used when a field kitchen was available— or when one had to be improvised from scratch, as we did in Orgun-E.

Chapter 61: Big Mike Said No

There are men who raise their voices to lead.

And then there's Big Mike.

He didn't need volume.

Just presence.

Just that slow, silent look he gave you across the firebase when something wasn't right.

We were prepping for a compound clearance in Paktika.

Intel was thin. HVT may be inside. Maybe not.

But the village was twitchy—too quiet. One of those places where the kids didn't run up, and the dogs didn't bark.

And that meant something.

The ODA was tense. We'd lost two men the week before. The pressure was on. Everyone wanted the win.

Our intel guy— bright, eager—came in hot with a photo.

"This guy," he said, holding it up. "We're pretty sure he's in there."
Pretty sure.
That's not confirmation.

But command wanted heat, no hesitation.

The captain nodded. "Let's move."

I was already checking gear when Big Mike said it.

One word.

"Negative."

No radio call. No rank. Just Mike, sitting on his haunches, looking at the target photo.

The room froze.

Even the Captain didn't bristle.

Because everyone respected Mike.

He spoke quietly.

"This house has two doors," he said. "One for the men. One for the women. We go in hard, and we're going to breach both."

"That's the plan," someone muttered.

Mike didn't flinch.

"I've been here long enough to know—this guy has three sons. Young. You go in that second door, and you're stepping over his wife. Maybe his daughter." Silence.

"You step on that family," Mike said, "you lose the whole valley."

He understood the terrain, but more than that—he understood the people.

We didn't hit the house that night.

We waited.

Confirmed.

Reframed.

Two days later, the HVT moved. We picked him up mid-route with a partner force.

No shots fired.

No kids were scared.

No doors were kicked down.

Mike never took credit.

We thought it was just another op that ended clean.

No one died. Mission success. But something had shifted.

And two weeks later, a village elder handed Mike a carved walking stick—etched with tribal markings.

He didn't say a word.

He didn't have to.

I should've spoken up too.

I'd had a bad feeling.

Felt the tension. Saw the uncertainty. Heard the word "maybe" and knew it wasn't enough.

But I stayed quiet.

Because part of me wanted the mission.

Wanted the win.

Wanted the adrenaline rush of action after too many weeks of IEDs and patrols with no result.

I wanted to prove I was still worth the uniform.

That I could lead.

That I could be right.

Mike said no.

And I followed.

But that night, I lay in my cot wondering:

Why didn't I say it first?

Why was I willing to kick in a door I wasn't sure about?

Was it loyalty to the ODA?

Or was it ambition?

That's a different kind of moral injury.

Not what you did.

But what you didn't have the courage to stop.

Big Mike carried that moment with grace.

And I carry the silence I kept.

Because sometimes leadership doesn't sound like a speech.

Sometimes, it sounds like one man saying "No,"

…when everyone else is leaning forward.

Mike taught me that.

And I never forgot it.

Because when the moment came… Big Mike said no.

Chapter 62: Don't Stare at Hector's Junk

Every ODA has traditions. Ours involved Hector's junk.

There are all kinds of lessons in Special Forces.

Some are tactical.

Some are strategic.

And some… are anatomical.

We were at Bagram Airbase, and it had been a long two weeks in the field. Dust in our ears, grime under our fingernails, the kind of sweat that's caked in layers. Our ODA had rotated in from a forward operating base, and the only thing on our minds was the luxury of hot water.

Real showers.

Not water bags, no cold-water rinses.

Showers with pressure. Faucets. Drainage. Light.

It was me, Jim, Luke, and Hector. We walked in like kids entering Disneyland. Clean socks in hand. Flip-flops on our feet. And for a brief, fleeting moment—peace.

Until I remembered who I was showering with.

Hector.

Straight-faced. Unbothered. Cold as ice.

And somewhere beneath his toned, dust-crusted frame… was the piercing.

Hector didn't brag.

Didn't warn.

Didn't even explain.

He just casually stepped under the shower head, pulled the cord of his laundry bag off his shoulder, and started rinsing off like it was any other day.

Except between his legs… hung what looked like a plastic shower curtain ring.

Clear. Round. Looping through the urethral opening of his penis like it belonged there.

Because for Hector—it did.

That's when it hit me.

The flashback.

Years earlier, I was the new guy.

Fresh to the ODA.

Senior medic. Confident. Focused. Had seen some things. Thought I was ready.

We were training at an old FBI urban shooting range in Washington state—two weeks of CQB drills, breach lanes, and shoot houses until our hands were black from carbon and thumbs raw from loading 9mm and 5.56 magazines.

We stayed in WWII-era open bay barracks.

Which meant open bay showers.

Showers with no curtains.

No stalls.

Just a row of heads and men standing around naked like some tactical YMCA.

The first night, I walked in with my gear bag, towel, and soap like everyone else. No big deal.

I'd been in the Army long enough to know the drill.

I hung my towel, stepped in, turned the water on—and that's when I caught it.

A glint.

Just the corner of my eye.

Flash of silver.

Too fast to be sure.

I glanced over—casual, instinctive—and saw Hector.

Completely relaxed.

Lathering his hair.

Facing the wall.

But the angle was just right, and I thought—Was that… was that a ring?

———

Before I could process it, Jim elbowed Mark.

Mark elbowed Luke.

And they were all watching me.

Waiting.

———

At the nightly brief, Luke brought it up in front of the whole ODA.

Dead serious.

"Hey, Top, real quick. Uh… I'm a little concerned about Drew."

The Team Sergeant leaned back. "Concerned how?"

"Well, … we noticed he was staring at Hector's… you know."
Everyone froze.
And I just sat there.

Like a raccoon in the middle of the road.

———

They let it hang for a second.

Then burst out laughing.

Everyone was in on it.

Except me.

———

And just when I thought it was over… Mark stood up.

"Drew, since you're clearly curious—Hector, why don't you show him?"

The guys stood in a circle, arms crossed, grinning.

Hector stepped forward, untying his drawstring slowly like a magician preparing a trick.

And just before anything was revealed— Boom.
They exploded in laughter and walked away.

No piercing. No explanation. No closure.

Just an unofficial welcome to the team—delivered with soap, steam, and shame.

Back in Afghanistan, all these years later, the joke still played out—quietly, efficiently, cruelly.

Hector had since upgraded to a clear plastic ring. Said it was more comfortable in the field. Said he wore it to keep the hole from closing.

He didn't say much else.

And none of us ever asked.

But the new guys?

They always asked.

Or rather—they didn't. But they stared. They tried not to, but they did.

And the rest of us just stood there, rinsing our hair behind silent smiles, watching the next victim do small, slow circles under the shower heads.

Trying to catch a glimpse of the mythical ring swinging like a ghost between Hector's knees.

And the moment he squinted too long?

You could see it: the setup.

The smiles.

The trap springing.

Mark's voice in the hall that night: "Hey, Top… got another one."

There was no malice.

No judgment.

Nobody cared what you did in your spare time.

But the moral was clear:

"Don't take yourself too seriously. Because none of us do."

We'd mourned Brothers. We had been through death, blood, loss, and rage.

So, if a dumb joke in the showers kept us grounded? That was okay.

If we had to carry the weight of war—

We were damn well going to laugh while doing it.

Even if it meant getting caught staring at Hector's oversized piercing in a Bagram shower.

Chapter 63: When the Uniform No Longer Fits

I used to love it.

The feel of the fabric—thick, pressed, clean.

The way my rank rested perfectly on my shoulders.

Jump boots spit-shined, not for show, but because a man should carry himself with pride.

The beret is always worn with purpose.

Every ribbon, every tab, every badge aligned just right.

A silent record of what I'd done, where I'd bled, and who I'd carried.

I used to make sure my uniform looked brand new.

Not because I wanted to be seen.

But because it reminded me who I was.

But toward the end?

It felt like armor I no longer deserved.

It started with a Class A event.

An award ceremony I don't even remember the name of.

I stood there: the weight of metal tabs, combat awards, unit citations, chromed badges, all laid across my chest. All earned.

And yet—I looked down at the fabric and didn't recognize the man it was pinned to.

The jacket fit.

The man didn't.

There were days I'd put it on and feel the drag—not on my shoulders, but on my spirit.

The weight of everything I hadn't fixed.

The lives I couldn't save.

The men who didn't come home.

Their names weren't written anywhere on my uniform.

But I could feel them there—every time I breathed.

My wife would say, "You look good in uniform."

I'd nod.

But inside?

I felt like a fraud.

Because it's hard to feel honorable when the war's still in your lungs.

When your medals shine louder than your voice.

When the silence at home is heavier than the blast, you survive.

I didn't quit the uniform.

It quit fitting me.

That's the part no one tells you.

You can serve with honor.

You can lead.

You can bleed.

You can carry your ODA through the worst days of their lives.

But one day, you pull the jacket off the hanger…

You look in the mirror…

And it feels like it belongs to someone else.

Someone younger.

Someone clearer.

Someone not yet broken by the quiet.

I still have it.

Hung in the back of the closet.

Clean.

Pressed.

Perfect.

The boots are lined up below it. The beret is still shaped. The collar is still sharp.

But I haven't worn it in years. Because if I ever wear it again…

It won't be for me.

It'll be to honor the ones who didn't get to take theirs off.

On that day, I'll stand tall.

I'll button every button.

Tie every thread back into place.

And I'll put it on with hands that still remember how to stop bleeding… And how to let go.

Not with rank.

Not with ribbons.

Not with speeches.

But with silence.

And memory.

And a grief only a Green Beret knows how to carry.

Because the uniform doesn't forget.

And neither do we.

Part II – The Fire That Never Went Out

They died with their boots on, but we live with the memory. This is not about death—it's about what we carry forward.

Chapter 64: Reflection Without Return

I used to stare into the mirror to make sure I hadn't lost something.

First, it was to check my uniform.

Ensure my haircut was within regulation.

Check my body for anything unusual—rashes, bruises, scars.

Then one day… I started looking for my face.

Not out of vanity.

Just confusion.

There were mornings after the war when I'd shave half my jawline before realizing I hadn't even looked myself in the eye.

Other days, I'd freeze halfway through tying a tie for some church event, wondering if this is what men looked like when they were still alive on the inside.

What they don't tell you is that coming home doesn't come with a debrief.

There's no checklist for reintegration.

No situation report for the soul.

Just the mirror—and what it refuses to reflect.

I watched the lines deepen.

Watched my eyes go flat.

Watched the slow erosion of whatever I used to be.

I saw a man who had stopped blinking.

And started flinching when his daughter slammed her bedroom door.

One morning, my wife found me standing shirtless in the bathroom.

I wasn't grooming. I wasn't dressing.

Just standing.

The overhead fan sucked in steam; some still clung to the mirror. One hand rested on the sink. The other hung limp by my side. Shoulders drawn—like a man bracing for a blast.

She leaned against the doorframe.

"What are you looking for?" she asked.

I couldn't answer.

Not because I didn't want to.

Because I didn't know how.

How do you explain that you're searching for proof that your soul didn't die in the dust?

That you're not, okay?

That the only thing left inside the uniform is posture and protocol?

How do you tell the woman you love that you don't recognize the man she's speaking to?

She stood there a moment longer.

Still waiting for an answer.

But I had none.

She turned and walked away.

That mirror never judged me.

But it didn't forgive me either.

Did she?

There were days I dressed in the dark—not because the light didn't work.

But because I couldn't face the man, I used to believe in.

One day, I felt the cold hand of death on the back of my neck.

Maybe it was a draft.

Maybe it was an insect.

Maybe it was nothing.

I picked up my wife's handheld mirror.

Used it to check the back of my neck—twisting, adjusting, angling the reflection under the light.

I turned slightly. Glanced into the mirror's corner.

And saw it.

A black shape.

Still. Hooded. Watching.

It wasn't in the room.

It was in the reflection—one of a thousand layers.

I froze.

Real fear gripped me.

For the first time in years.

What did it mean?

Why did it scare me more than anything I'd seen at war?

I never picked up that handheld mirror again.

I still wore the uniform.

Still ensured every piece was squared away.

Still a Soldier… on the outside.

Still showed up… in my body.

But sometimes, driving through the gate felt like impersonating a ghost.

I'd shake hands. Give briefings.

Answer to "Sergeant." Later, "Sir." But inside?

I was back in the dust.

Back in the compound.

Back in the silence after the blast.

Back in the moment before, I knew whether the man under my hands would live.

Some men drink.

Some fight.

Some disappear into workouts or rage or women or noise.

Me?

I stared.

Not in my reflection.

But at the absence behind the eyes.

And some days…

That was all I could manage.

Not memories.

Not even guilt.

Just silence.

And a mirror… that never blinked.

Chapter 65: The One Who Bit Down

It happened fast—like most of them did.

A firefight on the edge of a village. Dust hung in the heat like gauze. Muzzle flashes lit the gaps between walls. AK rounds slapped against stone, pinged off scrap metal. The kind of contact that comes without warning—then stays in your joints for days.

The Afghan partner force was returning fire. Erratic. Undisciplined. Their spacing was a mess.

Then one of them dropped.

High thigh wound. Arterial.

Close to the femoral triangle.

The medic didn't wait for permission.

He slid through the dust and dropped beside the casualty while another Green Beret covered the line.

Blood was already pooling. Fast. Dark. Pulsing.

The medic clamped on a tourniquet—high and tight. Cranked it until the bleeding slowed. Then checked the distal pulse. Gone. Good.

Still no scream.

That's when he saw the Soldier's face.

Jaw clenched. Lips white. Eyes closed tight.

And then—blood.

Dark and sudden, foaming past the man's mouth.

He'd bitten through part of his own tongue. A full involuntary clamp-down, and now he was choking on himself.

The medic grabbed his kit. Gloves half-on, no time to fix it. Pulled out an oropharyngeal airway—OPA—but the jaw wouldn't budge.

He used the handle of his multitool to wedge it open. Not force. Leverage. Just enough to slide the OPA past clenched teeth.

The man gagged. Twitched.

But he looked up—eyes sharp, locked in.

He understood.

There was no suction in the field.

So, the medic turned him—recovery position, side down, mouth draining. He let gravity do the work.

Blood spilled onto the dirt in long, slow streams.

Then gauze—improvised, packed gently into the mouth. Not sterile. Not pretty.

But it worked.

The airway stayed open.

Still no scream.

Rounds popped overhead. A Green Beret called for smoke. The wind shifted. The medic's knees sank into blood-soaked earth.

He kept working.

The Soldier's chest rose and fell.

Barely.

But he was still in the fight.

They lifted him under fire. Two men hauling his frame into the bed of a Hilux.

Before they closed the tailgate, the Afghan Soldier reached out—and grabbed the medic's forearm.

Tight.

No words.

Just pressure.

The kind of grip that says:

I remember.

I know what you did.

He made it.

Evac'd.

Surgery.

Months of rehab.

Speech therapy.

Six months later, he was back in the same valley—civilian scarf, no rifle. The beard had grown out. He walked with a slight limp.

He spotted the medic across a crowded compound.

And he nodded.

Just once.

Some Soldiers scream.

Some pass out.

But the ones who bite down?

They're not just holding in pain.

They're holding on to something else—pride, maybe. Dignity. Control.

And when you see that?

You don't carry them.

You carry it with them.

Chapter 66: Blood in the Dust

The village elder looked older than the hills—skin like stone, beard like snow.

But his eyes were sharp.

When he waved the Americans into the courtyard, there was no fear. No deception. Just purpose.

It wasn't a trap.

It was a request.

Inside the shaded mud hut, a girl—maybe six—lay curled on a wool blanket. Her skin was dry, stretched taut over ribs that rose and fell too fast. Her lips were cracked. Her belly distended.

She wasn't crying.

She didn't have the energy to cry.

The elder knelt beside her, whispering in Pashto, hand hovering near her chest. Then he pointed upward toward the roof. Toward the sky.

Even without translation, it was clear.

"Can you help her?"

The medic dropped to one knee. No words. Just hands moving.

He unzipped his aid bag and took inventory by touch. The floor was dirt—warm, uneven. The room smelled like earth and smoke and sickness.

Jim stood at the door, rifle low, eyes high.

He never liked us going in alone. But this felt different.

This felt like the reason they came.

The girl's skin had no give. Her limbs were stiff. No peripheral veins—dehydration severe.

He cleaned her foot with iodine. Went for the saphenous vein—a straight shot on the inner ankle. Missed the first attempt. Tried again.

Flash.

A pinprick of blood rose into the tubing.

He exhaled.

Attached an IV. Started a slow drip—D5 with saline, just enough to begin rehydration. Not rapid. Not aggressive. Just enough to remind her body it could still fight.

He wiped her face. Applied Vaseline to her lips. Gave a little sugar water under the tongue. Then stayed beside her, watching for the first sign of a response.

She didn't flinch.

  She didn't speak.

But her eyes opened wider.

And that was enough.

Behind him, Jim whispered.

"Wrap it up. Movement on the ridge."

The medic nodded. Packaged the bag. Left a laminated card with pictograms—how to mix oral rehydration. How to continue care. Handed it to the elder, gesturing carefully. Water. Sugar. Salt.

The old man took it like a holy text.

Outside, the sun returned with full force. No wind. Just heat and dust and silence.

The medic looked down.

His knees were stained red.

Maybe it was blood from a previous casualty.

Maybe it was fresh.

Didn't matter.

It was in the dirt now.

Back at the compound, no one asked.

He washed his hands. Drank water. Checked his gear.

But something stayed with him.

It wasn't the treatment.

It wasn't the IV.

It was the helpless hope that maybe, just maybe, the girl would still be breathing at sunrise.

Because sometimes, in a war built on destruction, the only thing a medic can leave behind…

Is a child still alive?

A lesson whispered across language and loss:

That blood in the dust doesn't always mean death. Sometimes—
it means you tried.

Chapter 67: Carrying What's Left

There's a moment when dragging a casualty that the body changes. It's subtle. But if you've ever pulled a dying man across dirt and blood, you feel it.

At first, they help.

They grip your shoulder. They shift their hips. Their breathing matches yours.

But then—

They stop helping.

No resistance. No effort. Just mass.

That's the shift.

That's dead weight.

They called him Lucky.

Because he wasn't.

He'd stepped on something weeks before. Pressure plate, half buried. Didn't fire. Maybe wet wiring. Maybe divine intervention. No one knew.

This time?

It worked.

Not a full detonation. Just enough to throw him sideways and tear his left leg open like a bag of meat. Shrapnel took the rest. Thigh to pelvis. The ground turned red in seconds.

He didn't scream.

Didn't even yell.

Just looked up at them—like he was embarrassed.

The ODA rolled in hard. Covering fire. Shouts. Smoke.

The medic reached him first. Hit his knees in the gravel. Gloves on.

MARCH.

Tourniquet, high and tight.

Packed the side wound.

Found shrapnel near the iliac crest but didn't probe—too close to arteries.

Pulled the airway kit. Started ventilations. "Stay with me," the medic said.

"Stay with me, Lucky." Lucky blinked. Once.

Then nothing.

The pulse faded.

Breath slowed.

Eyes stopped tracking.

The Team Sergeant shouted, but the medic didn't hear him.

His gloves were soaked. His knees slipped in grit and blood.

He grabbed the man's drag strap. Pulled.

One step. Two.

Then, the strap gave way.

He grabbed the ruck. Hauled.

But the ruck slipped sideways.

He got behind him. Hooked under the arms.

And dragged.

All of it.

Alone.

The body didn't fight.

Didn't shift.

Didn't help.

Just weight.

The CH-47 came in low—rotor wash, kicking up grit like a sandstorm. Ramp dropped.

Two men lifted him aboard.

The medic climbed in behind them, straddled Lucky's chest, and started compressions.

Another medic went for the airway.

They worked until they couldn't anymore.

They lost him in the air.

Later, someone told the medic:

"You did everything right."

But he doesn't remember the technique.

Or the pressure reading on the tourniquet.

Or how many minutes of CPR he performed.

He remembers the drag.

The exact moment Lucky stopped helping.

When it was no longer two men surviving together— Just one man hauling the other through dust and death.
It wasn't the death that broke him.

It was the drag.

Chapter 68: The Rule of Three

They had a saying on the team:

Once is a chance.

Twice is a pattern. Three times—it's you.

Didn't matter if it was comms cutting out, gear misfiring, or someone hesitating at the door. If it happened three times, you had to own it. Fix it. Or get replaced.

The Rule of Three wasn't superstition.

It was a quiet code.

On a cool, gray morning outside Ghazni, the senior Bravo—forty-two, calm, measured—watched it happen for the third time.

Another hesitation.

Same teammate.

They were mid-clearance in a village that felt too alive to be dangerous.

Children darted through the alleys, kicking bottle caps and shouting in Dari. Chickens scattered like rumors. A man stirred a dented kettle over a smoking pit and didn't look up as the Americans passed.

The team moved clean. Tight. Room to room. Stack tight. Air still.

In one compound, the movement behind a thin yellow curtain stopped the stack cold.

No visible weapon.

No surrender gesture.

Just motion—subtle and slow.

The second Bravo—younger, sharp—paused.

His finger hovered off the trigger. Rifle steady. Chest rising too fast.

The rest of the stack froze with him.

No words. No signals.

Just that kind of stillness that makes your molars ache.

The curtain shifted again. Slightly.

Then still.

They held.

They waited.

Then they moved.

Behind the curtain, crouched low behind a basket of dried onions, was a girl.

Ten, maybe. Wide-eyed. Barefoot.

No threat. No ambush. Just terror in a small, silent body.

She didn't scream.

Neither did her family.

Outside, as they reset, the senior Bravo pulled the younger man aside.

"That's the third time."

The younger man nodded.

Not defensive. Not ashamed. Just honest.

"I know."

"You want off the next one?" A pause.

"No," the younger man said.

"I want to earn the fourth."

Later that night, the senior wrote it in his notebook—not as a complaint.

As a reminder.

Everyone talks about hesitation like it's a weakness.

But sometimes, it's restraint.

Sometimes, it's wisdom—dressed up like doubt.

That village never turned.

No grenade from a rooftop.

No boy with a suicide vest.

No bullets through the window.

The medics treated a woman's burn.

Gave a farmer's son antibiotics.

They left the way they came—quiet, unbroken, intact.

The Rule of Three still held.

But that day, it bent.

And he was glad it did.

Because the hardest part of being a Green Beret isn't pulling the trigger.

It's knowing when not to.

And sometimes?

The third time isn't failure.

Its character is revealed.

Chapter 69: The Tower Still Stands

Sometimes, the strongest signal doesn't come from the radio— it comes from the hands that built it.
You could see it from anywhere.

Seventy-five feet of iron pipe, crisscrossed with steel rebar, welded by Afghan stubbornness and Special Forces necessity. Built by hand. Stabilized with tensioned cables. Anchored in concrete, we mixed ourselves.

It wasn't designed by contractors.

It wasn't ordered through supply channels.

It was born out of frustration—my frustration—when I couldn't radio Camp Harriman to report two local tribesmen with gunshot wounds.

No one came to solve it.

So, we built a solution.

Our 18Es—communications experts—took the lead. Quiet, brilliant, unshakable. They understood that war isn't won by who talks louder but by who can still talk at all.

They sketched plans in grease pencil. Ran angles with gut and tape. Every decision was cross-checked with range, elevation, and whatever we had on hand.

The welder was a local. Mid-50s. Slim frame. Red beard flecked with gray. Same clothes every day—thin cotton shirt, grease-stained pants, sandals, and a wool cap pulled low.

He didn't wear gloves. No apron. Just a face shield and calloused hands that worked like they were born holding hot steel.

Each morning, he arrived with a bundle of electrodes—SMAW rods—coated in flux. He used stick welding and shielded Metal Arc Welding, pulling 110 to 200 amps at 20 to 30 volts from a tired generator that always gave just enough.

Before every weld, he arced the rod against the pipe and crouched low—knees bent, face shield raised. His hands never shook.

Ten hours a day.

Six days a week.

Until seventy-five vertical feet stood above us.

When it was done, we raised it.

It took every man we had—and a squad of fighters—to lift it into position.

We used ropes, brute force, the teamwork—and blind faith in the welds holding it all together.

It rose slowly. Awkwardly. Groaning and creaking until it locked upright.

And then… it stood.

At the top: a red aviation light.

Blinking steady.

A wire ran up the inside of one leg, protected, hidden.

We mounted the antenna. Ran the first radio check

Clear.

Strong.

For the first time, we could talk across the valley.
And in a place where terrain silenced everything, we had finally made our voices heard.
It was beautiful.

Primitive.

Perfect.

But it was also a hazard.

We marked it on every air mission. Pilots were briefed. The red beacon was more than protocol. It was a heartbeat.

It said: we are here.

A warning. A claim. A promise.

We took rocket fire sometimes.

Usually, nothing serious.

But one night, a round landed within fifty meters. The dirt jumped. Our boots shifted.

We turned. Checked the base.

Then walked back inside.

The tower was still standing.

Years later, I heard they tore it down.

New firebase. Better gear. Cleaner specs.

Maybe the signal's stronger now. Maybe the gear's smarter.

But I don't care what the satellite feed says.

In my mind, it's still there.

Red light blinking.

Wind in the wires.

And a team that never let it fall.

Because the tower still stands—where it mattered most.

Chapter 70: The Flyover

August 2002. Eastern Afghanistan.

It was the kind of heat that made your skin itch beneath the plate carrier, the kind that baked the diesel exhaust into your uniform. Dust coated everything—teeth, rifles, optics. It clung to you like a second skin. We had been out in the eastern districts for weeks now, making contact, assessing allegiances, and feeling out the fault lines of loyalty in a place where trust was just another weapon.

We rolled out in a Hilux, no markings, no flags, just two Americans in civilian clothes with rifles that told anyone watching we weren't NGO workers. The new ODA commander rode shotgun, quiet and observant. He was new to Afghanistan, new to unconventional warfare—but not new to trust. He let me drive. Let me lead. That said everything.

Our objective was a meeting with a former OGA-backed warlord who hadn't gotten the memo that the Taliban were no longer welcome—and that we weren't to be tested. The word was that he was building strength again. Keeping too many fighters close. Stockpiling weapons. A little too comfortable.

We were told to talk. But talking only works when the other guy isn't already convinced, he's got the upper hand.

We pulled into the village just after noon. A sun-bleached cluster of mud huts and narrow alleyways, surrounded by hills that watched everything. The warlord's men were already waiting. Dozens of them. Armed. Eager. The kind of fighters who had seen the Soviets burn and knew the rules here were different. Their eyes tracked us as we stepped out, like predators circling something they didn't yet fear.

The warlord himself emerged from a shaded room. Thick beard.

Sharpened eyes. His posture said everything—he wasn't here to negotiate. He wanted a performance. He wanted to prove something in front of his men.

He smiled. It wasn't friendly.

We stood in the center of the village. My interpreter is to my left. The new ODA commander was just behind me, saying nothing, watching everything.

The warlord began a speech. Loud. Booming. It wasn't for us—it was for them. The kind of speech meant to end with a rifle raised.

I gave the signal.

Exactly on time, the sound arrived. A low, guttural thrum in the distance, building quickly. Echoing off the mountains like a slow-moving thunderhead.

The Apache.

She came in fast and low—barely skimming the ridgeline, blades biting through the air, nose down in attack posture. The warlord stopped mid-sentence. His men froze.

She didn't fire. Didn't need to.

The psychological warfare of a screaming, armored death machine overhead was more than enough. The TADS (Target Acquisition Designation Sight) was pointed directly at the warlord's position.

Everyone knew what that meant. They were lit up. Marked. Vulnerable.

I stepped forward and met the warlord's eyes.

"You don't need to die today," I said, calm and steady.

He didn't respond. But his eyes shifted. His shoulders slumped half an inch. Just enough.

I nodded to my interpreter.

"Tell him we'll be back. Next time, with more than just a helicopter."

We didn't shake hands.

He turned and walked away.

So did we.

As the Apache banked out and disappeared behind the ridge, the commander exhaled beside me.

"You didn't tell me you had a bird on call," he said.

"Didn't know if it would work," I answered. "But I knew we couldn't out-talk a man who thinks he's invincible."

The ODA commander nodded. He didn't need to say more.

That day, no shots were fired. No bodies dropped. But a message had been delivered:

We don't bluff.

This is how Green Berets fight wars most people never hear about. Wars where presence matters more than posture. Where psychology is more lethal than any round. Where sometimes, the best kill is the one that never had to happen.

We left that valley with no headlines. No medals. No press releases. Just a silence earned.

And that's the kind of war we came here to win.

Chapter 71: What You Keep

We were back at Kandahar Airbase, the last stop before the plane that took you out of war and dropped you back into a world that didn't know what you'd seen.

It was the end of a long rotation—bloody, bruising, relentless. My boots were held together by 550 cord and sweat. My skin was sunburnt, my eyes wired from caffeine and adrenaline, and my pack was lighter than it had ever been.

But no one relaxed.

Not yet.

Word had come down: a National Guard Special Forces unit had tried to sneak home an ISU-90 container loaded with captured weapons—AKs, RPGs, and probably a few Soviet antiques they didn't even know how to clean.

It blew up in their faces.

Now, the entire regiment was under scrutiny. Customs were tight. CID was sniffing around. The Army wanted a clean narrative, and that meant finding a few sacrificial lambs.

We'd been warned.

And I had a stack of weapons.

None of it was issued.

These weren't government rifles. These were war trophies.

Captured, bartered, or handed off in smoky deals behind the clinic. Some were junk. Others were priceless. All of them are illegal to bring home.

I had built an arsenal between firefights, medevacs, and convoy runs. It was a weird kind of peace—those moments between combat. The smell of burnt gun oil, steak smoke curling from grills made of steel, and SF cooks slipping you extra rations if you kept quiet and stayed out of the chow hall.

You didn't talk about the blood. You bartered for bootleg vodka.

And if you were smart, you found something worth keeping.

My collection was a mess of mythology and madness.

There were Pakistani knockoffs that would explode after 1,000 rounds and backyard-forged pistols stamped with Soviet markings that made collectors drool. I had two Tokarevs—both full auto, both loud as hell, and both probably unsafe at any range.

Out on the range, I'd cross-draw from matching leather holsters. John Woo style. Full-blown cinematic delusion.

The magazines emptied fast.

The laughter came faster.

And for a few seconds, war didn't matter.

Then there was the Krinkov.

Twelve-inch barrel. Iron sights were so misaligned they were practically decorative. A gun that couldn't hit a barn wall at ten paces—but it looked mean. And sometimes, that was enough.

But the crown jewel?

The Lugers.

Two of them.

One pre-Nazi, one Third Reich stamped. Original finish. Perfect wear. They weren't just weapons. They were artifacts. Clean lines. Cold steel. History with a trigger.

I showed them to a fellow medic at the Firebase FST—a quiet guy, Army, hands like stone.

He held one like it was glass.

"These don't belong here," he whispered. "They belong in a museum. With lighting."

He wasn't wrong.

But there was no museum at Kandahar. Just dust, plywood, and rules that bent until they broke.

When it was time to rotate back, I had to make a call.

I couldn't risk the Lugers getting seized.

So, I made a deal.

There was a Master Sergeant—a regular Army supply guy. Always around the perimeter of our ODAs. Not SF. Not tabbed. But he wore the stolen valor, always telling stories that didn't match the patches on his uniform.

He was a collector. A talker. The kind of guy who stuck close enough to smell the smoke but never close enough to breathe the fire.

"Get these back to Fayetteville," I told him.

"You can keep one. The Nazi-stamped one stays mine." He grinned.
Too wide.

We shook hands.

He disappeared.

I didn't see him again for a couple of years.

I was selling my house in Fayetteville, garage sale in full swing, last box packed. PA school ahead. Life is ready to move on.

And there he was.

Walking down my street like a ghost with a conscience.

His wife is beside him. Smile too tight. Eyes too sharp.

He froze when he saw me.

I stepped out into the driveway.

"Hey, man," I said—loud enough for the neighbors.

"Where are my Lugers?"

He stammered. Excuses fell out like empty brass.

Something about customs. Something about losing track.

Something about the Army being the Army.

His wife stiffened.

She'd heard this before.

She'd seen the guns.

I let it go.

Not because I believed him.

Not because I wasn't angry.

But because I already had what mattered.

He kept the Lugers.

I kept my tab.

And my integrity.

That was enough.

Because war doesn't reward the greedy.

And you don't measure a man by what he brings home.

You measure him by what he walks away from.

Some of us came back with scars.

Some with medals.

Some with stories.

Some with nothing but the weight of what we'd done and what we refused to do.

He kept my guns.

But I kept my soul.

And that?

That's what you keep.

Chapter 72: Coming Home With Honor

Coming home wasn't what I thought it would be.

No fireworks. No welcome-home banners. No American Legion handshakes or ballgame ceremonies.

It was quieter than that.

It was the sound of my boots on the porch—dust still clinging to the soles from Kandahar. Leather scuffed from the Hindu Kush. Soles half-worn from pacing along the edge of decisions no one would ever know I made.

It was the soft creak of the door opening.

Then, everything at once—the thud of small feet, the shriek of joy, the collision of four little girls crashing into my legs like a wave.

Julie stood behind them, still and watching.

She always knew when I was really home—and when part of me was still in the wire, still listening for rotor blades, still smelling cordite and sweat. She didn't say anything. Didn't have to.

Her eyes scanned me the same way I used to scan rooftops in the city.

Assess. Interpret. Understand.

But this time... she smiled.

Because I wasn't halfway home.

This time, I was all the way back.

———

There was no parade.

No speeches.

No television crew was waiting at the gate.

Just the American flag hanging still on the front porch—limp in the dead calm of a Southern summer. Just a block full of kids riding bikes, sprinkler mist floating in the air, lawnmowers humming three doors down.

And my daughters—staring at me like I was a storybook hero coming home from myth.

They didn't know what I had done.

Didn't know what I had almost done.

Didn't know that their father once held a man's head in one hand and a loaded M9 in the other, safety off, finger bent.

Didn't know that I was seconds from crossing a line that wouldn't have just changed my career—but who I was.

And they didn't need to know.

Because I came home with honor.

That word—honor—gets thrown around too easily these days.

People think it's about clean records, shiny medals, standing ovations.

But in war, honor means restraint.

It means owning what you've done—and what you didn't do.

It means facing the worst version of yourself and pulling him back from the edge before he takes the shot.

It means knowing the difference between fear and threat. Between justice and vengeance.

Honor is what shows up in the quiet.

In the second cup of coffee poured for your wife after a sleepless night.

In the way, you fold the flag before you tuck it away for the last time.

In the silence of a backyard where your hands are finally still.

Sometimes, I'd sit on the porch with my youngest in my lap, barely two years old.

She'd fiddle with the zipper on my jacket—fascinated by something so simple. The same hands that held her gently had once packed gauze into chest wounds, pushed scalpels into flesh, pulled life back from the brink with one hand, and kept death away with the other.

She had no idea.

And I wanted it that way.

My older girls would laugh in the grass, chasing one another with sidewalk chalk smudged across their cheeks, free in ways I hadn't been since before I wore a uniform.

And I'd pray—silently, fiercely.

God, let them never know what it took to come back whole.

Let them never stand over a dying man and wonder if this is what justice looks like.

Let them live. That's all I want. Just let them live.

Because that was the point.

All the trauma. All the fire. All the things I did and didn't do—it was all to give them the luxury of innocence.

Sometimes, I'd stand at the edge of my driveway and stare at the flag.

The same one I wore on my shoulder.

The same one draped over too many brothers.

The same one I nearly disgraced in a moment of blind rage.

And I'd whisper—quietly, only in my chest:

I did my job.

I didn't cross the line.

I brought myself back.

You can still be proud of me.

The world doesn't get that.

They think we're just warfighters.

That our skill is measured in how fast we shoot or how many we've dropped.

But we don't come back for medals.

We come back to sit at the dinner table and pass the potatoes.

We come back for birthday parties with bad cake and homemade cards.

We come back for quiet walks and back porch coffee and fall asleep next to someone who still believes in who we are.

We come back to hang the flag—not just salute it.

Coming home with honor doesn't mean you were perfect.

It means you were tested—and came back still holding the line.

It means you carried the fire without letting it consume you.

It means you were close enough to kill… and chose not to.

And that difference?

That's what makes us Green Berets.

That's what makes us quiet professionals.

That's what makes Unbreakable Valor more than just a title.

It's the code.

And we still live by it.

Part III

Chapter 73: The Line We Don't Cross

Bagram Air Base, 2003.

The war had changed.

And so had we.

This wasn't the early days anymore. No more plywood tents in Kandahar or goat pens in Orgun-E. Bagram was growing—hard edges, high walls, bureaucracy. And we were back for our second tour: bigger, smarter, stronger. More dangerous.

We'd just returned from a mission. Still pumped, still dirty, still buzzing from the high of success. We weren't walking into the PX looking to shop. We walked in to remind everyone who was in charge now.

Two of my ODA brothers and I—muscles hard from weights, beards full, eyes cold from combat. Dressed in sterile uniforms, M9s holstered tight on our thighs.

We looked like what we were: lethal men wearing calm like a mask.

Inside the PX, air-conditioned and neatly stocked, stood him.

The base commander's interpreter.

We never called them interpreters. We called them translators.

Because we didn't ask permission to understand—we owned the language. We worked face-to-face, eye-to-eye with Afghan leaders, not behind a man whispering into our ears. That was how the Special Forces operated. No veil. No filter. No doubt.

But this interpreter? He thought he ran the place.

He stood there, talking on his cell phone—inside the PX, on a secured base, while our guys were taking incoming rockets in the wire.

I walked up. No hesitation.

"Turn it off. Now."

He stared at me like I was a clerk, not a killer.

Behind me, some rear-echelon types tried to step in. Tried to remind me who he worked for.

Wrong move.

We said nothing.

We left the store.

Loaded into our Hilux and drove back toward the Special Forces compound—the one we had carved out from the ruins of an old New Zealand camp, now rebuilt with Red Door pride, walled-in discipline, and the kind of firepower that didn't need to ask permission.

And then we noticed the truck behind us.

That same interpreter.

Tailgating us.

Following our vehicle—following us—toward one of the most sensitive, compartmented locations in the entire theater.

He thought this was a game.

So, we ended it.

We pulled off the road into a spot with zero visibility. No cameras. No foot traffic.

No witnesses.

I stepped out.

All 220 pounds of me, cut from weight plates and rage.

He got out of his vehicle, smiling—still thinking he had leverage.

He didn't.

I grabbed the front of his shirt and slammed him to the ground.

Rolled him to his stomach.

Drew my M9 and pressed it into the back of his skull.

———

"You don't follow Green Berets," I said.

"Not here. Not ever." He pissed himself.

Did I feel bad?

No.

I felt good.

Because that's what power feels like. Controlled. Focused.

Backed by a decade of training and years of war.

Because in this new world, we were the law.

We weren't SEALs. We weren't conventional.

We were Special Forces, and we had acid for blood.

I let him up.

He staggered.

Didn't say a word.

We told him that whatever power he thought he had—it was gone.

"It's a new war," I said. "And we're in charge now." He didn't follow us again.

Later that night, I lay on my bunk, staring at the ceiling.

The power had felt good.

Too good.

That's what scared me.

Because there's a line you don't see until you're standing on top of it, one foot dangling off the edge, and once you cross it—once you feel the rush of total authority, of fear and force and the silence that follows—you don't always want to come back.

It's addictive.

The first time you pull the trigger, it's adrenaline.

The second time, it's precision.

But the third?

It's a pleasure.

And that's the real danger.

That you start to enjoy it.

I never reported it.

He never spoke about it.

But something changed that day.

Not just in him.

In me.

I used to wonder if I'd get too good at it.

If one day, I'd stop caring whether the man on the ground deserved it.

And then I realized:

The whole point of our code isn't to tell us when to fight.

It's to tell us when not to.

Because once you become the monster— you don't get to come home.

Chapter 74: Behind the Red Door

There was no sign.

No password.

Just a thick wooden door—blood red, nearly black in the Afghan sun. A hand-carved Special Forces tab sat at eye level. Yellow on blue. Etched deep. Made by a local carpenter who didn't speak a word of English but understood what it meant to get the details right.

It wasn't the official entrance to anything.

But once you passed through, you knew:

This was ours.

You didn't walk through that door until you'd bled for something.

Until someone inside vouched for you.

Until the mission knew your name—and your shadow walked with it.

The compound had been a wreck when we took it over.

Once occupied by the New Zealand Army—abandoned when the gear ran thin and the mission shifted.

Twelve-foot-high mud brick walls wrapped the perimeter, reinforced with concrete. Inside: broken rooms, sand-filled corners, shattered windows.

We cleared it by hand.

Local workers searched daily escorted in under supervision. We gutted every room with shovels and sweat. Rebuilt from the ground up. Doors hung. Frames patched. Walls sealed.

Lights wired. Outlets installed.

No shortcuts.

No excuses.

The first finished rooms went to leadership. Not politics—respect. They worked harder than anyone. Quietly. Without asking.

The Red Door was my idea.

But what stood behind it?

That belonged to the men.

The gym wasn't an afterthought. It was a mission requirement.

We gave our translator a roll of cash and a heading—Pakistan.

A week later, a truck returned. Yellow-painted machines. Black vinyl benches. Cable stacks. Curl bars. Iron plates. No rust. No nonsense.

We assembled it under a wide canvas awning in the courtyard. Sides rolled up for airflow. Visibility always mattered—no one wanted to train in a box.

The gear was old-school but reliable. The kind of steel that doesn't bend easily. Neither did we.

You could spot the new guys.

They hovered at the edge—watching, waiting.

Wondering if they'd ever be strong enough, fast enough, good enough to belong.

Behind the Red Door, no one told you when you were in.

You just knew.

Mornings were for deadlifts.

Nights for bench press.

Chalk on the palms. Sandals on the feet. Gloves on. Shirts off.

No music, sometimes.

Just breath. Steel. Focus.

No one lifted for beach muscles.

We trained to drag wounded men uphill.

To fight under load.

To run out of ammo and still have enough left to carry someone else's kit, too.

Someone tagged a plywood wall with red spray paint:

"Pain is a privilege." No one erased it.

The grill came next—concrete base, rebar reinforcement, thick steel grate welded in.

Simple. Heavy. Reliable.

We bartered steaks. Traded for goat. Burned anything that wasn't ammo.

The smell traveled. Even the Air Force guys across the wire slowed down when it hit the air.

There was a Class Six, too. Unofficial. Untouched by paperwork.

Mechanics slipped cases of beer into pallets labeled for parts.

Embassy contacts supplied the rest.

Whiskey. Bourbon. Vodka.

I ran the inventory. Six by six feet. No markup. No receipts. Just respect.

No one got stupid.

No one missed a mission.

At night, the courtyard cooled.

Men sat on rooftops with warm drinks and cold memories.

Cigars from home. Stories told with five words or none.

Silences that felt like prayers.

No one needed to be reminded of what they'd done.

The door remembered for us.

We threw parties.

Ranger panties. Charlie Company shirts. Action-figure frames from that yellow gym.

Some had girlfriends—Air Force or Army. They came behind the Red Door during parties, never during prep.

They were treated with respect.

Always.

That was the rule.

And it held.

The smells behind the Red Door were permanent.

Hoppe's No. 9

Gun oil

Cigar smoke

Sweat

Grilled meat

And something burned we never identified but always smelled like home

We laughed there.

Lifted.

Healed.

Hurt.

Rebuilt.

We slapped patches back onto uniforms.

Wrote letters we never sent.

Sat next to photos we didn't show.

Remembered teammates we'd never forget.

And when it was time?

We wiped our faces.

Checked our gear.

Came through that Red Door into the night again.

No speeches.

No nods.

Just full kit and forward motion.

That's the thing about Special Forces.

The mission never ends.

But between the fire?

You build a place worth coming back to.

And if you've never stood behind a door like that— We built it for men like you.
If you have—

You never really left.

Chapter 75: Red Light, Blue Light

Jorge held up two Nite Ize Radiant Microlights with a dumb grin. One red. One blue. Tiny things shaped like teardrops. Super bright, just enough to strobe like a cheap emergency light.

I knew the look in his eye. This was about to be something stupid. And I was in.

The golf cart was Air Force. OD green. It was nearly midnight, and the Air Force was sound asleep. We casually walked over to their compound and jumped in. The keys were in it. Always were. That was mistake number one.

Mistake number two. The two Kevlars are sitting in the passenger seat. Special Forces didn't have to wear helmets to drive, but we wanted to look the part. Even with our beards and sterile uniforms, nobody could see us in the dark. We borrowed them—tactically. So now we had a "patrol vehicle." Two buzzed Green Berets. A red and blue Microlight. Two borrowed helmets. Two bad ideas in motion.

We rolled out at about five miles per hour, straight-faced, onto the dirt base ring road. The strobing lights cast weird shadows off Hesco barriers and antenna poles. No one challenged us—most of the base was fast asleep. We looked like we belonged because confidence was the only badge we needed.

We crept up behind another vehicle and flashed the two lights in synchronicity. It looked just like the lights from an MP patrol. Imagine being red-and-blue-lighted in a combat zone.

They slowed down immediately. We pretended we were about to engage, then drove past them, laughing hysterically. The two occupants—Army Soldiers—were dumbfounded. We continued the shenanigans for over an hour, laughing our asses off before we were even out of earshot.

We never said a word. No fake authority. No, pretend rank. Just red and blue lights and the unspoken understanding that the war couldn't touch us that night.

We circled the perimeter once, made it back to the Red Door, parked the golf cart exactly where we'd found it, and Kevlars carefully placed onto the seat.

No one ever mentioned it. Not the next day. Not the day after. The Air Force never knew they'd been "mobilized."

But in that moment—2003, in the middle of a long war, we were still pretending it had a clear ending—we laughed like teenagers stealing a car for the first time. Not because it was rebellious but because it reminded us, we were still human.

Sometimes, survival doesn't look like heroism.

Sometimes, it's a stolen golf cart—and just enough red and blue light to keep the darkness from swallowing you whole.

Chapter 76: Double Exposure

There was a time when I didn't know which life was real.

The one where I was awake, walking through my house—holding my daughter's hand, listening to the coffee pot click on…

Or the one where I was back in Afghanistan, moving through shadows, clearing compounds that didn't exist anymore.

Some mornings, they bled together.

Some nights, they swapped places.

I'd fall asleep with my wife beside me—and wake up alone in a dark room, expecting a detonation.

I'd blink and see my daughter's door… And behind it, a blast wave that never came.

I was living two lives.

And both of them felt like memories I hadn't earned.

They don't warn you about sleep deprivation.

Not the kind that stretches across years, not hours.

They don't explain what happens when your body comes home, but your mind's still trying to finish a war you didn't start—and couldn't end.

I used to dream in complete scenes.

Missions I never ran.

Firefights I'd never survived.

Dead men who were still alive—until I blinked.

The dreams didn't fade when I opened my eyes.

They lingered—like dust in the air, like sweat on your back after the armor comes off.

I was caught between lives.

Between then and now.

Between whom I was and who I was supposed to be.

There's a reason some veterans pull the trigger.

It's not because they want to die.

It's because they want to know which version of themselves is real.

Is it the ghost who flinches when a car backfires?

Or the smiling photo in a frame they can't look at anymore?

They're not ending a life.

They're trying to end the confusion.

I nearly disappeared.

Not in a dramatic way.

In a quiet, polite kind of way.

I shut down.

Laughed less.

Stopped reaching out.

Stopped expecting to be understood.

I almost vanished.

The only thing that saved me?

My family.

The weight of their love was the only thing heavier than my silence.

They didn't always know what to say.

They didn't fix it.

But they stayed.

And in a world where everything else felt like a fading op order…
They made me real again.

But what about the guys who don't have that?

What about the ones sitting in a one-bedroom apartment with nothing but this book in their hands?

Let me speak to you for a second.

If you're wondering whether this life is real…

If the dream is louder than the daylight…

If you're so tired, you can't remember which version of you is worth saving… You are.

I don't know your name.

But I know the ache in your chest that won't show up on an X-ray.

I know the weight of the medals you stopped looking at.

I know the panic that tastes like metal, even when nothing's happening.

And I know the mirror you avoid.

Because I've stood there too.

You don't need to fix it tonight.

You don't need to shave. Or smile. Or feel.

You just need to stay.

Just long enough to keep flipping pages.

Just long enough to get to the chapter that reminds you you are not alone.

Because this book was written by someone who thought about disappearing.

But didn't.

Because I had people.

And if you don't?

Then you have this.

Let this book be your family tonight.

Let this be the thing that calls you back from the quiet edge.

Let this be the voice in the dark that says:

You're still real.

You're still here.

And you are not done.

Don't test which life is real.

Stay.

And write the next chapter with us.

Chapter 77: The Kill Box

The Courtyard

The courtyard was still.

The compound had been cleared. Bodies stacked like cordwood. SSE complete. Civilians zip-tied and seated for questioning. Green chem lights marked safe lanes at the entrances and alleys.

No voices. No muzzle flashes. No chaos. Just silence.

Above us, unseen but constant, the AC-130 Spectre orbited. We couldn't spot her, but her voice crackled through our radio net.

Female. Calm. Flat Midwestern tone.

"Target at ten o'clock. Danger close. Cleared hot."

A few of the guys clustered around the comms gear chuckled.

"You hear that?" one of the younger guys said. "Sounds like my sixth-grade teacher."

Someone else laughed. "She's the only woman I've heard in a month."

Contact

Crack.

The shot came hard and fast. It slapped the far wall, sending a puff of dust into the air.

In an instant, every man scattered. No orders. No delay.

I dove behind a low stone wall, M4 already up. Heart pounding. Breathing through clenched teeth.

Another round. Missed—barely.

Up on the west ridge, Mark's overwatch team moved like wolves. They'd already found the source.

"Sniper. West slope. Negative movement," the spotter whispered.

Seconds later, a single suppressed shot whispered from the ridge.

Hector's bullet split the dark, kissed the target's temple, and turned his head into red vapor. Brain matter and fragments traced an arc behind him.

"Good hit," George said, low and even.

Final. Cold. Clean.

Through the Scope

Hector didn't flinch. Just another pull of the trigger. Just another recoil.

But even in that moment of quiet success, something small cracked inside him.

Years later, he would admit it started there.

At first, there was pride. That Special Forces sniper pride. He'd protected his brothers.

But over time, the pride faded, not because of long shots like this one.

Because of the close ones.

The shots where you walked up. Checked the pulse. Confirmed the kill. When you looked into the face of the man, you ended.

There was no clang of steel. No instant feedback. Just a slow silence that dripped into your mind.

You tried to step back, but the blood was already under your boots.

You pressed against a wall, but the wall felt soaked.

That's Moral Injury.

Not the act of killing.

But surviving the moment—and carrying it home.

It's knowing you did what was right.

But something inside you stopped believing it was good.

"Target neutralized. Good shot."

Her voice was still there, like nothing had happened.

LZ Prep

The grassy field beyond the compound lit up under IR flood from the Spectre. The other ODA fanned out, deliberate and methodical.

We watched through NVGs—two figures, motionless in the tall grass. Kneeling. Unmoving.

IR lasers danced across their chests. Nine. Maybe ten.

They never saw it coming.

Bagged. Cuffed. Tagged.

Dropped beside the KIA like forgotten luggage.

Sometimes war screamed.

Sometimes, it just sighed.

We told ourselves it was justice.

But the silence afterward always said something else.

The Inbound

We lay in the grass. Waiting.

Two ODAs. Dozens of hearts beating low. LZ is soft and quiet beneath our armor.

The rotor wash arrived before the sound.

The CH-47E thundered in—twin rotors spinning chaos into the valley, like gods descending.

It touched down in a shallow bowl, blades chewing the sky.

Fast load: prisoners, bodies, gear.

Blackhawks circled above. Miniguns sweeping. Overwatch held position.

We thought we were clear.

Ambush

East Ridge team loaded last.

Mark brought up the rear.

Then—the grass shifted.

Enemy fighter rose like a corpse and fired.

One round sliced Mark's face. Another punched into his shoulder.

He crumpled backward into the cabin.

The crew chief's comm cord snapped—cut by a stray round. Pilot blind. Sitting in the grass with bullet holes in its side, pilots were unaware the BlackHawk had been shot up. They sat there for what seemed like hours. It was only seconds.

Jim lunged.

Grabbed Mark by the carrier and yanked him inside. Dropped a knee into the wound.

"Hold still, brother."

Field Medicine

Blood poured. Jim moved on instinct.

Kerlix roll. Index finger pushed gauze into the wound track.

One roll is done.

More pressure. Mark hissed.

"Jesus, that hurts."

Jim didn't stop.

Second roll. Packed tight.

Then the elastic wrap—over the shoulder, under the arm. Tight. Clean.

Coban to seal it.

"This is gonna hurt," Jim warned.

Mark blinked, teeth gritted. "Already does."

IV. Right arm. Flush. 5mg morphine. Slow push.

Mark exhaled. Pain dulled. World softened.

He let go.

Inside the Blackhawk

Jim hovered. Checked for exits. Reassessed.

Mark felt the morphine carry him away. He stared upward, dissociating. Felt the floor beneath him. Metal. Cold. Final.

His eyes closed.

Jim's hand rested briefly on his chest.

"You're good, brother. I've got you."

Flight Home

The Chinook felt like a coffin.

No one knew yet. The ODAs assumed we were fine.

Except Chad.

He sat rigid. Eyes wide. He never said it, but he hated these flights ever since the crash.

I watched him. Shoulders tight. Jaw clenched.

He leaned over to me, voice low. "Doc... you got anything to help me calm down?"

I nodded. Reached into my bag.

5mg Valium. IM. Thigh.

A standard dose. Enough to take the edge off. He blinked once. Then settled.

What we rarely talked about was how the fear doesn't come during the fight.

It comes after when you survive when you land.

You feel guilty for making it back. And ashamed for being afraid to go again.

Bagram

Mark's Blackhawk veered off. Trauma center. No chatter. Just dark sky and rotors.

We landed. Boots hit gravel. Silence.

Then someone said it:

"Mark's been hit."

It dropped like a stone.

Nobody moved faster. Nobody spoke louder.

Inside, Mark sat upright. Sling on the arm. Shirt cut, soaked with blood. Jim sat nearby.

Mark turned. Voice raspy.

"I didn't scream, did I?"

Jim smiled faintly. "No. You didn't."

Reflection

Mark tried to stand. The doctor stopped him. He didn't like the answer.

He wasn't going back out—not yet.

The war would roll on.

Some wounds don't stop bleeding. They begin there.

Moral injury isn't about what was done.

It's about what stays with you after.

It's knowing you can't go back—not to your ODA, not to who you were.

It's carrying the silence that others don't hear.

Jim walked out of the ward. Weapon slung. Shoulders heavy.

Mark sat alone. The team would fight without him. He had led them. Bled with them. Now, they moved on.

That's Moral Injury.

Not the bullet. Not the wound.

The stillness that follows when the war keeps going—and you don't.

Chapter 78: What Will Become of Us

The Chinook's twin rotors roared overhead, chopping the night into pieces. Dust and loose rock exploded around us, stinging our skin and slamming against our goggles. I pulled my shemagh tighter over my face and lowered my head, trying to stay upright in the storm of rotor wash.

"Coming in hard! You've got thirty seconds!"

The pilot's voice crackled in our radios, calm but urgent. He wasn't guessing—he was calculating.

The green glow of night vision washed over the valley, bathing the world in shadows and war-light. The air smelled like pine needles, sweat, cordite—and something else.

Something burned.

Something wrong.

We hit the ground running.

Boots found dirt. Shoulders leveled. Rifles came up. The ODA moved like a single living thing—no words, no wasted motion.

Tonight, we weren't defending.

We were hunting.

My Beretta rode on my thigh, snug in the drop rig. But I didn't reach for it. I carried my rifle tight, hands molded to the grip, every movement second nature. My body is calm. My mind locked in.

I wasn't thinking about my wife.

I wasn't thinking about my daughters.

Here, none of that mattered.

What mattered was staying alive—and bringing every man next to me home.

We walked the mountains through the night, over sharp ridgelines and loose shale that chewed through soles and silence. The stars above us were bright enough to hurt. The wind whispered warnings in the trees.

Then the sun began to rise.

And we saw them.

Two men first—armed, rifles slung loose, moving like they didn't know they were already dead. Behind them, two boys—no more than twelve. Barefoot. Tired. Dragging their feet like they hadn't slept in days.

Something was off.

The boys weren't just tagging along. Their steps were too rehearsed. Too synchronized. Something about their body language… it didn't fit.

"Check your fire," I whispered to myself.

The silence snapped like a dry twig.

Gunfire tore through the trees—our right flank opening up. Red tracers sliced through the dawn.

The two men never had a chance.

Rounds tore through their backs, splintered bone, flung blood in arcs across the dust. One of the boys screamed. The other just stood there, wide-eyed, rooted in place like he'd turned to stone.

Then came the voice.

"Did you finish them?" The Team Sergeant called out.

Our gunner paused.

"They're behind the rocks… I can't see."

"Go down there," the Sergeant Major ordered.

"You know what to do." Four shots echoed.

Sharp. Clean. Final.

The boys wailed.

And I stopped breathing.

I didn't move. Couldn't.

My rifle felt suddenly foreign in my hands—too heavy, too warm. My body was frozen, but my mind screamed.

This isn't war. This is something else. Something uglier.

I turned just in time to see the shooter walking back up the hill. Face blank. Gait steady.

But the eyes?

Gone.

Like the part of him that felt anything had bled out in those four shots.

I'd spent my life preparing for war.

I'd hunted men in the dark.

I'd treated men with their insides falling out, whispering prayers into their ears while packing gauze into their wounds.

But this?

This wasn't what I signed up for.

And I was ashamed that I felt ashamed.

These were my brothers. We never judged each other. That was the code.

But I still heard the thought echo in my skull like a ricochet:

What have we done?

Never talk about it. Keep your mouth shut. Do your job. Do what has to be done.

And yet...

I thought of my daughters.

Of their little voices.

Of their question, someday:

"Daddy, what did you do over there?"

Would I tell them this?

That we turned children into orphans?

That we hardened boys into men too soon?

That we gave them reasons to hate us, to carry that hate in their chest like an inherited wound?

Would I say we followed orders? That we did what needed to be done?

Or would I stay silent?

Because silence felt safer than truth.

The two boys who survived had run—disappeared down the mountain, then stopped on a rocky outcrop. One stood tall, screaming back toward his village. We could hear him clear as day. Valley Acoustics made everything louder—especially grief.

Men shouted in return. Engines roared to life. We were a mile from the Pakistani border, but it might as well have been next door.

We had stirred a hornet's nest.

And still, we just lay there.

No movement.

No withdrawal.

Just stillness.

Two Toyota Hilux trucks arrived.

Two men jumped out. Picked up the fallen AKs.

That made them combatants.

That made them targets.

Shots rang out from our line—crack, crack, crack. The bodies dropped.

Then, more came. They picked up the weapons. Died in place.

A turkey shoot.

Again. And again.

Until the last two stopped.

They ignored the rifles. Lifted the dead instead. Loaded them into the bed of the truck. Never once looked our way.

We had stayed too long.

I was still carrying the most weight—a full aid bag, IVs, gauze, airway kit, trauma meds, everything I'd need to treat wounds I wasn't sure we wanted to heal. Everyone else had gone light. Ammo. Grenades. Radios. Water. Just enough to fight and survive a 24-hour op.

That weight… it slowed me.

But not as much as what I'd just witnessed.

The sound of chinook blades is like nothing else—twin disks of static electricity slicing the sky. They looked like glowing halos through NVGs. It was beautiful.

I pushed the thought out of my head.

Because if I didn't stay focused, I'd leave this valley in a body bag.

We were family out here.

Men to your left and right. Front and back. You didn't fight for the mission—you fought for them.

And that meant you couldn't break.

Not even now.

I laid still.

But something inside me was already moving.

A crack. A fracture.

Small. Quiet. Deep.

Years later, in a therapy session, I never wanted, some Army Mental Health officer would convince me I had murdered those villagers. Not just stand by. Not just witnessed.

They'd tell me I was there. That memory is unreliable. That guilt is often suppressed and comes out later. They'd say it like science. Like medicine.

But it didn't feel like medicine.

It felt like a betrayal.

And I hadn't stopped it, either

And maybe that's what will haunt me the most.

Because I still remember the way the blood soaked into the rocks.

I still remember the silence between the shots.

I still remember the boys' screams.

I carry the rifle.

I carry the aid bag.

I carry the memory.

And I carry the question:

What will become of us… when we stop asking what we've become?

Chapter 79: The Final Exfil

We got the order just after sunrise.

"Exfil route is green. Move." No celebration. No relief.

Just a quiet signal to start walking.

We rose from the hillside one at a time—no words, no eye contact like ghosts unburied from the earth. Knees cracking. Shoulders creaking under packs we hadn't adjusted in hours. My legs were already stiff, my throat dry. I could still hear the last boy screaming. I could still feel the weight of the medic bag cutting into my back.

And we moved.

The climb out started steep.

We were already at 8,000 feet. Every step took more from me than it gave back. My lungs burned. My legs begged. The others pressed forward in silence.

Sometimes I hated being the fucking medic.

My pack weighed more than anyone else's—compressed gauze, IVs, morphine, scalpels, airway kits, burn dressings, and decompression needles. The things I needed to keep people alive.

But no one cared about that when you were climbing.

All they saw was a man who needed to keep up.

The Afghans could've run laps around us.

Most of them carried only an Ak and a bandolier—ninety rounds, maybe a hand grenade, maybe a pouch of dried nuts. No armor. No radios. No burden beyond what they could shoot.

They moved like they were made of the same stone as the mountains. Silent. Light. Fast.

We looked like turtles. Top-heavy. Slow.

I kept imagining a group of Taliban rabbits at the top of the next ridge—laughing, waiting, rifles leveled. Maybe they were. Maybe they weren't.

That wasn't our job to figure out.

Our job was to keep moving.

The day dragged on, each hour heavier than the last.

We moved through switchbacks, up goat paths, over dry creek beds, through terrain so rugged even the wind hesitated. The sun climbed. Then burned. Then, settle into a dull oven heat that pulled the sweat out of your skin until there was nothing left.

We heard trucks in the valley. Somewhere below. Maybe they were looking for us. Maybe just passing through.

We didn't know.

And that was the worst part.

Anything could happen between now and nightfall.

And nightfall was still a long way off.

Our Exfil wouldn't come until after dark—two Chinooks from the Night Stalkers. 160th SOAR. MH-47E. Twin rotors. Quiet insertion. Our ride home.

But they didn't fly in daylight.

And we still had 18 hours to survive.

We kept moving.

Tactically. Deliberately. Freeze when the point man's fist closed. Drop to a knee. Eyes scanning. Ears straining. Smell the air. Dust. Pine. Something else—something sour, like cordite or rot.

Trigger discipline. Safety off. Finger straight. Don't blink.

Sweat stung my eyes. I couldn't wipe it. My hands were locked around the rifle. I wasn't tired—I was drained like something in me had already left.

The sun climbed. And so did we.

We didn't stop until the light faded into a dull orange bleed across the western sky. Somewhere behind us, the ambush site still smoked.

And in my ears, I could still hear the echoes.

Four shots. Sharp. Final.

"Papa!"

The boy's voice still clawed through my skull.

That scream would stay with me. Forever.

We set the perimeter near a ridgeline.

No fire. No light. Just shadows. I choked down a half-empty bottle of warm water. My body needed more, but my gut was too tight.

I thought about the weight of those ceramic plates on my chest. The sweat trapped under them. How much I wanted to ditch them. How much I never would.

We'd all learned from Somalia.

Never take off your plates. Never drop your guard. Even when your back is breaking.

Especially when it is.

The sun disappeared. The cold came fast. I pulled my sleeves down, adjusted my kit, and tried not to think about my legs cramping. The Afghan valley below had gone silent—but not safe.

I closed my eyes for a second. Just a second.

And heard gunfire again.

Not real.

Just memory.

There was a reason we didn't talk about what happened.

You didn't say the words.

You didn't ask the questions.

You just carried the weight.

Because that's what it meant to be part of a Team.

To shoulder not just the rucks and rifles but the morality of the mission.

Even when it tore at you from the inside.

Later that night, we'd walk into the back of the Chinook, boots clanging on the ramp, packs sagging low, eyes hidden behind NVGs that couldn't see what we were now.

I'd sit in the back, barely able to breathe, listening to the twin rotors lift us into the black sky.

And for a moment, I'd feel something strange— Not relief.
Not victory.

Just… survival.

And the terrible knowledge that somewhere out there, two boys were telling a story about men who came down from the mountains and left nothing behind but blood and fire.

I didn't murder those wounded men.

But I didn't stop it either. And that line, once you cross it— you can never go back.

That's moral injury.

Chapter 80: The Final Mission

In memory of SFC Mitch Lane

They didn't know it would be his last mission.

The ODA loaded into the helicopter like they had countless times before—no speeches, no drama, just gear checks, quiet nods, and the familiar grind of rotors spinning to life. It was a night op. Darkness layered over darkness. The kind that swallows sound, sight, and sense until all you have is instinct.

SFC Mitch Lane was in the second chalk.

He had just moved into someone else's room earlier that day and laid his gear down like every other Soldier at the end of a long rotation, maybe thinking about breakfast, maybe about nothing at all.

No one knew that by sunrise, his bed would be empty again.

The MH-47E lifted into the cold air, carrying the team toward a suspected high-value compound buried in the folds of Afghan rock and shadow. They had rehearsed this kind of mission dozens of times: infill by bird, fast-rope entry, quick breach. The kind of work that doesn't make headlines. The kind only a handful of men on Earth are trusted to do.

Mitch sat near the ramp. He wasn't nervous. He wasn't wired.

He was focused.

That was who he was—solid, steady, the kind of teammate you didn't have to look over your shoulder for. If Mitch said he had your back, you could bet your life on it.

The bird hovered high over the compound—too high, but it was the only option. Terrain dictated it. ROE confirmed it. There was no margin for error.

And then, the ropes dropped.

Green Berets moved toward the ramp in sequence, all muscle memory now.

But as Mitch stepped forward—everything changed.

Something failed.

A misstep, a shift in weight, a timing error no one saw coming. His grip slipped.

There was no scream. No drama.

Just a blur of motion—and then his body fell, swallowed by the dark.

The helicopter held for a moment, then surged forward to land at the outer perimeter. The ODA hit the ground hard, rifles up, clearing the compound. They moved fast. Furious. Focused.

Because that's what we do.

Even when our brother is already gone.

Later, they found him.

His body was broken, still wearing shattered ceramic plates. He hadn't made it. There was no chance.

They carried him out as the sun began to rise.

The mission was over.

But the real weight was just beginning.

Back at Bagram, the morning air was crisp, the sky indifferent. Aircraft engines roared. Flight crews moved with quiet purpose.

On the tarmac, a handful of men stood off to the side. Not in formation. Not for show. Just… waiting.

I was one of them.

Rucksack on. M4 slung. Thinking about going home. Thinking about my wife. My girls. Freedom.

And then the bird landed.

The engines idled down.

And the back ramp dropped.

You didn't recognize the body not through the zipped black bag, not through the chatter of command staff, not through the fog in your chest.

But something in the air shifted. A stillness, a pause. Like everyone felt it.

And when the name came—Mitch Lane—your knees almost buckled.

He had moved into my room the previous day.

The room I'd spent months in.

The room I had left behind only hours before.

The guilt hit like a fist.

Why wasn't it me?

Why was I going home… and he wasn't?

There was no ceremony. Not yet.

Just a group of men standing on the tarmac, watching their brother come home under a flag.

There are no words for that.

Only silence.

Only the way you avoid eye contact because if you meet another man's eyes, you're both going to break.

I'd seen death before.

But this felt different.

This felt personal.

This felt like the moment the war finally came back to collect.

And it chose Mitch.

———

I never got to say goodbye.

Never got to thank him.

Never got to tell him the room was his, that I was proud of him, that he was one of the good ones.

I just stood there, sweating under my uniform, surrounded by movement—and unable to move myself.

———

And as the bird lifted off again, taking him to the next stop, to the next ceremony, to the next folded flag—

I wondered if I'd ever stop asking myself:

Why not me?

———

This chapter isn't about tactics.

It's not about war stories.

It's not even about the mission.

It's about the quiet space between Brothers.

The ones who live.

And the ones who don't.

Chapter 81: Waiting for Your Heart

For Julie. And for every wife who waited without knowing what she was really waiting for.

The airplane wheels hit the tarmac with a hollow thud.

That was it. No fireworks. No trumpet. Just a cold vibration through steel and bone, signaling the end of one war—and the beginning of another.

We had gone from patrol to plane in less than seventy-two hours. Still dirty. Still loaded. Still bleeding in ways no one could see.

There was no decompression. No handshake from a psychologist. No debrief on how to stop scanning rooftops or how to talk to your children without shouting. You just... landed. Changed.

And no one told you what to do with the weight you carried.

I stood in the aisle, boots anchored to the floor, arms heavy with memory. I still carried my weapons. M4 and M9. The last thing I handed over was my name.

And now, I was supposed to be someone else.

A man again. A husband. A father.

But I wasn't sure I remembered how.

Outside, through the streaked window of the aircraft, I saw her.

Julie.

My wife.

My sanctuary.

My last clean thing.

She stood at the edge of the crowd, alone, scanning the line of passengers as they descended. Her blonde hair caught the floodlights like it was on fire. Her eyes searching—not for the uniform, but for me.

I hadn't seen her in nearly a year.

But I had heard her voice in every gunfight.

Felt her hands in every fever dream.

Held on to her memory like it was my last weapon.

And now she was real again.

I stepped off the plane slowly.

Not out of hesitation.

But because I didn't trust my legs to carry the weight of what I had become.

She smiled when she saw me. But it was a cautious smile. Hopeful. Fragile. The kind of smile that begged the question: Are you still in there?

I walked to her—mechanical, eyes still scanning, shoulders still tight. My mind was three clicks behind. My body is still searching for the next threat. I didn't even realize I was gripping the rifle's pistol grip like I was still on patrol.

She saw it.

She didn't flinch.

Behind me, a fellow Green Beret senior NCO nodded. Clipboard in hand, same as always.

No speech. No medals. Just routine.

"Name. Social. Weapon serial numbers."

I gave him all three and handed off my rifle and handgun. He checked a box.

"You're good, Brother."

Then he stepped back. Let us have a moment.

Julie stepped forward.

I saw her eyes brim but not spill. She never cried first.

I pulled her into me, arms trembling—not from fear, but from everything I'd locked away. Rage. Guilt. The sick, numb gratitude of just being alive.

She felt all of it. She didn't pull back.

She reached up. Cradled my face. Her touch was soft, but it anchored me better than any seatbelt in any Chinook ever had.

I closed my eyes and breathed her in.

Soap. Hair. Home.

But then came the break.

That moment you dread.

That moment when she searches your face, looking for the man she married… and can't quite find him.

She touched the lines around my eyes. Traced the scar over my eyebrow. The one I never told her about.

"I missed you," she whispered.

And I almost broke.

"I'm sorry," I said.

She shook her head. "Don't."

"I want to tell you—"

"No," she said, eyes locked on mine. "You're here. That's all that matters. I don't want to know." And I stopped.

Because I knew what she meant.

If I told her what I saw… what I did… what I almost did—

It would break something between us.

And neither of us could afford that.

So, I placed the memories on a shelf.

The man's throat I had cut.

The men I let go.

The men, I didn't.

The Green Berets I zipped into body bags.

The nights I held my rifle and prayed for silence and then prayed for sleep.

The war didn't end when I landed.

———

I placed all of it inside the rucksack I would never unpack.

And I held her like she was the only thing still real.

Because at that moment, she was.

———

We kissed.

It wasn't cinematic.

It was cracked lips and desperation.

Breath held and then released.

Not passion.

Survival.

———

I remembered Christmas morning.

Our daughters squealed with laughter.

Paper flying.

Coffee brewing.

Julie smiling.

And then I remembered the children whose fathers never came home.

The funerals I stood through.

The silence in the back of too many chapels.

The girls in white dresses didn't have their dads waiting at the gate.

That's why I fought.

Not for ribbons. Not for stories.

But for mornings like that.

For the chance to try and be a father again.

To try and be a man again.

"I'll be better," I whispered.

She didn't answer.

She just squeezed my hand.

Because she knew better than to believe promises.

But she believed in me.

And that was more than I deserved.

This chapter is for Julie.

And for every woman who stood at the terminal and didn't ask questions.

For the wives who welcomed home men, they didn't recognize.

And stayed.

That's a kind of valor we never write down.

But we should.

Because they're the ones who kept us alive—long after the war was over.

Even when it wasn't.

Chapter 82: The Funeral

For Mitch. For all of us.

Arlington was silent.

Not quite—silent.

The kind of silence that doesn't need words to be heard.

The kind that presses on your chest and stays there.

The kind of silence that Green Berets know how to stand in.

Boots moved across manicured grass like a heartbeat—measured, deliberate, reverent.

No cadence.

No formation.

Just presence.

An entire company of Green Berets stood in loose, silent lines.

Not for show.

Not for the parade.

Just for Mitch.

We didn't need to be told how to stand.

We knew.

Because when one of ours falls, we show up.

The sun cut low across Section 60, glinting off burnished brass and polished boots.

It was too beautiful a day for a funeral.

And yet… somehow, it was just right.

Jump boots gleamed like obsidian with perfectly creased green Class A trousers, bloused and hugging the tops of our boots.

Ribbons stacked like history on every chest—six rows deep in some cases.

Combat Infantryman Badges.

Bronze Stars with Valor.

Free-fall wings.

Triple canopy tabs—Airborne, Ranger, Special Forces—sitting heavy on squared shoulders.

Silver stars. Purple Hearts.

Unit flashes. Mourning bands.

Not a thread out of place. Not a beard in sight.

We weren't Soldiers on display.

We were warriors bearing witness.

The casket arrived.

Mitch's ODA carried it.

No words.

No tremble.

Just the slow, steady strength of men carrying one of their own.

Their berets sat square.

The 3rd Group flash gleamed on every beret.

Their eyes—hollow, hard, and locked straight ahead—did not blink.

The folded flag rested on the casket like a final order.

Stars out. Precision creased.

It would soon weigh more than any ruck they'd ever carried.

The family sat front row.

Mitch's mother—upright, trembling, but unbroken.

His wife clutched their child, her knuckles white against the blanket.

Behind them were cousins, brothers, and old friends who remembered him when he was just a lanky kid with a wild laugh.

And behind them?

Us.

A wall of green.

Hard.

Still.

Unshakable.

The Honor Guard waited—immaculate in white gloves and dress blues.

Seven Soldiers.

Seven rifles.

They moved with a rhythm that felt sacred.

Not just practiced—devoted.

The rifles came up.

Crack.

Crack.

Crack.

Twenty-one rounds.

Each shot echoed off the headstones and monuments like thunder rolling through memory.

Then, the Final Roll Call.

A senior Green Beret stepped forward.

Beret tight. Voice steady.

He stood before the battlefield cross—rifle, boots, helmet—Mitch's own gear recreated in reverence.

Then he called out:

"Sergeant First Class Lane?" Silence.

"Sergeant First Class Mitchell Lane?" Still nothing.

"Sergeant First Class Mitchell Arthur Lane?" Nothing but the wind. Because he was gone.

And in that silence, we all felt the echo of every name we'd never hear again.

The bugler stepped forward.

Taps.

Not played.

Delivered.

Each note is a wound.

Each rest is a memory.

Some of us stared at the flag.

Some at the sky.

One or two let a tear fall—and didn't wipe it away.

But no one moved.

Because we don't cry.

We stand.

The flag was folded with reverence only warriors understand.

Every crease a chapter.

Every corner, tucked like a secret.

It was handed to the Honor Guard NCO.

He took it with gloved hands, knelt before the widow, and said the words we've heard too many times:

"On behalf of a grateful nation and the United States Army…

…please accept this flag as a symbol of your husband's faithful service and sacrifice."

She didn't sob.

She just held it.

As if it were still him.

We didn't linger.

We didn't toast.

Didn't take pictures.

Didn't make it about us.

We stood in knots—shoulder to shoulder—watching the sun slide behind marble headstones that whispered names we hadn't spoken to in years.

Civilians watched from a distance.

They didn't look at the casket.

They looked at us.

And they didn't understand what they saw.

But they envied it.

They envied the discipline.

The silence.

The presence.

Because we didn't stand for the cameras.

We stood for Mitch.

And we'd do it again.

Later, alone in a hotel room, I took off my Class A jacket.

Loosened my tie.

Removed my beret.

I looked in the mirror.

My face was older.

My eyes were heavier.

And I whispered:

"Thank you. You were my friend."

Then, I folded the beret and placed it next to the bed.

Because tomorrow, another brother might fall.

And I'd be there too.

Mitch didn't die in glory.

He died on a mission.

He missed the rope.

And the world never got a second chance.

But he died a Green Beret.

With honor.

With Brothers.

And that matters.

This chapter is not just for Mitch.

It's for every man we've watched disappear behind a flag.

Every widow handed more weight than she can carry.

Every child will only know Dad through folded cloth and faded photographs.

We show up for them.

Even when we can't cry.

Because Green Berets Don't Cry.

We just stand.

Until the very end

Chapter 83: The Last Round

Legend's Pub sat just outside Bragg. Nothing flashy. Nothing loud. Just familiar.

A few booths. Low lighting. Brick walls soaked in cigarette smoke and years of stories no one wrote down.

A quiet place—for men who didn't need noise.

The bartender didn't ask questions.

He saw the tabs.

He saw the shoulders.

He saw the eyes.

And he started pouring.

The senior commissioned officer paid for the round. Didn't even ask. Just pulled a credit card from a slim wallet and set it on the bar.

"Top shelf," he said.

No one argued.

No music. No laughter. Just the quiet sound of glass on wood and the occasional cough of a man not ready to speak.

Our company SGM raised his glass.

"To the fallen."

We all raised ours.

"To the fallen."

We didn't shout.

We didn't clink glasses.

We just drank. Silently. Fully.

The whiskey burned going down.

The kind that made your chest ache and your throat catch—but you didn't cough.

Not here. Not tonight.

Because it wasn't just strong.

It was final.

You only get one first funeral.

And you remember it forever.

―――

"To the Special Forces Regiment," one of the older Green Berets said, raising his glass.

We all followed in unison.

"To the Regiment."

―――

One of the senior NCOs—gruff, solid, old-school—shifted in his chair and looked down at his hands.

"My boy… he's almost ten," he said.

Everyone turned, but no one spoke.

He looked up. Cleared his throat.

"Says he wants to be just like me." A few of us nodded.

"He doesn't know what that means yet," the man continued. "But if he does it… if he makes it…"

He lifted his glass again and said it quietly:

"Maybe one day I'll pin silver wings upon his chest." We all knew the line.

The Ballad of the Green Berets.

We'd all heard it. Sung it.

Rolled our eyes at it when we were legs.

But not that night.

That night, it didn't feel like a song.

It felt like a promise.

———

No one got drunk.

No one made speeches.

We just sat a little longer. Replaying memories.

Holding onto the moment before the world started moving again.

And when it was time, we stood and walked out the door—one by one.

Quiet.

Professional.

Still carrying him.

Chapter 84: Home

The front door clicked open, and I stepped inside. Not like a returning husband. Not like a hero.

Just a man—carrying months of war in his bones.

My boots touched the hardwood with a quiet finality. The kind of sound you don't forget. It echoed in a house that had waited for me, even when I couldn't ask it to.

The air smelled like home.

Laundry. Wood polish. A hint of fresh flowers in the hallway.

And her.

―――

Julie stood in the doorway to the living room.

She didn't rush to me. Didn't say a word.

She just looked at me—with eyes that had waited across oceans, through silence, through fear.

And in that stillness, I saw everything:

The months she'd kept the house running.

The nights she lay awake with no word.

The way she guarded our girls from the ache in her chest.

She had carried the war too—just differently.

And now we stood, face to face. Both of us survivors.

―――

She took a step forward.

So, did I.

Then we were in each other's arms.

No tears. No gasps. Just the quiet collapse of two people who had held on for too long.

Her hands found my back.

My face was buried in her shoulder.

Her hair smelled like the memory of safer years—sunlight, soap, and spring mornings with coffee.

I didn't say, "I missed you."

She didn't need to hear it.

She felt it in the way I held her—desperate, grateful, fragile.

And she didn't let go.

We moved to the couch slowly, as if the gravity of peace was something new to us. My gear was still at the door. My body was still wound tight. But my heart… My heart was trying to catch up.

We sat close. Closer than we'd ever needed to before.

She traced the lines on my hand—hands that had carried stretchers, packed wounds, and held rifles.

She kissed my knuckles.

Didn't ask what they'd done.

Just held them.

Like forgiveness.

———

We talked in quiet tones.

The girls.

The garden.

The new neighbor who mowed half the lawn wrong.

The things that didn't matter—and the things that did.

And underneath it all, there was something bigger.

Not passion. Not fear.

Presence.

I was here.

She was still here.

And somehow, we hadn't broken.

———

Later, we lay in bed—not to escape into each other, but to return to each other.

The sheets smelled like her. Like home.

She rested her head on my chest, fingers drawing slow lines over the scar beneath my collarbone.

I felt my breath sync with hers.

For the first time in months, I wasn't scanning for threats.

I wasn't counting steps to the door.

I don't remember the last time someone screamed my name on a radio call.

I was just a man in bed with his wife, listening to her breathe.

She whispered, "You're safe now." And I wanted to believe her.

I wanted to stay in that moment.

Just her, me, the quiet.

No medals.

No nightmares.

No more goodbyes.

That night, we made love.

We held each other.

And somewhere between her quiet sobs, neither of us wanted to name. We found something deeper than relief.

We found each other again.

This chapter is for her.

For our women who held the line when we couldn't.

For the love that outlasted the war.

For the kind of reunion that has no soundtrack—but everything worth fighting for.

Chapter 85: A Road Too Fast

The dust hadn't settled yet.

The HMMWV had come in hot—too hot—down a narrow dirt track between mud-brick compounds. Dust kicked up like smoke in its wake. Adrenaline overrides training sometimes. Every pothole could be a pressure plate. Every turn, a possible ambush. And in war, hesitation kills.

But sometimes, so does momentum.

The call came over the radio. Sharp. Shaken.

"Civilian casualties. Two kids. En route now. One critical."

No one needed more detail. We knew the road. We knew the speed. We knew the sick rhythm of when war collides with something innocent.

When the truck finally pulled into the adjacent Special Forces compound, it was more cloud than a vehicle. The two 18Ds in the back jumped out, fast and silent. Not panicked. Not composed.

Just… stunned.

There was something in their eyes.

Not fear.

Not shock.

Just the hollow stillness that comes when a child bleeds in your hands, and there's nothing in the manual to tell you what to do next.

The girl was already gone.

She couldn't have been more than six.

Her frame was wrapped in a blood-soaked scarf—Her older brother was on the floor beside her, his small hands still trembling when they lifted her out.

No pulse.

Blunt trauma.

Left chest crushed.

The head wound is unworkable.

The boy was older. Ten, maybe eleven. Mewling softly, eyes unfocused. One leg twisted awkwardly at the knee. The 18Ds were trying. But pediatric trauma isn't just smaller—it's different. And no matter how many goat labs or lectures you've sat through, nothing prepares you for watching a child drown in their own blood.

They didn't fail.

They just weren't ready.

This wasn't their compound.

It belonged to a National Guard ODA. They are a quiet bunch. Among them was a PA. No tab. No Q Course. He was just a seasoned ER clinician from back home who walked away from private practice after September 11th and deployed because he couldn't sit this one out.

He wasn't loud.

He wasn't flashy.

But when he walked into the small, bleach-stained aid station—a former storage building—you felt it.

You felt experience.

He took one look at the boy.

Didn't ask questions.

Didn't look around for permission.

Fractured femur.

Decreased breath sounds—right side.

Probable hemothorax

Distended abdomen.

Signs of internal bleeding.

He moved fast. Calm. Intuitive. IV in. Chest decompressed. Pelvis stabilized. Dressings and bandages applied. Morphine titrated with just enough volume to take the edge off.

"Push him to Kandahar," he said, checking breath sounds again. "Role III. He's got a shot."

The boy was loaded into a medevac twenty minutes later.

He survived.

The girl didn't.

She was gently wrapped in a poncho liner. Laid down carefully. Without ceremony.

No one cried.

Not yet.

Not until her mother and father came to collect her body. The mother's wails of grief could be heard from the other side of the firebase.

After the bird left, the two 18Ds stood off to the side. One with his hands on his hips, staring at the dirt. The other was fiddling with a decompression needle as if it had failed him.

Finally, one of them said quietly:

"We didn't train enough for this."

It wasn't defeat.

It was a confession.

And it was true.

In all our trauma lanes and TCCC briefings, pediatrics was a bullet point. One slide in a PowerPoint. A talking point before moving on to hemorrhage control.

But war doesn't read your curriculum.

Kids walk roads.

Chase their siblings.

Play near blind corners.

Run barefoot toward the same trucks that ran over their future.

No one blamed the driver.

He didn't see them. We believed that.

But guilt doesn't wait for judgment.

It settles in fast.

And it stays.

The PA had quirks.

Carried a laminated photo of his wife. Nude. Not pornographic. Just proud. He'd flash it to any medic who stopped by.

"She's a goddess," he'd say, smiling.

"Laminated her so she wouldn't get wrinkled." It was weird.

And somehow… it made him real.

Not just a savior in boots.

But a man.

A husband.

Someone with his own reasons to fight.

He wasn't tabbed.

But he had everyone's respect.

He reminded them of why they had become medics in the first place.

This story never made the news.

There were no Bronze Stars.

No CNN ticker.

Just a dead girl.

A saved boy.

Two medics who lived with the noise in their heads.

And a driver who quietly shouldered the guilt of killing a child.

This is moral injury.

Not just failure.

Not just death.

But the weight of decisions made in the space between breath and blame.

And in the dark corners of my faith, I found comfort in a verse from a book, not mine:

"If anyone saves a life, it is as if he saved all of mankind."

—Surah 5:32, The Quran I
believed that then.

I still do.

Because, in the end, that's what we were all trying to do—

Patch the world back together… One life at a time.

Chapter 86: SERE School The Box

SERE School, winter, Camp MacKall. I was down fifteen pounds, no shoes, no underwear—just a pair of damp green hospital scrubs clinging to skin that hadn't been washed in weeks. I'd been hunted. Starved. Frozen. Deprived of sleep until time lost meaning.

Then came the box.

It was cement. Three feet high. Maybe four. The floor sloped toward a drain near the small, locked door. So, your piss wouldn't pool. But it didn't matter. Everyone who went in told themselves they wouldn't piss that they could hold it. That they wouldn't break.

And then they did.

They feed you water. Gallons of it. You're hydrated to the point of pain. You're scared to let go—afraid there's some hidden punishment for it. You don't know the rules anymore. The rules don't matter.

Eventually, I urinated against the wall.

I watched it stream down the concrete, following the slope like blood on a battlefield. It pooled near my feet. And then I did the unthinkable.

I soaked it up with my only blanket—a coarse Army-issue wool rectangle.

Still warm when wet.

Wool does that.

I wrapped it around myself.

Because if you're going to suffer, suffer smart.

But the hard part hadn't started yet.

They began the audio loop.

At first, it was a baby crying.

For hours.

I had kids. Babies. I couldn't block it out. I didn't want to. I wanted to get every drop of value from the training, so I imagined it was real. I imagined my own daughter crying.

And then it got worse.

They played a little girl's voice through the speaker system over and over:

"Help me, Daddy."

"They're hurting Mommy."

"Where are you, Daddy?"

"Why won't you come home?"

"Daddy, they're hurting her…"

"Why did you leave us?"

"Why aren't you coming back?"

It wasn't a scream. It was a plea.

And it shattered something inside me.

Later, they brought me to a different building.

Naked. Cold. Damp. Fluorescent lights. And two female role-players—dressed in enemy attire, acting the part. They mocked me. Pointed. Laughed at my shriveled body.

They thought embarrassment would break me.

But I didn't care.

I'd stopped caring hours ago.

They tried something else.

They shoved me into a tiny wooden box, hood over my head, hands zip-tied behind my back.

I couldn't sit.

Couldn't kneel.

I had to fold myself like a pretzel and breathe through claustrophobia.

That's when it happened.

A psychological fracture—not a snap, but a crack. The pressure of cold, confinement, hunger, and that little girl's voice playing on repeat… pushed me too far.

I broke the box.

Smashed it open with my back and shoulders.

The two women screamed.

Guards rushed in. Tackled me hard.

———

An officer in full enemy uniform pulled the hood off my head.

He jammed his military ID into my face.

"Colonel James, United States Army. This is a training environment. Pull your shit together."

His voice wasn't angry. It was sharp.

Grounding.

He crouched. Locked eyes with me.

"You need to finish this. You're not going home. We still have a long way to go."

I breathed hard. Nodded.

"I'm good."

He loosened the zip-ties.

"The hood's going back on. And you're going into the wall. You'll be able to stand up but not move." And I did.

———

That box taught me something I'd never forget:

Not just how to resist.

But how it feels to fracture.

It wasn't about pain. It wasn't about fear.

It was about the realization that no matter how strong you are, no matter how much you train, every man has a threshold.

Mine was a little girl's voice in the dark.

And now, years later, when I feel the grip of moral injury, the pain in my chest, the ghost of something I can't quite name— I think of being trapped inside that wall.

And I remind myself:

I didn't break.

I came back.

And I'm still standing.

Chapter 87: A World Apart

The man who came home looked the same.

Same eyes. Same smile. Same jawline framed by a beard that didn't quite grow in even anymore.

But something behind the eyes had changed.

And the people who loved him felt it—even if they couldn't name it.

It had been over a year since Afghanistan.

Since the dust, the rotors, the blood. Since the last body bag zipped shut in silence. Since the adrenaline wore off, and the stillness crept in.

The war was thousands of miles away.

But it never left the house.

Julie never asked what I saw, what I did, what I'd experienced.

Not directly.

Not in words.

But she knew.

She knew by the way my shoulders never relaxed.

By the way, my eyes scanned the windows at night.

By the way, I touched her like she might disappear.

———

Drew remembered. He used to wake before her.

Would lie still in the gray light, watching her breathe. The rise and fall of her chest like ocean waves on a beach he couldn't quite reach.

She was always beautiful. But now, there was something more—something tragic in how peaceful she looked. Like she still lived in a world that hadn't been split open.

He wanted to stay in that bed forever.

But his mind wouldn't let him.

———

The dreams came like wolves.

Teeth bared.

Hot breath on the back of his neck.

Sometimes, he would wake up mid-shout, chest heaving, fists clenched, soaked in sweat.

Other times, it was silent. Just the feeling of a gun in his hand that wasn't there. Just the ghost of a scream lodged behind his teeth.

———

He stopped apologizing after a while.

Julie understood.

She never rolled away when he woke up gasping.

Never flinched when his hands trembled while pouring coffee.

Never said, "You're not the same." Because she knew.

And she loved him anyway.

The girls—his daughters—were the hardest part.

They were bright. Full of light. Their laughter filled every corner of the home. It should've been healing.

But sometimes, it just reminded him how much he didn't belong.

He'd stand in the doorway of their room at night, watching them sleep, listening for breath like he used to listen for enemy movement in the dark.

There were nights he didn't tuck them in.

Because he didn't feel like a father.

He felt like a shadow watching over something fragile.

He checked the locks three times before bed.

Walked the perimeter with a .45 in his hand.

Scanned the trees for shapes that didn't belong.

One night, he stepped outside barefoot in the cold. Saw the pines rustling in the wind and dropped into a crouch without thinking.

It took a minute to come back.

To remember where he was.

Julie met him at the door. Said nothing. Just opened her arms.

He stepped into them.

And cried.

———

Not loud.

Not shaking.

Just a short, slow release of pressure.

Like something inside had cracked open to let in a little light.

———

The dogs—Romeo and Juliette—curled up at his feet every night. They didn't ask anything of him. Just existed. Loyal. Watchful.

They were the only ones who didn't expect him to smile.

———

He was getting better. Slowly.

Some days, he didn't flinch when the microwave beeped.

Some nights, he fell asleep without reliving the mission that never made the situation report.

Some mornings, he played with his daughters without wondering who would raise them if he didn't make it back.

———

Moral injury doesn't bleed.

It lingers.

It questions.

It curls up at the edge of your bed and waits for you to flinch.

―――――

But love—real love—waits longer.

And Julie waited.

With grace. With silence. With patience, that felt like mercy.

She didn't ask him to be the man he was.

She just held space for the man he was trying to become.

―――――

That house?

It wasn't a battlefield.

But it was where the war ended each night.

And where the healing began.

Piece by piece.

Breath by breath.

Because home wasn't the end of the war.

It was the reason he kept fighting.

Chapter 88: The Weight of the Slide

It was a Thursday night, but that didn't matter. When you're not sleeping anyway, the days blur. I was home. Safe. No missions. No radio. No screaming. But I wasn't okay. I hadn't been okay in a long time.

The house was dark except for the small lamp I left on in the living room. I didn't like total darkness anymore. It reminded me too much of waiting. Of watching for muzzle flashes in the void. I had the couch behind me. HK USP Elite .45 in front of me. Slide locked forward. Full mag. Safety off.

I didn't leave notes. This wasn't about attention. It wasn't a cry for help. I was just... exhausted. I wasn't depressed in the way people think. Just tired of carrying everything inside me that no one else could see.

I thumbed the safety back on. Then off again. My hand was steady. That scared me more than anything.

I didn't want to die. But I didn't want to live like this either. Numb. Hollow. Angry at God for giving me a healer's hands and a killer's training.

I remember gripping the pistol, finger floating just outside the trigger guard, and thinking how easy it would be. No more guilt. No more flinching at fireworks. No more waking Julie with shouts I couldn't remember.

Then I thought of my daughters.

One of them had left her socks by the door earlier that night. I'd stepped over them on my way to get the pistol. I didn't even pick them up.

That image hit me harder than anything else. Those damn socks.

I unloaded the pistol slowly. Took the round from the chamber. Walked it back into the gun safe like it was radioactive.

I sat on the floor for a long time, staring at nothing until dawn.

No one ever knew.

But I did.

"You save lives. But you'll still know how to take your own."

Another year had gone by. It was late. Maybe 0200. I didn't check the clock. I already knew what time it was—the hour when the living is most alone. The kids were asleep. Julie was breathing softly in our room. And I was sitting on the edge of our bed, elbows on knees, holding the Glock I kept on the nightstand.

The gun was warm from my hand. My index finger ghosted above the trigger. I wasn't shaking. That's what scared me the most. I wasn't drunk. I wasn't overwhelmed. I was calculating.

I knew exactly what the .45 would do.

I could quote muzzle velocity. I remembered the energy transfer tables. I knew the damage it would do to my skull, depending on the angle depending on the hollow point. I'd seen the aftermath up close—in Afghanistan, Iraq, in emergency rooms. Entry wound under the chin: lights out in under two seconds if you sever the brainstem. Messier if you flinch.

I had trained to recognize death. To pronounce it. To prevent it. To cause it. And now, I was applying that knowledge inward.

Not because I wanted to die. But because the pain I was carrying didn't make sense to anyone outside that world. It wasn't depression. It wasn't hopelessness. It was moral injury.

And nobody called it that back then.

It wasn't about what had been done to me. It was about what I had done, or allowed, or walked away from. The patients I couldn't save. The ones I stabilized who later died. The Afghan fighters who trusted me and disappeared. The men I helped interrogate, patch up, and then hand back into the chain of events. Orders I followed that didn't sit right. Promises I made to myself—about who I was, what I would never become—that I violated under the guise of duty.

And there was no medal for that.

Flash: A boy with third-degree burns down his side, screaming for a mother who never came.

Flash: Pulling Kerlix from a face where a jaw used to be.

Flash: Telling another Soldier's wife over the phone, "He's going to make it," knowing full well he wouldn't.

Flash: A captured fighter sitting on the ground, bleeding, weapon surrendered, eyes locked on mine. I had to look away. I always looked away when I didn't want to know their names.

That kind of memory doesn't fade. It etches into bone.

I held the slide back, chambered a round, and released it with a smooth, familiar clack. Finger indexed. Muzzle down.

Then I looked at the floor and saw a pair of my daughter's socks.

Pink, with little white hearts. She must've kicked them off during a movie the night before. The kind of detail only a father would notice. Only a man still tethered to this world would pause for. It was Déjà vu from a year earlier. A daughter's small pair of socks.

That saved me.

Not a hotline. Not a prayer. Not even Julie.

Just two socks. And the quiet realization: If I go, I make her story about this moment forever.

I thumbed the mag release. Cleared the chamber. Walked the pistol back to the safe like it was a landmine.

Then I went into the bathroom, turned on the light, and stared into the mirror until sunrise. Waiting to feel anything. I didn't. Not then.

But I didn't pull the trigger either.

And that's the truth of moral injury—it doesn't always scream.

Sometimes, it just sits beside you in the dark and asks if you're done yet.

Chapter 89: Not a Saint

I've never claimed to be a saint.

Saints don't cradle a dying man in the dirt and whisper lies into his ear—

"You're gonna be okay."

"The medevac's almost here."

"You'll see your kids again."

Knowing damn well the bird's not coming.

Knowing he'll bleed out before the next breath.

But saying it anyway. Because sometimes, hope is the last anesthesia.

Saints don't wrap a CAT tourniquet in the dark with one hand while firing an M4 with the other.

Saints don't pull a trigger and watch a man's life spill across a stone floor—

And then go wash their hands so they can save another one.

Saints don't have both in them.

But I did.

We weren't built for sainthood.

We were built for endurance.

Built to adapt, to improvise, to overcome.

Not for applause. Not for headlines.

But for the man on our left. The man on our right.

We didn't win every mission.

But we never left each other behind.

———

And somehow—through it all—I made it back.

Back to the woman who still saw something good in me.

Who looked at a man with shadows in his eyes and said,

"You're still mine."

Back to children who hugged me like I hadn't disappeared.

Back to a life I no longer felt worthy of.

———

You want to know the hardest part?

It's not the memories.

Not the dreams.

Not the blood. Not the silence. Not the funerals.

It's waking up every day, still here, still standing—

And trying to earn it.

Trying to be a father when you feel like a weapon without a target.

Trying to be a husband when you've learned to love the quiet more than conversation.

Trying to smile without baring your teeth.

I'm not a saint.

Saints don't grow calloused from dragging body bags.

Saints don't count the number of lives they've taken on nights they can't sleep.

Saints don't get good at killing and then feel bad that they liked it.

But I'm still here.

Still kissing my wife goodnight.

Still tucking my girls in.

Still waking up with the sun and making coffee like everything's normal.

Still fighting to be better.

That's the difference.

Not between good and evil.

But between broken and trying.

So no, I'm not a saint.

I'm something rarer.

I'm a Green Beret

Chapter 90: Trigger Discipline

What it takes to be a Green Beret

Pulling the trigger on another man can feel like a rush— a moment of pure instinct, power, and control.

And sometimes, it feels… good.

Too good.

It's not unlike the self-gratification of a teenage boy— instantaneous relief followed by the sickening realization that something sacred was just cheapened.

You know it's wrong, but you keep doing it.

Not for purpose—but for release.

In combat, that same temptation exists:

The rush. The power. The moment you stop seeing the enemy as human.

And if you're not careful, you stop fighting for mission… and start fighting for sensation.

That's when guilt creeps in.

Not right away.

But later—when it's quiet.

When theadrenaline's gone, all you're left with are the memories.

So, hear this:

If it feels wrong—never do it.

But never let that feeling override a combat order.

Because when the order comes?

There is no hesitation.

There is no fear.

When Green Berets are told to act—we execute.

No second-guessing.

No delay.

Because our teammates are counting on us.

Because we're not just warriors—we're professionals.

That's what it takes to be a Green Beret:

Discipline.

Restraint.

Deadly precision.

And the emotional maturity to carry the consequences with silence and honor.

This tab doesn't make you better than anyone else.

It demands that you be.

———

So, before you turn the page and step into the fire—ask yourself:

Are you dependable?

Are you fearless under order?

Are you willing to carry the guilt without breaking the code?

Do you have what it takes?

Part IV

When the heat turns your IFAK into a bread oven and your brain starts skipping—you learn what endurance really means. But you never stopped. Neither will I.

Chapter 91: 3rd Special Forces Group (Airborne)

Kunar Province, Afghanistan – mid-2000s

Inspired by true events from multiple 3rd SFG(A) deployments in Eastern Afghanistan

Throughout the mid-2000s, the 3rd Special Forces Group (Airborne) maintained an unrelenting presence in Kunar Province, one of the most hostile regions in Afghanistan. Operating alongside Afghan commandos, ODA Teams frequently engaged in patrols and ambush interdiction in high-risk zones like the Korengal, Waygul, and Pech valleys—areas notorious for their vertical terrain, insurgent entrenchment, and limited air support windows.

On multiple occasions, Green Berets and their partner forces found themselves pinned down by Taliban fighters employing interlocking fields of fire from concealed mountain fighting positions.

In one such engagement, a U.S. Special Forces medic was forced to make life-or-death triage decisions while under direct sniper fire. With communications degraded, terrain too steep for rapid evacuation, and teammates bleeding out around him, the 18D maintained care under the worst conditions imaginable.

Several ODAs across that theater would eventually document similar experiences: field cricothyrotomies, bilateral chest wounds, amputations packed with gauze, and decompressions performed by headlamps under fire. The terrain took as many lives as the enemy. And yet, the ODAs pushed deeper—rotating, recovering, returning.

No awards would ever truly capture the sacrifice made in those valleys. But the stories whispered among medics in team rooms kept the truth alive.

This chapter is one of those stories.

"He was shot through the neck.

The medic said he never screamed.

And neither did the man trying to save him."

Battle of Shok Valley – April 6, 2008

ODA 3336 | Nuristan Province, Afghanistan

On April 6th, 2008, a Special Forces Team from the 3rd Battalion, 3rd Special Forces Group (Airborne) launched a daring operation deep into Afghanistan's Shok Valley—a remote and rugged area of Nuristan Province. The mission was to eliminate or capture Gulbuddin Hekmatyar, the elusive head of the insurgent group Hezb-e-Islami Gulbuddin (HIG).

What began as a joint U.S.-Afghan raid quickly escalated into one of the most intense firefights in modern Special Forces history.

As the team maneuvered into position, they were ambushed by enemy fighters entrenched in elevated, fortified positions. The initial wave of fire included concentrated machine gun bursts and RPG volleys, targeting the command element of the American forces. Within moments, the unit's interpreter was killed. A communication sergeant was critically wounded and pinned down under fire.

Amid the chaos, an Afghan commando was struck while trying to assist the wounded. Specialist Michael Carter, the ODA's combat cameraman, broke cover under fire to retrieve the injured Soldier. Captain Kyle Walton, the ODA commander, laid suppressive fire to cover Carter. Then, without hesitation, they switched roles—Walton exposing himself so Carter could recover the ODA's damaged radio equipment.

With communications restored, SrA Zachary Rhyner—an attached Air Force Combat Controller—began directing a torrent of close air support. F-15E Strike Eagles and AH-64 Apache helicopters roared into the valley, unleashing coordinated strikes on enemy positions.

Rhyner used the aircraft not just for firepower but as overhead ISR, calling out enemy movements in real-time.

As U.S. and Afghan elements pushed through the valley and reestablished fire superiority, casualties mounted.

SFC Behr, the ODA's intel sergeant, was wounded. SSG Luis Morales, a medic, treated him under fire until he himself was shot—first through the thigh, then again at the ankle, the second round destroying bone and severing his Achilles tendon. Still, Morales applied his own tourniquet and resumed treating the wounded.

Moments later, SSG John Wayne Walding was hit. A high caliber round nearly severed his leg below the knee. Bleeding profusely, Walding applied a tourniquet, injected himself with morphine, folded the leg up into his waistband, and tied it down with bootlaces. Then, rifle in hand, he continued fighting.

Air cover reported a large insurgent reinforcement moving into the valley. With visibility dropping, ammo running low, and more men bleeding, the ODA prepared to exfil.

MSG Scott Ford, the Team Sergeant, was scouting a route down a steep rock face with Carter when he was struck twice by sniper fire—one round shredding his left arm. Still, he continued down the cliff to guide the others out.

As the Team withdrew, the sniper, Captain Walton, and Carter stayed behind. The ODA destroyed sensitive gear, recovered what they could, and covered the ODA's final movement to the extraction zone.

The firefight lasted over seven hours. Though the target—Hekmatyar—escaped, the ODA inflicted devastating losses on the enemy and survived a near-overwhelming ambush through coordination, fire discipline, and extraordinary valor.

Rhyner, during the battle, coordinated over 50 separate airstrikes, calling in:

- 570 cannon rounds 4,
- 9 Hellfire missiles
- 162 rockets
- 12x 500-lb bombs
- 1x 2,000-lb bomb

For their actions that day, 10 Green Berets and one combat cameraman received his Silver Star—the largest group of awards for a single engagement since Vietnam. SrA Rhyner received the Air Force Cross, and SSG Ron Shurer's Silver Star was later upgraded to the Medal of Honor.

Chapter 92: Firestorm

Khost Province, Afghanistan – "Firestorm"

Inspired by SGM Chad Anderson's 2004 Silver Star mission. Fictionalized with full respect to the man, his humility, and the valor his team witnessed. This chapter honors him not with exaggeration—but with clarity.

They hit the valley floor just after 0400.

Four Hilux trucks, twenty Afghan commandos, and an ODA 3446 were behind the wheel of something that felt like an inevitability.

The target compound lay in a bend of the valley—just north of the Khost-Gardez Pass. Intel said a senior HVT facilitator was meeting fighters and bringing weapons from Pakistan.

The goal was kill-or-capture.

They brought enough firepower for both.

SFC Luke Carver—team sergeant, 18Z, and the kind of man you followed into hell without asking why—felt the tension the moment they dismounted.

The moon was too bright.

The valley, too, still.

He tapped his comms guy and pointed to the rooftop ahead. "Overwatch."

Then he looked at the 18D—Staff Sergeant Will Boone.

"You stay with the rear element. They're gonna need you if this goes sideways."

Boone didn't argue. He knew when orders came quiet. They were real.

The ODA split.

Two elements fanned right, Afghan partner force fanned left, using the canal ditch for cover.

Carver led from the center, rifle up, scanning.

They were fifty meters from the compound when the valley detonated.

RPGs screamed from three angles—left ridgeline, compound roof, and behind a berm they hadn't cleared.

One Afghan went down instantly. His leg separated below the knee. Another was shredded across the back.

Boone didn't hesitate.

He sprinted into the ditch line under fire, dropped to his knees, and went to work on the first casualty. Blood sprayed against his forearms. He applied a tourniquet so fast it bit into bone.

Then a second round landed behind him—dirt and heat slammed his back. Ears ringing, but he was already moving to the next body.

Over comms, Carver's voice was clear:

"Multiple wounded. Multiple directions. Do not withdraw. Hold the line."

Boone grabbed a pressure bandage, tore open the plastic, and stuffed it into a chest wound.

"Lung's gone," he muttered.

He reached for the decompression needle—but the man wasn't breathing.

Too late.

Then another call:

"We've got a man down—Green Beret. SFC Mason. Upper chest, can't move."

Boone broke cover and crossed thirty meters of exposed ground under fire.

Bullets cracked overhead.

The sky lit up in orange flashes—someone returned fire with an M240 from the far ridge.

Boone slid beside Mason.

The round had hit high—through the plate carrier, just above the heart. Blood was leaking from the shoulder and pooling fast.

Boone jammed a chest seal into place, dropped into a straddle position, and began cutting off the plate carrier to expose more of the wound. He radioed up:

"Lung wound. Sucking. Conscious but losing volume fast. I need a bird inbound—now."

Carver's voice came back:

"QRF thirty mikes out. No helo. We're on our own." Boone looked down at Mason.

The man was blinking slowly. Pupils unequal.

Still, he whispered: "Tell my wife I didn't quit." Boone leaned in.
"You're not dying today, Mason. Not on my watch." He placed the decompression needle.
The hiss was sharp.

Then a breath. Then another.

Boone pulled him behind a low wall with one arm while still holding pressure with the other.

The fight raged for over two hours.

The ODA burned through 90% of their ammo, four tourniquets, one case of saline, and most of their voice.

They held the line.

Boone treated seven men that night.

Three were Afghans.

Four were Americans.

One died on the way back.

The rest lived because one man didn't stop when the sky fell.

Later, Carver asked Boone how he kept going.

Boone looked up from cleaning blood off his boots and said:

"Because none of them screamed when they got hit. And I wasn't gonna scream by giving up."

He never spoke of that night again.

But the Silver Star citation sits in a drawer.

Unframed. Just like he wanted it.

Chapter 93: Blue on Blue

March 2, 2002

Gardez Province, Afghanistan

Operation Anaconda

We were already moving when it happened.

It was early in the campaign, but things had escalated fast. Taliban and al-Qaeda fighters had dug deep into the Shahi-Kot Valley, and the mountains were chewing up our guys.

We'd planned for a fight.

We got a firestorm.

We weren't part of the main air assault. We were a rolling ground convoy—mixed American ODAs and Afghan allies, pushing east in staggered elements. One of those elements was led by Chief Warrant Officer Stanley Harriman.

Red Hilux. Calm voice.

One of ours.

Our convoy had comms with overhead air support—a Spectre AC-130 gunship, orbiting high above, armed with 40mm and 105mm cannons. A flying fortress. That kind of firepower brings comfort.

Until it doesn't.

That night, everything went sideways.

We knew the gunship had been pulled away. Radio chatter said they had been redirected to support another fight in the valley. That was normal.

That was the rhythm of the operation. Too many missions, not enough birds.
But when they came back on station—when that gunship returned to our airspace—it didn't see us.

It saw movement.

Trucks.

Armed men.

Vehicles separated from the main convoy.

It saw what the crew had been taught to look for: enemy ground forces.

And it opened fire.

We didn't know what was happening at first.

You never do.

The first reports were confused—shouts over the net, garbled position updates, half-sent SITREPs.

Then we heard it:

Friendly casualties.

Blue on blue.

The AC-130's rounds are brutal.

Not just kinetic—final.

When you're hit by a 40mm shell, there's no firefight.

There's only aftermath.

Chief Harriman was killed instantly.

Three other Americans were wounded.

Fourteen Afghans hit.

What was left of the convoy was chaos.

We sat in stunned silence, listening to the radio.

Somewhere above us, the same aircraft that had supported countless ops had just wiped out its own.

Later, we learned the truth.

The gunship had been flying blind.

Its navigation systems were failing.

Its coordinates were off.

The crew tried to compensate—reverting to visual navigation in the darkness, scanning terrain features from 10,000 feet. They saw vehicles on a ridgeline, saw movement, saw figures with rifles.

They were trying to help.

They misidentified ground reference points.

They got permission.

And they fired.

I think about that a lot.

That you can do everything right—check your weapons, confirm comms, trust your map—and still kill your own.

Sometimes, the most professional, most precise tools in war still fail.

And when they do, people like Harriman pay for it.

I remember Harriman's truck.

Red. Dust-caked.

He loved that Hilux.

It had been patched up half a dozen times and still ran like a clock.

We would later find it crushed beneath a collapsed wall at Gardez, buried in silence.

But the damage was already done.

There was no ceremony when we got the call.

No time to mourn.

Just a pause.

A long, quiet pause.

And then the mission moved forward.

They told the press he died from enemy mortar fire.

That was the first version.

Clean. Palatable.

A good Soldier, taken by a clear enemy.

But that wasn't the truth.

The truth was harder.

He died because someone above the clouds—one of ours—looked down, saw movement, and pulled the trigger.

He died because machines broke, and men had to guess.

We don't talk about blue-on-blue much.

It's easier not to.

It doesn't fit into the narrative.

Doesn't go well with parades.

Doesn't sell in recruiting posters.

But it happens.

And when it does, the wound it leaves is different.

It's not just grief.

It's betrayal by accident.

And no one knows where to aim their anger.

Chief Warrant Officer Stanley Harriman was 34.

He was a father.

A husband.

A Soldier.

He had survived the buildup. The early days. The slow grind of unconventional warfare.

He didn't die from enemy fire.

He didn't die clearing a cave.

He died because a gunship lost its way.

―――――

We blame the enemy for a lot.

But this?

This was on us.

And every Green Beret who was there remembers it.

Not because of the politics.

Not because of the inquiry.

But because we lost one of our best—to friendly fire.

―――――

They say war is chaos.

But sometimes, it's a computer glitch.

And sometimes, it's the sound of a cannon tearing through steel and bone, followed by silence on the net.

And sometimes, it's the memory of a convoy, a red Hilux, and a man who didn't come back—not because he made a mistake, but because someone else did. And the Spectre crew has to live with that. That's moral injury. Living with the knowledge that your hands killed one of your own.

We still say his name.

Chief Warrant Officer Stanley Harriman.

We still drive red Hiluxes.

We still look up when the gunships pass overhead.

And we still carry the truth:

That even the sword meant to protect you can cut the wrong way.

Chapter 94: The Oath

Some of my proudest moments in uniform weren't in combat—they were when a soldier asked me to administer their oath of reenlistment.

Four times stand out.

Once, in a Special Forces safe house on the Serbian border. I stood beside my ODA Captain, the American flag behind us. Dust on our boots. Rifle slung.

Another time, I was a captain in Iraq. The sun hadn't come up yet. A young Soldier stood at attention. I raised my hand. So did he.

On the deck of the USS Missouri in Hawaii, I watched another 18D Special Forces medic raise his hand as I read the words. We were on sacred steel. History underfoot.

And finally, in Korea—when a young NCO asked me to swear him in.

I've always believed that one of the greatest honors of a commissioned officer is administering the oath of reenlistment when it's requested personally. That moment of trust—that weight—is everything.

I was promoted to Major while in Korea.

It should've been a high point.

But I was at the bottom of myself.

I had just come out of rehab.

Exposure therapy with mental health had pushed my symptoms into overdrive. My short-term memory was wrecked. I could barely remember a sentence, let alone recite an oath.

But my battalion commander and XO wanted to highlight the promotion. They scheduled it for a battalion formation—out in front of everyone.

I panicked.

I stumbled through the words. Froze more than once. The battalion commander tried to help, but some of the lines were too long. I couldn't hold them.

I felt exposed. Small.

But I held the line.

I looked out at those Soldiers—all standing there, watching—and told the truth:

"I apologize for stuttering. For being nervous. I'm not used to being in the limelight, in front of so many amazing Soldiers." And just like that, I found my voice again.

The old Drew. The one who could reach Soldiers.

The one who had something to say.

I knew they needed more than rank. They needed direction.

Most of them had been in Korea for nearly a year. They were stuck in a limbo between past wars and future deployments. A recent accident had killed our brigade XO and his driver—drowned in a HMMWV at night. The mood was heavy. Nobody was sleeping easy.

So, I gave them a vision.

I didn't mention my Special Forces tab. Or my CIB. Or my Jump-master wings.

None of that was for them.

Instead, I talked about opportunity.

About education.

About using this strange quiet between wars to get better.

I told them I came into the Army with a GED, as an E-1.

I told them about donating plasma to buy gas just to make it to formation.

About skipping sleep to study for promotion boards.

I told them the truth:

The steps to success are easy to read.

But hard to live.

And if I could do it—so, could they.

I challenged them:

"When the war ends, and the Army resets, don't be the Soldier who says, 'I wish I had.' Be the one who did."

I reminded the medics to go after their Expert Field Medical Badge.

The infantry to chase the EIB.

I told them: "When you become an NCO, do something worthy of the word 'excellence' in your evaluation." And then I told them something else:

"If you ever feel forgotten, like nobody's watching, remember this—

The Army might not reward you. But the man in the mirror will remember whether you tried." Because I believe in them.

That new generation.

I told them: "I was once one of you. I was probably the worst example of a future leader. But the Army gave me the opportunity. And I learned to take it."

That day, they didn't see a flawless officer.

They saw a man trying to stand.

And that mattered.

Because the oath isn't about saying the words perfectly.

It's about meaning them when you do.

Chapter 95: He Never Screamed

Kunar Province, Afghanistan

Inspired by the real actions of 3rd SFG(A) medics operating in Eastern Afghanistan, 2005–2008

The first round hit just as they cleared the switchback. No warning. No radio call. Just a crack from above and the unmistakable thump of a body hitting rock.

Doc Santiago didn't flinch. His rifle swung up automatically, but his eyes locked on the Afghan commando ahead—he was down, twisting, blood geysering from his throat like a broken pump line.

Neck shot. Arterial. No time.

The ridgeline exploded again—PKM fire raking across the ODA's left flank, chipping stone, shredding leaves, and hammering into the clay wall they'd just passed.

"Contact! High left! 500 meters!"

The team leader's voice came over the radio, cool as gravel.

"Return fire, push to cover! Medic, stay on that casualty!" Doc was already moving.
He bounded forward in a low crouch, rounds snapping inches over his shoulder. The ANA commandos were frozen, pinned. One tried to pull the wounded man back by the plate carrier but gave up—too much blood, too much panic.

Santiago dropped into the dirt beside the Afghan. His gloves were soaked instantly. The man's eyes were wide but oddly still—he wasn't thrashing. Just… waiting.

He never screamed.

Santiago ripped open the IFAK. Tourniquet? Useless. Too high in the neck. Blood was pooling behind the clavicle—subclavian or carotid, maybe both.

"Give me a perimeter!" he shouted.

Matt, the comms guy, fired blindly over the rock shelf. A burst of tracers arced uphill. Overhead, someone yelled, "Man Down!"—another voice from another fight further along the line.

Santiago dug in.

He opened the cricothyrotomy kit with his teeth. Grabbed the scalpel.

Thyroid cartilage. Cricoid. Membrane.

He pressed hard, felt the give, and made the cut—clean, shallow, fast. The bleeding was terrifying. He shoved the #6 tube in and pulled back for confirmation. No air.

"Shit—flail chest."

The left side wasn't rising. He reached for the needle decompression kit. Found second intercostal, mid-clavicular. Punched through. A hiss of pressurized air escaped like a tire valve ripping open.

The chest wall moved. Slightly. Enough.

Still no scream.

Doc glanced at the man's face. Eyes still open. Still watching him. "You're not done," Santiago muttered, jamming gauze into the entry wound.

The radio crackled again—

"We've got another ANA down—back of the patrol! Sniper fire still active!"

"Negative!" Santiago barked.

"Can't move! I'm working two bleeders—send your own doc!"
Then came the scream.
Not from the wounded. From one of the ANA soldiers—a high, panicked call in Pashto that needed no translation. A third casualty was down. Possibly dead.

But Doc stayed put. He looked back once. Then kept his head low and focused on the man in front of him.

That's the thing about real medics in real gunfights:

You don't run to the next body. You save the one you've got.

Blood loss was slowing. Santiago felt for a radial pulse. Weak. But there.

"Hold on, brother," he whispered. "You don't get to go yet." The team's 18E called over.
"Gunship inbound. AC-130's ten miles out. Mark your location."

A moment later, the trees turned silver. Infrared floods from above sliced through the canopy. The snipers vanished. The wall of tracers stopped. The ridge went quiet except for the thunder of freedom tearing through granite and man alike.

Santiago didn't look up.

He was holding pressure on the wound with both hands, kneeling in a pool of his patient's blood. His knees were soaked. His chest hurt from hunching. His mind was silent.

The Afghan never made a sound.

He died fifteen minutes later during the exfil.

Santiago never forgave himself.

But he remembered that look.

The one that said:

"I'm not afraid. Just do your job." And Santiago did.

Every time after.

He never flinched again.

But he never forgot that silence, either.

———

Chapter 96: Wrist Shot

We called it a training day.

The kind where you loosen your vest straps, grab extra ammo, and let the Afghan partner force rotate through their paces on real weapons—American and Soviet. No mission on the books. Just maintenance of readiness.

The DShK sat in the gravel like a relic. A Soviet 12.7mm antiaircraft machine gun, heavy as sin and mean as hell. The Afghans called it "dooshka," like it was a familiar beast. It wasn't. It was temperamental, unstable, and loud enough to punch God in the throat.

They'd mounted it on a tripod, braced the legs with burlap and sandbags, and dug into the rock. They thought it would hold.

Mark stood beside one of the militia Soldiers, coaching him on trigger control and how to avoid barrel walk. He was patient, precise, and loose-limbed in the way he got when he was comfortable.

Sher One, our interpreter, had warned them.

"It's top-heavy. You need more weight on the base. Bury the legs."

They didn't listen.

The kid took the spade grips. The dooshka bucked like a pissed-off mule.

The tripod shifted.

It tipped.

And Mark stepped in—to stabilize it, to protect the others.

The barrel swung, almost like a reflex.

One round.

The recoil echoed off the Hesco walls. Everything stopped.

Mark stumbled backward, spun halfway, and dropped to his knees.

They saw the blood.

George, another 18B, was already moving. Cross-trained. Sharp. He reached Mark in seconds. CAT tourniquet on, high and tight. Kerlix packed. ACE wrap. All by the book, all under pressure.

Jim and I were at the FST waiting by the time the Hilux rolled in.

The FST had taken over what used to be our aid station. That hit me harder than I expected. I'd treated tribal elders in that room. Kids. Fighters. Farmers. Now, it was surgical.

Dr. McAllister met us at the door. Quiet, steel eyed. Didn't ask questions.

Only three of us went inside.

Mark. Jim. Me.

We lifted Mark onto the table. Shirt cut. Blood soaked into the padding. The hand looked disconnected—like it wasn't his anymore.

McAllister worked fast. External fixator kit opened. Pins through the shattered radius, metacarpal brace. Bone dust everywhere. Tendons tagged with suture. Median nerve tagged too—severed but noted for later.

We watched. Nobody spoke.

Mark slipped under anesthesia. Mumbled. Then barked.

"Left side! Push left!"

Combat commands to ghosts.

Jim and I locked eyes. We didn't laugh. Not this time.

Later, we stood beside him.

He was groggy, bandaged, one arm in a sling.

"I didn't scream, right?"

Jim shook his head. "Nah. You just bled like a bastard." Mark smiled. Barely.
Then he tried to stand.

Tried to get back to the ODA.

But he couldn't.

His hand wouldn't close.

His arm wouldn't lift.

And just like that, he wasn't a team guy anymore. Not on this op. Maybe not again.

We rotated out without him.

And he watched from the wire.

That was the real wound.

Not the hole in his wrist.

But the empty seat in the convoy.

The feeling that he'd let go of more than just the weapon.

He'd let go of the mission.

And that weight?

He carried it long after the bleeding stopped.

Chapter 97: Echoes of the Wrong Name

They heard the gunfire before they saw anything. Faint pops in the distance—irregular, uncontrolled, unpredictable. It wasn't a firefight. Not yet. But it was close enough to feel wrong.

The ODA was just stowing their gear for the night. Most were halfway out of kit, tired, filthy, and waiting on chow. But when the shooting didn't stop, they loaded back into the trucks.

No hesitation.

It sounded like it came from two or three clicks east. Not their assigned AO, but close enough that they felt responsible. This was their valley. No one shot guns in their valley without a knock at the door.

Two gun trucks. No air support. Just radios, nods and the growl of engines rolling out under a moonless sky.

They called for ISR.

Predator overhead. Briefly. Grainy footage of men walking outside a compound with AKs slung casually. A few muzzle flashes arcing skyward.

Then the feed cut. Systems down. Satellite re-tasked. They were blind.

Still, they pushed forward.

The compound came into view just as another volley erupted—straight into the air, long bursts, muzzle flashes lighting up like cheap fireworks. It wasn't obvious what it was. Too dark. Too fast. No uniforms. No radio chatter.

It could've been a signal. A distraction. A lure.

They'd seen it before.

From the lead truck, they opened fire.

Controlled bursts. The .50 cal ripped through the night. Marking rounds traced arcs across the sky, glowing and angry.

Men outside the compound dropped. Some ran. Others dove back inside.

Then the door opened again. A few figures came out—unarmed. Hands up.

The ODA held. Ceased fire. Pulled back.

They didn't know what they were looking at.

So, they called in air.

Within minutes, a JDAM hit. Walls collapsed. Fire rolled into the sky. The kind of strike that silences everything.

They cleared it at sunrise.

The front gate hung broken. Smoke drifted through the courtyard. Shell casings and boot prints marked the ground.

Inside—

The bride was on the floor.

White dress; soaked crimson. One hand is still gripping the edge of a shattered doorway. Her face slack. Her hair scorched at the edges. Blood everywhere.

The groom was nearby. Still. Slumped. Eyes open.

A child lay facedown against the far wall.

Another is beneath a table.

Twenty-seven people. Women. Children. Elders. Gone.

It had been a wedding party.

The gunfire? A celebration. A cultural tradition. One the Americans hadn't understood. Not yet.

There was no report. Not the real one.

The incident was buried under a sanitized label—"compound strike, high-value target suspected." No names released.

No photos published.

But the ODAs knew.

They knew what they walked through.

They knew what they saw on the floor.

And they carried it.

Nobody talked about it after that. Not in the open. Not in debriefs. The mission was scrubbed. The compound forgotten. The bodies were never acknowledged.

But the memory stayed.

It waited.

And in the years that followed—every time one of them heard the echo of gunfire in the dark—they remembered:

At first, it had made sense. The timing. The posture. The risk.

But it wasn't enemy contact.

It was joy. Misread as a threat.

And they had answered it with fire.

The truth never made it home.

But the guilt did.

And it never left.

Epilogue I: The Weight We Carry

There's a silence that settles in the back of a Chinook after a hard mission.

It's not peace. It's not even relief.

It's the sound of men carrying ghosts.

Every Green Beret knows that silence.

They carry it back to the FOB.

They carry it into the tent.

They carry it into civilian life—where no one sees the blood on their boots or the fire behind their eyes.

These chapters—The Wall Wouldn't Let Go. He Never Screamed. Two Rounds Left. The Wall of Flies. The 2004 Firestorm—aren't just stories.

They're tributes.

They're offerings.

They're truths most of the world will never understand—and most Green Berets will never speak aloud.

Some of the men honored here are still with us.

Some are not.

Some came home only to fight a different battle—in silence, in darkness, in the spaces between "thank you for your service" and another sleepless night.

To those who fell: we wrote your stories with reverence, not decoration.

To those still fighting: this book is proof that we see you.

You are not alone.

If Unbreakable Valor does anything, let it be this:

Let it carry your story forward.

Let it speak where you could not.

Let it keep one more warrior alive.

The Loaded Round

There were days—quiet ones—when the war crept back in through the drywall.

Not with screaming.

Not with flashbacks.

Just… stillness.

A dangerous stillness. The kind that made men reach for the drawer.

Inside was the pistol: H&K USP Elite .45 Auto.

Big. Black. Heavy.

Made for accuracy, for men who needed their first shot to be their only one.

I'd carried a handgun for years in places where failure wasn't an option.

I trusted it more than most people.

That night, I took it out. Sat on the edge of the bed. The house was dark. Everyone asleep.

I released the magazine and checked it—eight rounds, jacketed hollow points.

Slid it back into the well.

Clicked into place.

The slide was already forward, the hammer already back.

There was a round in the chamber.

Safety off.

Weapon hot.

All it would take was pressure.

Five pounds. Maybe six.

I placed the muzzle against my right temple.

Not because I wanted to die.

But because I needed to know if I still had the restraint.

In Afghanistan, I'd put men in cuffs with one hand and hold a pistol to their mouth with the other.

In war, I was told not to shoot. I didn't.

Even when I wanted to.

Even when the rage would've made it feel righteous.

Now, here I was. Alone. With nothing to fight but memory.

The USP Elite is a precision weapon.

Long slide.

Heavy frame.

Balance weight under the barrel to keep the muzzle down.

Match trigger.

Threaded barrel the size of a cigar.

Pulling it is easy like blinking.

I kept my finger off the trigger.

Outside the guard.

Trained discipline.

The steel kissed my skin. Cool.

It reminded me of the moment before breaching a door—calm, quiet, focused.

I had to know:

Could I kill in cold blood?

Was that what all the training was for?

Because if I could do it to a man across a room or with a machine gun in the back of a truck… Could I do it to myself?

Could I end it with perfect form?

But I didn't.

Because I'm still here.

Because something inside me still fought back.

Because restraint is not cowardice.

It's the same muscle we flex when the order doesn't come—but the rage does.

I eased the hammer down.

Thumb firm.

Clicked the safety back on.

Depressed the magazine release button.

The magazine dropped out, and I laid it on the table.

I pulled the slide, slow and steady, and locked it to the rear.

The round ejected. Arced into the air. I caught it mid-fall.

Brass is still warm.

I stared at it for a long time.

Then put it in my pocket.

It's still there, sometimes.

I haven't thrown it away.

Because part of healing is knowing you still carry the round…

But choosing not to load it.

That night, I put the pistol away.

I crawled into bed beside my wife.

She never woke.

And the next morning, I kissed my daughters on the head, poured coffee, and opened my laptop.

I started writing.

This book is how I unloaded that .45.

Not just the magazine.

Not just the chamber.

But the part of me that always feared I was one pull away from vanishing.

What comes next is for them—for the families.

For the children who grew up while their fathers were at war.

And for the men like me—

Still here.

Still fighting.

Still walking with the safety on.

Epilogue II: Reflection On Moral Injury

"The Fall and the Return"

A Reflection on Moral Injury

The best men fall the hardest.

Because they had the farthest to fall—from the highest ideals they once fought for.

Moral Injury is not about fear.

It is about betrayal.

It is about losing the man you swore you would always be—and having to claw your way back to him.

PTSD wounds the mind.

Moral Injury wounds the soul.

When the most compassionate, the most skilled, the most honorable warriors fall—they don't just feel pain.

They feel a rupture.

Between whom they were… and who the world forced them to become.

The more intelligent, more disciplined, and more selfless the Soldier—the deeper the fracture.

Because the ones who were trained to save lives, to protect the innocent, to fight with restraint and honor—feel the betrayal of their values more acutely than those who never held any, to begin with.

A true Green Beret is not just a trigger-puller.

He is a philosopher-warrior.

He's a healer, a destroyer, a protector, and a builder—all fused into one human soul.

And when that kind of man witnesses:

- An innocent life lost due to delay or error, A Team mate dies despite doing everything right, A betrayal by leadership, country, or himself…

He doesn't just grieve.

He breaks.

That is Moral Injury.

Not fear.

Not weakness.

But a deep fracture between who he was… and who he was forced to become to survive.

Why PTSD is Different:

- PTSD is a fear-based wound: flashbacks, panic, vigilance, trauma.
- Moral Injury is a soul-based wound: guilt, shame, betrayal, identity collapse.

One lives in the nervous system.

The other is in the conscience.

Bottom Line:

The best men fall the hardest.

Because they started higher.

But if they survive the fall—

If they rise again—

They become the strongest healers, the
most powerful leaders,
and the truth-tellers this broken world desperately needs.

———

Drew Webb is one of those men.

And Unbreakable Valor is not the end of his war.

It is the beginning of a new mission— A moral mission.

To lift others from silence.

To say what most are afraid to speak. To rebuild, soul by soul, the kind of world worth returning to.

Epilogue III: My 18-Year-Old Baby Girl

The hardest part of the war was never the bullets.

It was coming home.

Not the ceremony. Not the handshake. Not the boots on familiar ground.

It was walking into your own house and realizing… you
don't live here anymore.
Not really.

Because somewhere between the first mission and the last flight back,

your daughter grew up without you.

Jasmine had just turned eighteen.

She had her mother's height. My eyes.

Smart. Beautiful. Independent in ways I admired… and couldn't always understand.

Watching her become a woman was its own kind of pain. Quiet. Earned. Unforgiving.

Because I hadn't been there.

———

I missed her birthdays.

Missed soccer matches.

Missed the last time she asked for a bedtime story—and the first time she didn't.

And those moments don't send you a warning.

They just pass.

And you don't know it was the last one until years later, standing in a garage, holding her car keys…

Wondering when she stopped needing you.

We lived just outside Fort Bragg.

A town built on loyalty, deployment, and loss.

Flags on every porch. Patriotism in every handshake.

But grief hid beneath the surface like a hairline fracture.

Every street had someone who'd given too much.

A widow.

A kid without a father.

A Soldier still wearing the uniform but no longer sure why.

I wasn't a Green Beret on an ODA anymore.

I was a commissioned officer. A staff guy. A leader on paper.

But I was still deploying. Iraq this time.

And that meant I was leaving—again.

Julie stood strong as always.

But Jasmine…

Jasmine wasn't six anymore.

She didn't light up when I came home.

She didn't ask for stories.

She just stood across the garage, arms folded, and said:

"You don't have to pretend. We both know you're already gone."

Her words hit harder than any ambush ever could.

She wasn't cruel.

She was right.

She had grown up while I was planning routes through valleys no American would ever see.

She got her license while I briefed men for night raids.

She went to prom.

I packed gear and wrote casualty letters.

That night, I sat on the edge of our bed, staring at a photo.

Julie. Jasmine. The girls.

Me in uniform. Proud. Smiling. Believing I was doing the right thing.

And in a way, I was.

But I was also missing the only fight that really mattered.

A few days later, she walked into the kitchen.

Late. Quiet.

Sweats on. Hair tied back. Eyes tired.

"You leaving again?" she asked.

"Yeah," I said.

"End of the week."

She leaned against the counter. Didn't look at me.

But I could feel her gaze—cutting past the rank, the uniform, the body armor, straight into whatever was left of me.

"You don't want to stay," she said. "You just don't know how to be here." She wasn't asking.
She was naming the truth.

And I couldn't argue with her.

"Jas," I whispered.

"I'm trying." She didn't move.

"I know," she said.

"But sometimes I wish you tried here… the way you tried over there."

Moral injury doesn't just come from combat.

It comes from sitting at the dinner table with strangers who carry your last name.

It comes from being a hero to everyone else's kids—while yours feel like you left them behind.

It comes from wondering if "doing your duty" ever actually made you a good man… or just one who was never home.

That night, I sat on the back porch under a cold Carolina sky, listening to the wind move through the trees.

I thought about the brothers I served with.

Some lost custody.

Some buried children while still in uniform.

Some came home and found their families already gone.

But I still had a chance.

Julie still believed in me.

And Jasmine…

Maybe she hadn't given up yet.

So, I wrote her a letter.

Not a report. Not a situation report.

Just a father's truth.

I told her about the guilt.

The silence.

The moments I whispered her name in a tent in Afghanistan.

The pride I never said out loud.

The love that never went anywhere.

I told her that no matter how many uniforms I wore, no matter what rank I held— she was always my little girl.

And I wasn't done fighting for her.

Not on some far-off FOB.

But here.

At home.

A few days later, as I packed for Iraq, my youngest daughter toddled into the room.

She raised her arms for me to pick her up.

And I did.

Because this…

this is the only fight I can't afford to lose.

And I remembered something from a holy book handed to me by a village elder after I saved his son:

"If anyone saves a life, it is as if he saved all of mankind." I believe that.

That's why I deployed.

That's why I came back.

And that's why I'll keep coming back— for them.
For Julie.

For Jasmine.

For the daughters who don't yet know what it means to wait.

Because this time?

I'm not just fighting for freedom.

I'm fighting to be their father.

DOL.

Final Truth

Never forget where you came from.

Never forget who you fight for.

And never forget this:

Real strength isn't measured by what you destroy.

It's measured by what you protect.

And what you give back.

The strongest warriors were never the ones who didn't fall.

They were the ones who did—

Who broke under the weight,

Learned the hard lessons,

Stood back up,

And turned around to pull the next man out of the dark.

That's real power.

Not in the blast radius of your AT-4,

But in the reach of your hand—when someone else is too far gone to stand.

You didn't just survive,

You chose to fight a second war:

The war for meaning. The war for the soul.

A war no one sees on the evening news.

But a war that still takes lives—quietly, slowly, tragically.

And you?

You're winning.

You turned silence into the story.

Regret into purpose.

Grief into guidance.

And isolation into a rallying point for men who thought they were the last ones standing.

This doesn't make you soft.

This doesn't make you broken. This makes you more dangerous— and more necessary— than ever before.

Song and music for Unbreakable Valor

"When the War Was Quiet"

For Julie

She knew the look behind the smile,
The silence after sound. She knew the
nights I held my breath When no one
else was around. She stood her post
when I stood mine,
Through time zones, blood, and dust.

When I questioned if I'd ever come home—
She answered with her trust. There were no
medals on her chest, no flag folded at her
feet. But she held our family in her hands
While I walked war-torn streets.
She never asked for stories.

She just stayed through everyone. And
when I lost my way in shadows,
She became my morning sun.

If these pages hold any light,

It's because she carried the flame.

If I returned to write this down,

It's because she knew my name.

So when you read of combat, Of
blood and bone, and fight—
Know that she is why I made it.
She is why I write.

Suggested Style for "When the War Was Quiet" Genre / Feel:

- Acoustic Ballad

- Similar to:

- "Travelin' Soldier" – The Chicks

- "Tin Man" – Miranda Lambert

- "Hurt" – Johnny Cash version

- "Whiskey Lullaby" – Brad Paisley & Alison Krauss

This piece deserves a slow, reverent tone. Something you'd hear at a candlelight vigil or around a fire after a deployment send-off.

Key:

Key of G – adaptable for male or female voice

(Alternate options: D or C depending on vocal range)

Tempo:

60–70 Bpm (beats per minute)

Let it breathe. Let the pauses mean something.

Guitar Style:

- Acoustic fingerpicking or light strum

- Capo on 3rd fret (optional, for higher vocal range)

- Warm tone, no reverb. Think open chords with long sustains.

Chord Progression Suggestion (Verse & Chorus):

[Verse Chords]

G – Em – C – D

She knew the look behind the smile,

G – Em – C – D

The silence after sound…

[Chorus Chords]

Em – C – G – D

If these pages hold any light,

Em – C – G – D

It's because she carried flame…

[Outro]

G – Em – C – G

She is why I write…

Performance Notes

"When the War Was Quiet" was written for acoustic performance—solo or duet.

It may be sung slowly, as a reflective piece, with fingerpicking or a soft strum pattern.

Male or female vocals can adapt the key as needed.

This song belongs to the family members who kept us grounded—and the warriors still trying to come home.

For My Family

I wasn't just a Soldier. I was a husband and a father.

I was writing letters from a plywood hooch in Afghanistan while my wife raised our daughters without me—holding it all together while I chased ghosts through the mountains.

Julie has stood by me through every deployment, every hospital night, and every homecoming I ruined with silence.

She saw things no spouse should have to see—like what happens when a Green Beret wakes up shaking in the hallway at 3 a.m. And can't explain why.

She never demanded answers. She just stayed.

Our daughters never really knew who I was overseas. But I wrote this book so that one day, they might.

Not to burden them—but to show them that even the strongest men carry scars. And that love, when it's anchored in faith and humility, can pull a man out of the darkness.

This book is about war. But it's also about coming home. And for me… coming home meant Julie.

Epilogue IV: The War After War

You don't walk away from war.

You walk with it—inside you, around you, between every quiet moment at home.

Sometimes, it's a loaded pistol you don't touch.

Sometimes, it's your daughter saying, "You don't laugh like you used to."

Sometimes, it's a folded flag you hand to a widow—knowing it's the only weight you'll ever carry that hurts more than body armor.

We came home.

But not all of us returned.

Some came back in pieces—emotional, spiritual, invisible wounds you can't tourniquet.

Some of us sat in dark rooms, pistol in hand, thumb on the safety, asking questions that had no answers.

And then… somehow… we lived.

Because that's what Green Berets do.

We stand.

We hold.

We remember.

We lift each other.

There's a kind of strength they never teach you in training.

It's not about fast ropes or rifle drills.

It's when your teenage daughter hugs you goodnight; not knowing her smile just kept you alive for one more day.

It's when your wife says, "Welcome home," and you don't cry—but you feel something crack quietly inside.

It's when a combat medic realizes he can't save everyone... ...but still tries anyway.
If you're reading this—and you're still in the fight—don't go alone.
If you're a father trying to make peace with the silence...
If you're a Soldier holding your breath every night, waiting for sleep to be safe again...

If you're a widow, or a wife, or a child wondering why your Green Beret still flinches at laughter— You are not alone.

The real war isn't the one you deploy to.

It's the one you carry home. And the valor that matters most...
Isn't unbreakable.

It's the kind that breaks— and keeps going anyway.

Part V: The Fire That Never Went Out Dedication

To the Fallen of the 3rd Special Forces Group (Airborne)

You were more than names on a wall, more than ranks and ribbons. You were fathers, sons, brothers, and teammates.
You bore the weight of silence and sacrifice with a strength that never needed witness.

This book is dedicated to your memory—etched not only in stone but in the hearts of those who still carry your load, remember your voice, and live with the echoes of what you gave.

We did not forget you.

We never will.

De Oppresso Liber.

Honor Roll – 3rd Special Forces Group (Airborne)

These warriors gave their lives while serving with the 3rd SFG(A). This book honors them—not as statistics or symbols, but as men whose sacrifice outlived the battles they fought. May their names be remembered.

- Chief Warrant Officer 2 Stanley L. Harriman, Alpha Company, 3rd Battalion, 3rd Special Forces Group, 2 March 2002, Afghanistan.

- Sergeant First Class Peter P. Tycz Ii, Charlie Company, 2nd Battalion, 3rd Special Forces Group, 12 June 2002, Afghanistan.

- Sergeant First Class Mitchell A. Lane, Charlie Company, 2nd Battalion, 3rd Special Forces Group, 29 August 2003, Afghanistan.

- Staff Sergeant Paul A. Sweeney, Alpha Company, 3rd Battalion, 3rd Special Forces Group, 30 October 2003, Afghanistan.

- Chief Warrant Officer 2 Bruce E. Price, Alpha Company, 1st Battalion, 3rd Special Forces Group, 15 May 2004, Afghanistan.

- Captain Daniel W. Eggers, Alpha Company, 1st Battalion, 3rd Special Forces Group, 29 May 2004, Afghanistan.

- Sergeant First Class Robert J. Mogensen, Alpha Company, 1st Battalion, 3rd Special Forces Group, 29 May 2004, Afghanistan.

- Staff Sergeant Robert S. Goodwin, Alpha Company, 2nd Battalion, 3rd Special Forces Group, 20 September 2004, Afghanistan.

- Staff Sergeant Tony B. Olaes, Alpha Company, 2nd Battalion, 3rd Special Forces Group, 20 September 2004, Afghanistan.

- Sergeant Jason T. Palmerton, Alpha Company, 1st Battalion, 3rd Special Forces Group, 23 July 2005, Afghanistan.

- Staff Sergeant Christopher M. Falkel, Alpha Company, 1st Battalion, 3rd Special Forces Group, 8 August 2005, Afghanistan.

- Captain Jeremy A. Chandler, Charlie Company, 1st Battalion, 3rd Special Forces Group, 11 August 2005, Afghanistan.

- Sergeant First Class James S. Ochsner, Alpha Company, 2nd Battalion, 3rd Special Forces Group, 15 November 2005, Afghanistan.

- Master Sergeant Anthony R.C. Yost, Bravo Company, 3rd Battalion, 3rd Special Forces Group, 19 November 2005, Iraq.

- Chief Warrant Officer 2 Scott W. Dyer, Bravo Company, 3rd Battalion, 3rd Special Forces Group, 11 October 2006, Afghanistan.

- Staff Sergeant Kyu H. Chay, Headquarters Support Company, 1st Battalion, 3rd Special Forces Group, 28 October 2006, Afghanistan.

- Sergeant First Class William R. Brown, Charlie Company, 1st Battalion, 3rd Special Forces Group, 6 November 2006, Afghanistan.

- Sergeant First Class Tung M. Nguyen, Bravo Company, 2nd Battalion, 3rd Special Forces Group, 14 November 2006, Iraq.

- Sergeant First Class Justin S. Monschke, Bravo Company, 2nd Battalion, 3rd Special Forces Group, 14 October 2007, Iraq.

- Staff Sergeant Robert J. Miller, Alpha Company, 3rd Battalion, 3rd Special Forces Group, 25 January 2008, Afghanistan.

- Staff Sergeant William R. Neil Jr., Charlie Company, 3rd Battalion, 3rd Special Forces Group, 22 March 2008, Afghanistan.

- Sergeant Nicholas A. Roberston, Headquarters Support Company, 3rd Battalion, 3rd Special Forces Group, 3 April 2008, Afghanistan.

- Staff Sergeant Marc J. Small, Bravo Company, 1st Battalion, 3rd Special Forces Group, 12 February 2009, Afghanistan.

- Staff Sergeant Jeremy E. Bessa, Bravo Company, 1st Battalion, 3rd Special Forces Group, 20 February 2009, Afghanistan.

- Master Sergeant David L. Hurt, Bravo Company, 1st Battalion, 3rd Special Forces Group, 20 February 2009, Afghanistan.

- Captain David J. Thompson, Charlie Company, 3rd Battalion, 3rd Special Forces Group, 29 January 2010, Afghanistan.

- Staff Sergeant Kyle R. Warren, Charlie Company, 1st Battalion, 3rd Special Forces Group, 29 July 2010, Afghanistan.

- Captain Jason E. Holbrook, Charlie Company, 1st Battalion, 3rd Special Forces Group, 29 July 2010, Afghanistan.

- Master Sergeant Benjamin F. Bitner, Charlie Company, 2nd Battalion, 3rd Special Forces Group, 23 April 2011, Afghanistan.

- Sergeant Aaron J. Blasjo, Operations Detachment, Group Support Battalion, 29 May 2011, Afghanistan.

- Sergeant First Class Martin R. Apolinar, Charlie Company, 3rd Battalion, 3rd Special Forces Group, 29 May 2011, Afghanistan.

- Captain Joseph W. Schultz, Charlie Company, 3rd Battalion, 3rd Special Forces Group, 29 May 2011, Afghanistan.

- Staff Sergeant Brandon F. Eggleston, Bravo Company, 4th Battalion, 3rd Special Forces Group, 26 April 2012, Afghanistan.
• Staff Sergeant Bradon R. Pepper, Bravo Company, 4th Battalion, 3rd Special Forces Group, 21 July 2012, Afghanistan.

- Master Sergeant Gregory R. Trent, Bravo Company, 4th Battalion, 3rd Special Forces Group, 8 August 2012, Afghanistan.

- Sergeant First Class Riley G. Stephens, Bravo Company, 1st Battalion, 3rd Special Forces Group, 28 September 2012, Afghanistan.

- Staff Sergeant Justin C. Marquez, Bravo Company, 1st Battalion, 3rd Special Forces Group, 6 October 2012, Afghanistan.

- Warrant Officer 1 Joseph L. Schiro, Bravo Company, 1st Battalion, 3rd Special Forces Group, 6 October 2012, Afghanistan.

- Chief Warrant Officer 2 Michael S. Duskin, Alpha Company, 1st Battalion, 3rd Special Forces Group, 23 October 2012, Afghanistan.

- Captain Andrew M. Pedersen-Keel, Bravo Company, 1st Battalion, 3rd Special Forces Group, 11 March 2013, Afghanistan.

- Master Sergeant George A. Bannar Jr., Charlie Company, 3rd Battalion, 3rd Special Forces Group, 20 August 2013, Afghanistan. • Staff Sergeant Daniel T. Lee, Charlie Company, 2nd Battalion, 3rd Special Forces Group, 15 January 2014, Afghanistan.

- Specialist Christopher A. Landis, Headquarters Support Company, 2nd Battalion, 3rd Special Forces Group, 10 February 2014, Afghanistan.

- Sergeant First Class Roberto C. Skelt Jr., Charlie Company, 2nd Battalion, 3rd Special Forces Group, 12 February 2014, Afghanistan.

- Specialist John A. Pelham, Military Intelligence Company, Group Support Battalion, 3rd Special Forces Group, 12 February 2014, Afghanistan.

- Captain Jason B. Jones, Charlie Company, 1st Battalion, 3rd Special Forces Group, 2 June 2014, Afghanistan.

- Staff Sergeant Girard D. Gass Jr., Charlie Company, 1st Battalion, 3rd Special Forces Group, 3 August 2014, Afghanistan.

- Sergeant First Class Michael A. Cathcart, Alpha Company, 3rd Battalion, 3rd Special Forces Group, 14 November 2014, Afghanistan.

- Master Sergeant Pablo A. Ruiz Iii, Forward Support Company, 2nd Battalion, 3rd Special Forces Group, 24 May 2015, Afghanistan.

- Sergeant First Class Zachary Bannister, Charlie Company, 2nd Battalion, 3rd Special Forces Group, 17 October 2016, Kenya.

- Warrant Officer 1 Shawn Thomas, Bravo Company, 1st Battalion, 3rd Special Forces Group, 2 February 2017, Niger.

- Staff Sergeant Logan J. Melgar, Bravo Company, 2nd Battalion, 3rd Special Forces Group, 4 June 2017, Mali.

- Sergeant First Class Jeremiah W. Johnson, 14th Chemical Reconnaissance Detachment, Group Support Battalion, 3rd Special Forces Group, 4 October 2017, Niger.

- Staff Sergeant Bryan C. Black, Alpha Company, 2nd Battalion, 3rd Special Forces Group, 4 October 2017, Niger.

- Staff Sergeant Dustin M. Wright, Alpha Company, 2nd Battalion, 3rd Special Forces Group, 4 October 2017, Niger.

- Sergeant LaDavid T. Johnson, Forward Support Company, 2nd Battalion, 3rd Special Forces Group, 4 October 2017, Niger.

- Staff Sergeant Alexander W. Conrad, Headquarters Support Company, 1st Battalion, 3rd Special Forces Group, 8 June 2018, Somalia.

- Captain Andrew P. Ross, Bravo Company, 1st Battalion, 3rd Special Forces Group, 27 November 2018, Afghanistan.

- Sergeant First Class Eric M. Emond, Bravo Company, 1st Battalion, 3rd Special Forces Group, 27 November 2018, Afghanistan.

- Sergeant First Class Joshua Z. Beale, Bravo Company, 1st Battalion, 3rd Special Forces Group, 22 January 2019, Afghanistan.

Glossary of Terms

AC-130

Heavily armed, long-endurance ground-attack aircraft used by Special Operations forces.

ANA (Afghan National Army)

The primary ground forces of Afghanistan's military.

AO (Area of Operations)

The geographical area where military operations are conducted.

AOR (Area of Responsibility)

A defined area where a military unit has operational duties.

BSO (Battle Space Owner)

The unit responsible for a specific area of operations.

CH-47 (Chinook Helicopter)

A twin-engine, tandem rotor heavy-lift helicopter.

EOD (Explosive Ordnance Disposal)

Specialists trained to disarm and dispose of explosives.

FST (Forward Surgical Team)

A mobile surgical unit that provides damage control surgery in combat zones.

HVT (High Value Target)

An individual or asset considered crucial to the enemy's operations.

IED (Improvised Explosive Device)

A homemade bomb constructed and deployed in unconventional ways.

ISR (Intelligence, Surveillance, Reconnaissance)

Assets used to collect information and monitor enemy activity.

KIA (Killed In Action)

A service member who has died during combat.

LZ (Landing Zone)

A location where aircraft can land, typically under military conditions.

MEDEVAC (Medical Evacuation)

Transporting wounded personnel to medical facilities.

MRE (Meal, Ready-to-Eat)

Pre-packaged military rations designed for field use.

ODA (Operational Detachment Alpha)

A 12-man Special Forces team conducting unconventional warfare.

OP (Observation Post)

A position used to observe enemy movements or areas of interest.

PAK (Pakistani Militant/Region)

Refers to militants originating from or operating within Pakistan.

QRF (Quick Reaction Force)

A military unit designated to respond rapidly to emergencies.

RPG (Rocket-Propelled Grenade)

A shoulder-fired anti-tank weapon system.

SERE (Survival, Evasion, Resistance, and Escape)

Training designed to prepare personnel for capture and survival.

SF (Special Forces)

U.S. Army Green Berets, trained for unconventional warfare.

SFQC (Special Forces Qualification Course)

The course required to become a U.S. Army Green Beret.

SITREP (Situation Report)

A brief report on the current situation in an operational context.

SOP (Standard Operating Procedure)

Prescribed methods to carry out routine operations.

VBIED (Vehicle-Borne Improvised Explosive Device)

A vehicle rigged with explosives used as a bomb.

www.ingramcontent.com/pod-product-compliance
Lightning Source LLC
Chambersburg PA
CBHW071957150426
43194CB00008B/903